STUDIES IN THEOLOGY AND EDUCATION

John L. Elias
Professor of Adult and Religious Education
Fordham University
Bronx, New York

ROBERT E. KRIEGER PUBLISHING COMPANY
MALABAR, FLORIDA
1986

Original Edition 1986

Printed and Published by
ROBERT E. KRIEGER PUBLISHING COMPANY, INC.
KRIEGER DRIVE
MALABAR, FL 32950

Copyright © 1986 by
ROBERT E. KRIEGER PUBLISHING COMPANY, INC.

Library of Congress Cataloging in Publication Data

Elias, John L., 1933–
    Studies in theology and education.

    1. Christian education—Philosophy—Addresses, essays, lectures. 2. Catholic Church—
Education—Addresses, essays, lectures. I. Title.
    BV1464.E45   1986   207   85–9887
    ISBN 0-89874-841-0
    10 9 8 7 6 5 4 3 2

TABLE OF CONTENTS

PREFACE

The studies included in this collection have their origins in a number of different settings. Some studies began as papers delivered at annual meetings of the Association of Professors and Researchers in Religious Education (APRRE): "Three Publics of Religious Educators," "The Role of Culture in Moral Education," "Religious Education in a Television Culture," and "Religious Education and Ideology." The audience for these was small groups of professional religious educators.

Other studies originated in lectures given to mass audiences of religious educators. "Parish Adult Education: From Rhetoric to Reality" was given to religious educators at St. Michael's College, Winooski. I presented "Ecclesial Models of Adult Religious Education" and "The Adult's Faith Journey" at the Religious Education Convention of the Archdiocese of Los Angeles. "Education for Power and Liberation" was my contribution to a Religious Education Symposium at LaSalle College, Philadelphia. "Social Imagination and Religious Education" was a paper presented at the Convention of the National Catholic Educational Association. "Theology and Models of Liberation Spirituality" was a keynote paper for a Conference on Peace and Justice at Marymount College, New York.

Three of these studies originated as papers prepared during my sabbatical in the United Kingdom. I gave the paper on "Traditions of Christian Education" to the Faculty of Theology, the University of Durham. "Religion and Adult Education in Britain" was presented at a conference for adult educators at the University of Surrey. The study on "From Militarism to Pacifism: Evolution in the American Catholic Church" was given at an Open Lecture sponsored by the Theology Department of the University of Birmingham.

The two remaining studies originated as publications: "The Theory-Practice Split" and "Paulo Freire: Adult Religious Educator."

The grouping of these fifteen studies in three categories indicates my major scholarly concerns in the past decade. *Foundational issues* have occupied my attention in attempting to understand the proper role for theory and practice and the influence of diverse publics on religious educators. I have also been interested in cultural influences on education, especially the powerful culture of television. A final foundational issue is the role that theology has played in the development of religious education theory.

My second preoccupation has been with *the religious education of adults*. I have long been concerned with the large gap that divides official church statements on adult education and the actual practice of the churches. I have attempted to bring to the fore the diverse forms of adult religious education by relating them to theological models of the church. Within one particular model, the servant model, I have found most helpful the work of Paulo Freire. In working with adults I have found it necessary to correlate a faith development theory with traditions of Christian spirituality. Finally, my understanding of the enterprise of adult religious education was sharpened by a study of its history and practice in the United Kingdom.

My third concern has been to relate religious education to *theologies of peace and justice*. As a preliminary task, it is necessary to understand the relationships among theology, ideology, and education. Any politically oriented education must deal with the realities of power and liberation. I have come increasingly to realize that the power of social imagination is of great importance both for theology and education. Any commitment to work for peace and justice entails a special style of life which may be termed liberation spirituality. The emergence of a liberation spirituality is seen in the evolution of a dynamic pacifism in American Catholicism.

I have grouped all of these studies under the general title of studies in theology and education. I have dealt with some issues from the perspective of Christian theology and with other issues from the standpoint of education. In a number of studies I have made explicit attempts to correlate the two standpoints.

I dedicate these studies to my students on both sides of the Atlantic in appreciation for their genuine encouragement and continuing friendship.

John Elias
Fordham University
St. Mary's College, Strawberry Hill, England

ACKNOWLEDGMENTS

I would like to thank the following publishers for permission to make use of previously published material:

The Religious Education Association: "Paulo Freire: Religious Education," *Religious Education*, January–February 1976; "Religious Education and the Television Culture," *Religious Education*, April–May 1981; "The Three Publics of Religious Educators," *Religious Education*, November–December 1983.

The United States Catholic Conference: "Ecclesial Models of Adult Religious Education," in *Christian Adulthood: A Catechetical Resource*, Vol. 2, 1983; "The Adult's Journey in Faith," in *Christian Adulthood: A Catechetical Resource*, Vol. 3, 1984; "Education for Power and Liberation," *The Living Light*, Spring 1976; "A Cultural Approach to Religious Moral Education," *The Living Light*, Fall 1980; "Parish Adult Religious Education," *The Living Light*, Spring 1982.

Lumen Vitae Center: "Ideology and Religious Education," *Lumen Vitae*, December 1982.

Educational Studies Department, University of Surrey: "Religion and Adult Education in Britain," The Education of Adults, Third International Seminar, 1984.

PART I: FOUNDATIONAL ISSUES

CHAPTER 1

THEORY AND PRACTICE IN
RELIGIOUS EDUCATION

It is the nature of philosophical problems that they are never answered to the satisfaction of everyone, in part because these problems touch upon the basic tensions and polarities of human existence. Thus, philosophers of every age have offered explanations of freedom and determinism, God and the world, individual and societal rights, virtue and vice, and truth and falsehood. The great works in philosophy are those that deal with these and similar problems in ways that are found helpful for persons beyond the writers' generation.

One of the most difficult problems that philosophers in every age have addressed is the relationship between philosophy and life, theory and practice. At the heart of this problem is the tension between knowing and doing—between knowing the truth and doing the truth, between knowing the good and doing the good, and between the contemplative and active life. For many philosophers, this problem is best expressed as the tension between theoretical wisdom and practical wisdom, or simply, as the relationship between theory and practice.

In this study I intend, first of all, to examine briefly the nature of theory by looking at the different ways in which theory has been related to practice, and to present a constructive approach to the relationship. Second, I will make this examination within the framework of the fields of education and religious education. Third, I will present some suggestions for closing the gap in the profession of religious education between the theoreticians and the practitioners.

OPPOSITION BETWEEN THEORY AND PRACTICE:
SUPERIORITY OF THEORY

Greek philosophers grappled with the issue of theory and practice in an attempt to determine what kind of knowledge was most worthwhile. The classical position in Greek philosophy is found in the writings of Aristotle.

Although a common interpretation of his thought is that theory and practice are in opposition, Aristotle's position contains more subtle variations than this interpretation allows.

Aristotle (1941 ed.) described three types of human life and activity: *theoria, praxis,* and *poesis. Theoria* (contemplation) was the speculative life in which one searched for truth solely by an intuitive and reflective process. To theorize was to achieve wisdom by understanding the most basic principles of life. The achievement of theoretical wisdom was the most complete form of happiness. Aristotle called the practical life *praxis* and described it as reflective engagement in some area of society. Praxis included two parts: action and reflection. To practice, for Aristotle, was to achieve practical wisdom, for example, in such areas as business, politics, and education. *Poesis* was Aristotle's term for the productive life. It entailed the making of artifacts or concrete things. Through it a person developed a craft, a skill, or an art.

Aristotle's description of these types of activities was partially determined by the social situation in which he lived and philosophized. Greek society was structured along the lines of classes whose life was characterized by the types of activities that he described. This type of analysis is also found in the work of Aristotle's disciple, Plato.

Despite Aristotle's careful distinctions, his legacy to medieval philosophy included a number of dualisms, notably the opposition between theory and practice and the superiority of theory over practice. Medieval philosophy continued and actually reinforced this tradition. Theory, which was the activity of the speculative or contemplative life, was highly valued because it gave true knowledge. Only the practical life afforded the experiences out of which opinions could be formed. But what one learned from experience was considered of little value when compared with what one learned from a contemplation of first principles, or the First Principle, God.

This classical position of Greek and medieval philosophy led to the notion that, in knowing and acting, it is always best to go from theory to practice. It devalued common experience and practice as sources of true knowledge. It exaggerated the value of theory and speculation in human life. It led to a depreciation and suspicion of manual work and practical involvement. In some cultures, this viewpoint led to rigid class distinctions that were devised according to what types of activities people engaged in.

In education the position that theory is superior to practice and that it is always best to go from theory to practice has led to a number of harmful effects. It has led to the belief that certain subjects (philosophy, mathematics, literature, and history) are in themselves more valuable than others (natural sciences, vocational education, technological education). For many years this viewpoint prevented the introduction of subjects of a practical nature into the school curriculum. The struggle between progressive education and liberal education in the United States and elsewhere has been largely centered on the issue of the relative importance of the theoretical and the practical.

The result of this viewpoint in religious education has been a relationship between theology and religious education which is rather one-sided. Theology is viewed as providing the theories, doctrines, and teachings for which practical-minded religious educators must find ways to transmit to students. This viewpoint emphasizes religious education as a purely content-oriented subject. It takes little account of the findings of social scientists and educators who write out of empirical research or practical experience.

THEORY AND PRACTICE IN OPPOSITION:
THE SUPERIORITY OF PRACTICE

In the middle of the seventeenth century, Francis Bacon, the British philosopher of science, introduced a new mode of thought to the Western world. Bacon (1876 ed.) argued that the surest way to knowledge was through an examination of facts gained from experience. This empirical or experimental mode of knowing was a principal element in the philosophies of empiricism and pragmatism which have been powerful influences in Anglo-American philosophy and education.

The empiric and pragmatic spirit is responsible for the bias toward the practical that characterizes American life and education. A basic premise of pragmatism is that we can determine what is good, true, or beautiful merely by examining practical consequences. Ideas are good and true to the extent that they help individuals to understand their experiences, solve problems, and lead to satisfying results. The emphasis on the practical is seen in the pragmatist's concern for reforming social institutions, for it is the power of action, not ideas, that is of most consequence in this endeavor.

Under the influence of empiricism and pragmatism, theory took on a different meaning. In the classical view theory was a description of reality, the way things are, and was derived from a contemplation of the essences of things. For the empiricists and pragmatists theory was more of an instrument to establish inferences about things that one experiences. Theory is like a road map or a tool for finding out about reality. Theories merely order experience and function as instrumental models for dealing with experience.

While Aristotle is associated with the view that theory is superior to practice, one of John Dewey's (1916) legacies to education has been the idea that practice is superior to theory. Dewey's rejection of metaphysics is a rejection of any organized body of knowledge that can determine before investigation what is true and good. He was deeply committed to the inductivism of the scientific method. His theories of knowledge, value, and education are rooted in the knowledge that comes from experience. One theorizes only out of this perspective.

The educational implications of the empiric and pragmatic point of view are seen in the educational theories that arose in opposition to classical or liberal education. These theories depended less on earlier accepted theories than on direct experience and observation. More attention was placed on methods and students in the educational process. The process of learning was analyzed in an empirical fashion. A science of teaching developed which was founded on a study of particular methodologies. The education of teachers became primarily training in practical skills rather than an education in classical educational theories.

Since Dewey's time, education in the United States has had a bias toward the practical. Although Dewey was a philosopher and a historian of education, these two disciplines are of minor importance in the education of teachers in today's schools of education. Courses in administration and methodology far out-number courses in philosophy and history. Research studies that deal with practical aspects of education are much more common than theoretical or philosophical studies.

The viewpoint that practice is superior to theory is one that has also found its way into the field of religious education. It is found mostly in classroom teachers and administrators of programs of religious education. These persons often feel that what is needed is some sure-fire method of teaching religion. One might write the history of religious education in this country by examining the search for *the* method that works. Often one finds a suspicion of theoreticians among practitioners on the grounds that theory is unimportant or irrelevant to educational practice.

THEORY AND PRACTICE:
A DIALECTICAL RELATIONSHIP

A preferable way of understanding the relationship between theory and practice is to view them not in a relationship of opposition or superiority but in a dialectical relationship. Hegel (1953 ed.) made one of the first moves in this direction when he rejected the separation of theory from practice and emphasized the unity of the two. He attempted to maintain the productive tension between practical life experience and the theories derived from the experiences of previous generations. Hegel utilized the dialectical relationships of the three movements of thesis, antithesis, and synthesis to show how theory and practice criticized each other and resulted in new truths.

Hegel's analysis of practice was criticized by Marx (1976 ed.) for being overly idealistic and contemplative. Marx argued that the dialectic between theory and practice was resolved by Hegel into a unity in which theory dominated. Marx preferred a more materialistic and historical view of the relationship. His approach to this relationship came from his analysis of the relationships among work, capital, and structures of society. For Marx, theory represented the consciousness that arises from practical involvement. Once a theory has evolved, it must inform further practice; thus a dialectical unity is posited between the two.

A weakness in Marx's approach to theory and practice is the limited way in which he defined praxis, and consequently, theory. By restricting his view of praxis to work, property relations, and revolutionary action, he advocated economic determinism and consequently a determinist view of the relationship between theory and practice. Domination by a capitalist system determines a consciousness or theory of reality (broadly described as alienation) that necessarily leads to a revolutionary praxis. Whatever one thinks of capitalist systems, it is clear that living in them does not necessitate a sense of domination, oppression, and alienation. It is also clear that people arrive at different theories or types of consciousness even though they are involved in the same praxis. Thus, the human mind adds more to theory than Marx appeared to have allowed.

Some of the weaknesses of Marx's theory are corrected by Jurgen Habermas (1973), a contemporary German philosopher of social theory. Habermas, in dialogue with Marxists, has placed more emphasis on theory as the critical reflection on self and society. He points out that particular interests, attitudes, and ideologies can influence theories. In developing his position for the relationship of theory to praxis, Habermas adds a broader range of human activities (science, art, religion, history, psychology) to work and property relations.

The dialectical approach to theory and practice has received its strongest educational development in the writings of Paulo Freire (1970; 1970a, 1973a). Freire advocates a dialogical approach to education in his theory of conscientization. His view will receive fuller treatment in the second part of this collection. Suffice it to say, for now, that the purpose of education for Freire is to bring people to critical consciousness of the social realities in which they are immersed. Critical awareness entails the denunciation of oppressive reality and the prophetic announcement of a utopian reality that is free of oppression. To conscientize others is to aid them in decoding reality and in stripping it of the deceptive myths that both distort a vision of reality and prevent cultural action for change. This conscientization is made possible through praxis—reflection and action on the world with the intent of changing it.

The dialectical approach to theory and practice is a challenging one for religious educators. A number of religious educators have begun to raise critical questions of religious education from this perspective. Thomas Groome has developed an educational methodology which is informed by these principles (1980). Monette has raised basic questions about the education of adults from a perspective of critical theory (1978; 1979). In other studies in this collection I will draw on this theory of dialectical relationship for dealing with such issues as ideology and political education.

Having argued that the dialectical relationship between theory and practice is the preferable position, I will now offer some suggestions on how this dialectic works out according to the different functions of theory and practice that have been described.

THE DIALECTIC BETWEEN THEORY AND PRACTICE IN RELIGIOUS EDUCATION

Education is rightly termed a practice in human life. As such, it can be likened to law, medicine, business, and sports. A practice is "any form of activity specified by a system of rules, which define offices, roles, moves, defenses, and so on, and which give the activity its structure (Rawls, 1971, p. 55)." The attempt to understand rationally the various aspects of a practice is called a philosophy or theory; thus, we have a philosophy or theory of law, medicine, and education. The question to be considered here is, what are the characteristics of the relationship that exists between theory and practice? At least four elements appear to be present in this relationship: explanation, direction, criticism, and imagination. Between theory and practice there needs to be maintained a critical correlation with regard to these four elements.

Explanation

One of the purposes of theory is to describe a phenomenon. A theory explains a practice such as education. Educational theories attempt to explain the ends and objectives of the practice of education. They help us to decide which activities are appropriately considered educational activities. Theories attempt to do in a systematic manner what common sense does in an unorganized way. Theories attempt to probe goals, relationships, methods, structures, and institutions, as well as norms and procedures of evaluation.

It is important to recognize that in the social sciences theories are at best conjectures that need to be examined and refined. They are like explanatory or tentative hypotheses that need to be examined and verified. The more rigid conception of theories in the natural sciences has even come under criticism by contemporary philosophers of science.

While it is generally recognized that theories are explanatory, the explanatory nature of practice needs to be pointed out. Practice helps us to understand a theory. Just as we learn about love by experiencing love, so we learn about education by experiencing education in various roles: teacher, student, administrator, or parent. One can begin to understand either by theorizing or by practicing. But practice impels thoughtful persons to a deeper understanding of theories, especially since there is rarely a one-to-one correspondence between theory and practice. Practice often supplies the concrete examples needed to give insight into a theory. It is often the case that practice comes before theory and gives rise to theory, according to the well-known axiom "Theory begins after sundown."

A conflict arises when theories contradict practice or practice contradicts theory. It cannot be decided beforehand whether practice is not rightly understood or theory has not been adequately applied. Teachers rather quickly learn that different methods are appropriate for different groups, and even at different times with the same group. Administrators know that what works in one situation does not work in another. The existence of such conflict points out how complicated a practice is and how we can never be satisfied with one theoretical approach nor with one practice. Both theoreticians and practitioners need to be open to challenge by the practices and theories of the others. Only by keeping the dialectical process open can advances be made.

The history of catechetical theory in Roman Catholicism illustrates this dialectic in religious education. A doctrinal approach which was found to be unsatisfactory to many teachers was replaced by a biblical-liturgical or kerygmatic approach. The attempt to put this approach into practice raised questions about the appropriateness of this method, which came from a preaching mode, to the classroom. Teachers attempted more experiential, secular, and personalistic modes of instruction. Theoreticians followed suit in the development of theories which explained such practices. In more recent times a call has been heard for the introduction of more explicitly religious material in religious education curricula. Thus a certain dialectic has existed between theory and practice in the last twenty years. I am sure that a similar pattern can be found in the history of Protestant religious education in the United States.

Direction

Education theories, like all other theories of practice, have the important function of directing action. There is a close connection between the explanatory function of theory and practice and the directive function. But it is helpful when dealing with a practice such as education to distinguish the two functions.

Whoever theorizes in education should not have the elaboration of theory in mind as the end product, but rather the development of guidelines for practice. The general goals of education are well known: the formation of character, the cultivation of intelligence, the promotion of knowledge, education for work and leisure, and education for citizenship and social involvement. Educational theory is organized along lines that direct practical activities: teaching, training, learning, evaluation, or administration. Because of this directive character, theories of practice, such as education, differ from scientific theories whose primary functions are to describe, explain, control, and predict. This distinction must be recognized if one is to avoid underestimating the importance of theories for practice.

Educational practice is also directive. It gives direction to both theorists and researchers. Practice directs theorists to facts, phenomena, and events which must be explained. It reveals the incongruities that are not accounted for in existing theories. Freire's experience in literacy education with peasants in northeast Brazil directed him away from a static view of education and toward a dynamic view of education as the development of critical political consciousness. Carl Rogers's (1969) experiences with patients directed him away from a behaviorist understanding of the person and toward a humanistic perspective in which freedom, relationship, and authenticity are highly valued.

The field of religious education needs a healthy tension in the matter of direction. Practitioners need to take direction from theorists and theorists must look in the direction of practitioners. I have attempted to remain open to these directions in my professional life. At the university I deal mainly with theories and attempt to direct students to examine these thoroughly. At the same time I am involved as a director of a parish adult religious education program and a parish adult catechumenate. More and more I find the two worlds coming together. My university classes are filled with many examples from my practice. At the parish level I attempt to utilize, test, and understand more fully various theories and models of adult religious education.

Criticism

Theories "criticize" practice. They test the practice of education according to accepted criteria and standards. Theories of instruction, learning, and evaluation question why these activities are organized in the way they are. They ask whether education achieves the goals it sets out to reach. Educational theories subject well-known educational practices to criticism. Theories ask about the fundamental rationale and assumptions of a particular curriculum or program. Theories raise questions about assumptions of curricula and programs.

The critical function of theory is seen in the three components of theoretical inquiry: analysis, evaluation, and synthesis. Analysis describes the concepts, definitions, models, arguments, and slogans that are used in educational practice. It subjects these to careful scrutiny. Evaluation is concerned with determining the validity of practices, whether or not practice achieves its stated goals. Synthesis attempts to put together the findings of practice into a fully integrated theory.

Practice also has potential for offering constructive criticism to theories. Practice may show that theories are inadequate for explaining or imaging reality. By putting a theory into practice, one often sees ways in which the theory should be modified. It is the failure of a theory to meet the test of practice that often leads to its abandonment. When people resist learning in encounter groups, simulation situations, and games, some modifications in the theories behind these is called for.

A mutual criticism of theory and practice is needed in the field of religious education. Curricula and programs need to be put to the test of theories, with probing into aims, objectives, and assumptions. Theories need testing by both formal and informal experimentation. Considering the number of scholars in the field of religious education, there is a great dearth of empirical studies that test theories. Most of the writing in the field is on a philosophical or general level. This is one reason to be saddened over the cessation of the journal *Character Potential* from the field of religious education because of its strong commitment to methods of empirical research. When one considers how long it took to generate the research base of Kohlberg's theory of moral development, one realizes how painfully slow is the process of developing a synthesis of theory and practice in just one area.

Imagination

Thus far, the relationship between theory and practice has been viewed primarily from a rational perspective. To complete this analysis, one must also look at theory and practice from the perspective of the imagination. At times, theories "imagine" or "construct" new realities or possible practices. Though theory most often arises from attempts to explain, criticize, and direct practice, in some cases it begins with a denial of present practice and with attempts to imagine new and different practices. Theory is thus often utopian in its rejection of present practices in the call for new and radical forms of practice. The theorizing of Plato in *The Republic*, of Rousseau in *Emile* (1956), of Thomas More in *Utopia* (1955), and B. F. Skinner in *Walden II* (1948) are examples of such imaginative theorizing. In the early 1970s Paul Goodman (1970) and Ivan Illich (1970) imagined a society in which formal schooling would be greatly reduced and informal modes of education would predominate. The debate over their proposals helped to clarify educational theory.

As theory imagines practice, so does practice often present concrete situations that serve to stretch the imagination of theorists. Dewey's theory of progressive education derived as much from his actual experience with extraordinary educational practice (described in *Schools of Tomorrow*, 1962), as it did from his intellectual immersion in the educational theories of Rousseau, Pestalozzi, and Hegel. Myles Morton's radical theory of adult education (Adams and Horton, 1975) arose from his imaginative educational efforts in dealing with social problems in the South of the United States. Imagination is often found in the person of action who develops concrete solutions to particular problems, creates a unique educational experiment, or fashions a new type of relationship with learners.

Imaginative theorizing is also found in the field of religious education. The best recent work of this genre is John Westerhoff's *Will Our Children Have Faith?* (1976). This work is somewhat modeled after Illich's program of deschooling in its proposal for eliminating the schooling paradigm of religious education and the imaging of an enculturation model. This work presents a vision of church education in which family, church, and community are central and in which programs are organized without the elements that are specific to schooling: classrooms, graded curriculum, formal teacher-student relationships, etc. Imaginative theorizing is also found in the writings of Edward Robinson (1977) and others (Durka and Smith, 1979) who have attempted to utilize esthetic and artistic models of religious education.

HEALING THE SPLIT BETWEEN
THEORY AND PRACTICE

Thus far the theory-practice problem has been discussed chiefly as an intellectual issue. The problem also exists at a more practical level in the field of religious education. In education, as in many other areas, there is a social division between theoreticians or researchers and practitioners. Theoreticians and researchers are usually found at universities, colleges, and seminaries, while practitioners work in other settings. When the two groups come together, it is usually the theoreticians and researchers who speak to the practitioners. Theoreticians usually write for the scholarly journals while practitioners write for the more practice-oriented publications. While a degree of social separation is certainly necessary for professional identity and growth, one can still question the degree to which this separation contributes to the crisis between theory and practice in the field of religious education.

Efforts should be made to close the gap between these two groups within the field of religious education. Closing this social gap may also help resolve some problems at the theoretical level. I should like to close this study by making some suggestions for greater collaboration between the two groups of religious educators.

Institutions of Higher Education

Those who teach religious education in schools of higher education should continually examine their teaching to see whether or not it is consistent with the sound principles and practices of education. It is also important for such academics to engage in teaching outside the higher education setting. Persons who are involved in such practical fields as medicine, business, education, politics, and counseling need direct practice to enhance and enrich their teaching. My professional work of teaching and writing has been substantially aided by my teaching and administrative work in local church communities. I know of other academics who have done the same with similar benefits.

Institutions of higher education might have expert practitioners of religious education attached to them at least on a part-time basis. The practical experience that many students bring to institutions of higher education should be tapped in creative ways, both formally in classes and informally through arranged meetings and sharings.

Within institutions of higher education there often exists a social split between theoreticians and empirical researchers. Those who teach theoretical foundations of education are often isolated from those involved in empirically based research. Through a creative effort in teaching, conferences, and collaborative scholarly work, this social split might be lessened. Collaboration between theoreticians and empirical researchers is necessary if research in religious education is to become theoretically sophisticated. Empirical research will also be strengthened by attention to theory development and theory testing.

Conferences

Each year there are many conferences in religious education: national, regional, and local. Conferences are usually directed either to professionals or to practitioners. What is necessary in the field are conferences where there is a good balance of theoreticians, researchers, and practitioners. A structure is needed in which all parties listen seriously to one another and take account of one another's perspective. Only through this kind of collaborative effort will academic professionals be able to work out the full import of their theories. The findings of researchers will be brought to the attention and criticisms of those who are best able to examine and, if suitable, draw practical implications. The experience and practice of persons working in the field will best be able to be used and subjected to criticism.

Journals

The social separation of theoreticians and practitioners in religious education is seen rather clearly in the publications in the field. Academics publish in and read professional journals and are rather critical of the more popular publications that are directed to and read by practitioners. Academics who write for nonscholarly publications are viewed with suspicion by some of their colleagues. There are certainly good reasons for both kinds of publications. But what might be called for on some occasions in such a practice-oriented field as religious education is a collaborative effort by professional academics and practitioners on particular issues. Creative editors could find ways to explore the same problem from both theoretical and practical vantage points. Collaborative writing between theoreticians and practitioners might also be encouraged.

CONCLUSION

Closing the gap between theory and practice in religious education is an urgent issue. The issue goes beyond the theoretical and social problem. At issue is the very nature of the profession of religious education. Because religious education is by its very nature a practice, the profession of religious education must develop both sound theories and sound practices, and it must constantly work for the integration of these at both theoretical and practical levels. This study has provided some thoughts on achieving this necessary integration. In our theorizing and in our actions, we need to maintain the dialectical tension between theory and practice. This can be done if we recognize that both theory and practice have powers of explanation, direction, criticism, and imagination. The integrity of both must be maintained in their integration. In education, theory without practice can become irrelevant and practice without theory can become mindless.

CHAPTER 2

THE THREE PUBLICS OF RELIGIOUS EDUCATORS

In recent years religious educators have given increasing attention in their writings to foundational issues in their field or discipline. Scholars have debated such issues as the appropriate name for the field (religious education, Christian Education, Jewish Education, catechetics), its disciplinary character (a unified discipline, an interdisciplinary field), different theoretical approaches, and the relationship of religious education to theology. Such discussions among a professional group of scholars is both a sign of troubles in a field and an opportunity for real development. Preoccupation with foundational issues may indicate a lack of clear direction, the existence of unresolved problems, the uncritical adoption of fads, or the splintering into separate groups. On the other hand, focus on foundational issues is an opportunity for recognizing the complexity of the field of religious education and for establishing the field or discipline on a firmer basis through both individual and cooperative efforts.

Given the description of religious education as a discipline or field of study which is seriously involved in a debate about foundational issues, my purpose in this study is to shed some light on the profession of religious education by attempting to draw a social portrait of the professional religious educator. By professional religious educators I mean those persons who have received advanced degrees in this area, who function as professors, administrators, and consultants, and who have or are eligible for membership in such organizations as the Association of Professors and Researchers in Religious Education (APRRE) and the American Academy of Religion (AAR). This social portrait is drawn by examining the relationship of religious educators to the three publics to which they are linked: the academy, the church or synagogue, and the wider society. My effort in this chapter is modeled after David Tracy's (1981) use of the sociology of knowledge to analyze the public nature of theology and the public roles and functions of theologians. This effort is also an attempt to address the issues raised by John Westerhoff (1981) on the various publics for the field of religious education.

All religious educators have a relationship to the three publics of the academy, church, and society, though usually they have a particular connection with one or two of these publics. They have been formed within academic institutions and are often situated within some institution of the academy; many address their writings to members of academic institutions. Professional religious educators have received religious formation within religious bodies and often maintain close relationships with such bodies; many, in their writings, address primarily issues that are essential in the life of religious bodies. Religious educators are shaped by the particular socioeconomic, political, and cultural worlds in which they live; some religious educators make the broader public a major focus of their professional writings.

An understanding of the relationships of religious educators to these three publics provides a heuristic tool for explaining certain differences among professional religious educators. In addressing the publics of the academy, the church or synagogue, and society, religious educators use somewhat different languages, modes of argument, and criteria for establishing positions. Their relationship to different publics may also be connected with different ethical stances (e.g., loyalty, free inquiry, and social commitment) and religious stances (believer or neutral observer). Depending on whether they are primarily associated with the publics of the academic community, religious bodies, or society, religious educators are likely to view their work as a distinct academic discipline (religious education), a pastoral or church activity (Jewish Education, Christian Education, Christian Religious Education), or a form of political and social education (education of the public or social action).

THE PUBLIC OF THE ACADEMY

Much of the scholarship and research in the field of religious education comes from professors and researchers who hold academic positions in various types of institutions of learning: seminaries for training ministers, departments of religion, religious studies, or theology in church-related colleges or universities, divinity schools, departments of religion in private or state colleges and universities. A reading of journals in the field and attendance at meetings of APRRE makes one at least vaguely aware of differences among religious educators who work in these institutions and who write both in and for these contexts.

Religious educators in academic institutions with close church relationships often experience a tension between the values of academic institutions and those of religious bodies to which they are related. John

Westerhoff gave expression to this tension in his statement that while teaching at Duke Divinity School he views himself as a catechist, at Duke University his self-understanding is that of a religious educator (1977). This is an indication of the multiple selves that religious educators have in addressing different publics.

The multiple selves of religious educators situated in academic institutions can be seen in their different self-understandings as theologians, professors of catechetics or Christian Education, or professors of education and religion. These different understandings find expressions in efforts to legitimate academic disciplines, since a major concern of religious educators in academic settings is to establish the academic legitimation of their field of study and scholarship. This self-understanding and legitimating effort often affects the choice of research topics, the modes of argument, ethical and religious stances, and criteria for determining meaning and truth.

In church-related academic institutions religious educators often assume the self-understanding of practical or pastoral theologians, since religious education in these institutions is often situated in departments of theology, and religious educators have mainly theologians as colleagues. For these religious educators, it is the connection with the discipline of theology that legitimates the discipline of religious education, which in these situations is often called catechetics, Christian Education, or Jewish Education. Most educators in these institutions are usually related primarily to the public of the church or synagogue. These educators often focus primarily on the presentation, reinterpretation and handing on of the religious traditions to which they belong. Their ethical stance is one of creative and critical fidelity to this tradition. Such educators are personally committed to and involved in their religious bodies.

Where religious educators are situated in departments of religion, religious studies, or religious education in church-related institutions, a self-understanding of being religious educators, as distinguished from theologians, is more common. In these settings the discipline of religious education is often legitimized as an interdisciplinary field of study drawing on religious and theological sources, social sciences, and education. In their writings these educators use the discourse not primarily of theology but rather of ordinary experience, philosophy, culture, and educational theory. The primary commitment of such educators is more often to the critical inquiry proper to an academic setting rather than to the pastoral work of religious bodies. The religious commitment of these educators to a particular religious tradition is often in tension with the demands of critical inquiry.

Finally, persons involved in religious education in departments of religion or education at state or private colleges and universities are more likely to view themselves simply as educators who have a special interest in the teaching of religion in churches or non-church institutions of society and with religion in the broader culture of the country. The primary commitment of this group is to the canons of their academic discipline and to the place of religion in the broader culture. The personal religious stance of these educators is often not relevant to their academic work. Generally speaking, though these educators might publish articles in religious education journals, their professional allegiance is not to such associations as APRRE but rather to associations in the general field of education or to such diffuse professional associations as the American Academy of Religion.

Though it may be risky to place religious educators into the categories developed in the explanatory hypothesis of this study, a few examples may help in clarifying how religious educators relate to the public of the academy. I think that Burgess (1975) correctly identified the theology of the church as the primary focus for such religious educators as Iris Cully, Howard Grimes, Johannes Hofinger, Sara Little, Randolph Miller, and Campbell Wyckoff. His inclusion of Gabriel Moran in this category is based on a reading of Moran's earlier works (1966; 1967). Other religious educators who appear to have the self-understanding of practical theologians include Berard Marthaler (1978), Michael Warren (1981), and John Westerhoff (1976). The academy to which these religious educators are related are divinity schools, seminaries, and theology departments of church-related institutions. It is these religious educators who often prefer to speak of their discipline as Christian Education or catechetics.

A second group has attempted to establish religious education as a discipline with less dependence on theology. Interestingly enough, a number of influential members of this group have connections with such private universities as New York University and the Teachers College-Union Theological programs. The group includes Mary Boys (1981), Gloria Durka (1979), Thomas Groome (1980), Maria Harris (1976), James M. Lee (1978), Charles Melchert (1977), Gabriel Moran (1981), and Kieran Scott (1980). I recognize that there are some wide differences among this group. Yet I believe that they can be thus classified because of their common attempt to situate religious education outside of practical theology and catechetics. Though some of these persons are situated in theology departments and not in departments of religious studies, it is clear that they do not attempt to make religious education primarily a theological discipline. Groome differs from the others in his theologically oriented effort to make a case for Christian Religious Education as an interdisciplinary joining of Christian theology and social theory. In this way Groome bridges the theological group and the religious educators group.

The third group interested in religion and education are identified with schools of education or departments of religion and do not possess a self-understanding of being religious educators. I would place in this group those scholars whose major thrust is the issue of religion and morality in all areas of society and culture. Many of the scholars who are primarily concerned with religion in the public schools would be within this classification. A representative example of such authors is found in Engel's collection (1974). This group has less interest in establishing religious education as a theological discipline or even as a discipline in its own right. The group is more concerned with religion within the general culture. Gabriel Moran appears to be the best bridge between the second and third groups in his efforts to develop a broadly based field of religion and education.

It is clear then that the academy to which religious educators relate is a complex one. There are major differences among religious educators at a denominational seminary, a church-related college or university, and a private or state university. There are various ways of achieving academic respectability in these institutions. The plurality of self-understandings that exists in the field among professors and researchers of Christian and Jewish Education, catechetics, religious education, and religion and education is not only a matter of semantics but also reflects how persons relate differently to the public of the academy. An examination of the other publics to which religious educators are related may confirm certain aspects of this analysis.

THE PUBLIC OF THE CHURCH

Most religious educators have some relationship to the public of the church or synagogue, at least in the minimal sense that their writings appear in journals that reach a church audience. For some religious educators, however, their own religious bodies appear as primary reference groups, with the academy and the wider society as secondary reference groups. These religious educators have the self-understanding of being primarily Christian or Jewish educators in addressing issues of church or synagogue education.

Those religious educators who identify with catechesis, nurturing theories of religious education, religious socialization or inculturation have the public of the church as their primary, though not exclusive, reference group for discourse and practice. The major concern in these theories is socialization in the traditions of a particular faith community. Often these educators have a theological self-understanding of their roles. They view the task of religious education as primarily handing on a faith that is often re-interpreted and re-presented. The ethical stance of such educators is primarily one of creative and critical fidelity to a religious tradition and secondarily one of the free and critical inquiry appropriate to the academy. Such educators are explicit in their commitments to and involvements in particular religious communities. Of course religious educators can be related in various ways to religious bodies, from loyal and critically conservative defenders of institutional decrees and doctrines to members of a loyal, critical, and at times prophetic opposition.

The involvement of religious educators in the public of the church takes various forms. Differences exist in social position and involvement among ordained ministers, priests, and rabbis, members of religious con-gregations of men and women in Roman Catholicism, and lay persons. Religious educators who teach in seminaries, divinity schools, and church-related colleges and universities have different self-understandings with regard to their religious bodies than do educators at secular or state universities. The history and character of such institutions are also impor-tant factors in shaping the understanding of these religious educators. Some religious educators are also deeply involved in developing curricu-lum and providing continuing education for members of their denomina-tion. Others serve in important positions in their denominational structure.

All religious educators who have a strong relationship to a religious body experience some tension in reconciling this self-understanding with the demands of the academy with regard to the canons of criticism and free inquiry within the academy. Though this tension is found in many educators, it was dramatically expressed in Moran's controversial article "Catechetics R.I.P. (1970)" and in Melchert's article "Does the Church Really Want Religious Education? (1974)." Both of these pieces are examples of attempts to be loyal both to the canons of the academy and of the church. Religious educators may also experience a tension between the demands of church or synagogue and those of the public of society, for example, on such issues as prayer in school, religion in public schools, tuition credits for private schools, and the general role of religion in social, political, and cultural spheres.

The resolution of the tensions that religious educators feel in attempting to remain loyal both to their religious bodies and to their academies cannot be easily resolved by simply wearing different hats on different occasions. Such an approach does not do justice to the complex social reality of religious educators. In terms of Tracy's analysis (1981), religious educators are:

> Intellectuals related to three publics, socialized in all three, internalizing their sometimes divergent plausibility structures, in a symbiosis often so personal, complex, and sometimes unconscious that conflicts on particular issues must be taken singly or "retail," not globally or "wholesale." (p. 26)

The complexity of the relationship between religious educators and the public of the church is also manifested in the different understandings of churches and synagogues. These understandings range from purely theological models to purely sociological constructs. Some religious bodies emphasize institutional structures while others stress communal aspects. Religious bodies also have differing conceptions of their relationship to the broader society. How religious educators have assimilated these conceptions of the internal meaning of church or synagogue and their relationships to society are influential in their self-understanding as related to the public of the church.

In addressing the public of the academy the religious educator is sensitive to the disciplinary nature of religious education. With reference to the public of the church or synagogue, religious educators are more concerned with the religious tradition to be mediated. Most religious educators are far removed from the view of seeing themselves as solely messengers of their church theologies and of the theological disciplines. They recognize that the educational mission of religious bodies is part of the process of development and growth for religious and theological traditions.

THE PUBLIC OF SOCIETY

The third public to which religious educators are related is society. In general terms, society includes the socioeconomic realm, the realm of politics, and the realm of culture. Religious educators are socialized in all three of these realms. All persons have social selves, political views, and cultural interests. All religious educators as intellectuals in one way or another address societal concerns, though some religious educators relate to this public in a primary fashion. Of the three realms within society religious educators are most related to culture, since both religion and education are parts of the culture of society.

One of the greatest dangers that religion has faced is that of privatization. A strong tradition within religious bodies and in other groups in society has been against the active involvement of religion in the broader life of society. Religion is still considered by many to be a private matter. In the past few years, however, we have seen a strong reaction against this viewpoint within both conservative and liberal religious groups. As religions face the issues of increased involvement in such societal issues as world hunger, nuclear disarmament, social analysis, and racial and sexual equality, many religious educators have directed primary attention to the public of society.

The *socioeconomic realm* has at times been the primary focus for religious educators. George Coe's *A Social Theory of Religious Education* (1917), one of the classic works in the field, confronted the issues of capitalistic and socialistic systems from the perspective of religious education. Many other Protestant religious educators were so influenced by his direction that a distinctive Social-Cultural Approach to religious education has been identified (Burgess, 1975). Moran has often included in his work social criticism and related this to religious education (1970; 1974). Those religious educators who are concerned with education as action-reflection or social praxis show great concern for the socioeconomic arrangements in society. The work of Suzanne Toton (1982) in establishing the responsibility of the religious educator toward world hunger is representative of contemporary work in this area. Probings of ideology, social class, the world of work and technology, and examinations of social and economic systems are increasingly found among some religious educators. In Part III I will review some of the attempts of religious educators to deal with the issues of both economic and political ideology in society.

The realm of *politics* is closely related to the socioeconomic realm. Under the influence of liberation and political theologies a number of religious educators have focused on the political potential of religious education. Religious education for political liberation has been the focus for the British religious educator Brian Wren (1977) and for William Kennedy (1979). These and many other educators have been influenced by the conscientization approach of Paulo Freire (1970; 1970a, 1973a). The political nature of religious education has been emphasized in the writings of Moran (1974) and Groome (1980).

The *realm of culture* appears to be the primary focus for a number of religious educators in their efforts to relate to the public of society. Culture in this context includes education and the arts. Many religious educators are deeply interested in religion as it relates to all aspects of culture: schools, mass media, family life, work, and leisure. The aesthetic dimension of religious education has been examined in depth by a number of perceptive religious educators (Durka and Smith, 1979).

Religious educators are related to the public of society when their work focuses on particular social, political, cultural, or social movements and the religious dimensions of these. The major focus of these religious educators is on praxis, understood as:

> Practice informed by and informing, often transforming, all prior theory, in relationship to the legitimate and self-involving concerns of a particular cultural, political, social, or pastoral need bearing genuine religious import (Tracy, 1981, p. 57).

Religious educators who are principally related to the public of society often are committed to and involved in a social, political, or cultural movement which is the focus of their professional life. Religious educators who make such issues as racial justice, nuclear disarmament, feminism, improved group relationships, ecological awareness, and other movements a major focus of their work are usually involved in practical ways in these public movements.

CONCLUSIONS

The purpose of this analysis of the profession of religious education is not to classify religious educators into rigidly defined groups. I recognize that all religious educators have as reference groups all three publics of academy, church or synagogue, and society. What is important to emphasize is the effects that these reference groups have on the stances and writings of religious educators. It is not my view that these contexts determine the stance of religious educators but that they help to shape the horizons of thought. Religious educators might do a self-analysis of their own reference groups in order to determine how these have helped to shape their approaches to religious education. My own approach to religious education changed considerably after I moved from a state college department of education with little connection with theological and religious studies to a school of religion and religious education with a strong theological and interdisciplinary thrust.

From this analysis, it is clear that each public of academy, church or synagogue, and society has a complexity of its own. There are many kinds of institutions within the academy, many theologies and politics of church and synagogue, and different realms within society. Though one can expect a certain amount of consistency among religious educators related to similar publics, inconsistencies are also present. Conservative seminaries often house liberal educators. Radical and reformist social thought is at times found among theological conservatives. These inconsistencies guard us against accepting totally any classification of persons in a profession. Often, however, it is the inconsistencies that make clear what is usually the case.

It is important to recognize that religious educators are primarily related to one or two publics and that this relationship may to a large extent influence approaches to religious education. It appears that the primary reference group for most religious educators is the public of the church or synagogue just as the religious is widely viewed as the domain of churches and synagogues. The task for such religious educators is to bring to their work the values that are more often associated with the publics of academy and society: the spirit of free and critical inquiry and a commitment to broader social, political, and cultural values. In the same manner religious educators committed primarily to the academy might broaden their perspectives to examine the actual practice of religious education in religious bodies and other institutions. Religious educators primarily committed to the public of society need the disturbing values of prophetic religion and the spirit of free inquiry and tolerance, lest they develop uncritical commitments to particular causes, movements, or programs.

The final conclusion of this analysis is related to Tracy's contention that the three publics of academy, church, and society are part of the legitimation for three distinct theological disciplines: fundamental theology, systematic theology, and practical theology. Might we not identify in the field of religious education three similar sub-disciplines which are related to the efforts of religious educators to address the three publics of academy, church or synagogue, and society?

Foundations of Religious Education comprises attempts to establish the discipline of religious education within the context of the public of the academy. It utilizes the methods of such academic disciplines as philosophy, history, theology, psychology, sociology, and anthropology to establish the basic principles that are common to all particular forms of religious education. Such a sub-discipline deals with such basic issues as appropriate language, analyses of basic theoretical approaches, histories of religious education, relationships between religious education and particular theologies or religious traditions, and issues pertaining to the demands of those who committed themselves to the professional pursuit of religious education. Important works in this area include those by Moran (1970; 1981; 1983), Burgess (1975), Knox (1976), Barker (1981), and Schmidt (1983). Many of the publications of Religious Education Press are works in this sub-discipline of religious education. Most of the papers given at the annual meeting of APRRE and subsequently published in issues of *Religious Education,* deal with these issues.

Confessional or Systematic Religious Education is a second sub-discipline within the field of religious education. This form of scholarship is addressed to the public of the church or synagogue and is directed primarily at presenting an organized approach to religious education that is faithful to a particular religious tradition. Utilizing Tracy's fruitful analysis of systematic or confessional thought as embodied in classic expressions or interpretations of a tradition, one can point to certain classic or near-classic expressions of religious education in the Christian tradition. All of these works have explicit connections with particular Christian theologies. Examples of such works include Horace Bushnell's *Christian Nurture,* George Coe's *A Social Theory of Religious Education,* Harrison Elliot's *Can Religious Education Be Christian?,* Randolph Miller's *The Clue to Religious Education,* Joseph Jungmann's *Handing on the Faith,* C. Ellis Nelson's *Where Faith Begins,* Shelton Smith's *Faith and Nurture,* and Gabriel Moran's *Catechesis of Revelation.* In each of these works there is an expression of religious education in a particular faith and theological tradition. The profession of religious education needs to keep such classics in print, just as educational classics are kept alive by Teachers College Press. Much is to be learned from these works and the theologies which they embody.

Confessional religious education is also found in a number of recent influential works. These include Groome's *Christian Religious Education,* Richards's *A Theology of Religious Education,* Moore's *Education for Change and Commitment.* In the next study I will devote attention to a study of some Christian classics in religious education.

Practical Religious Education is the latest sub-discipline to be developed. This form of religious education takes its starting point from a particular social, political, or cultural movement, cause, or problem. These forms of religious education are based primarily on personal involvement and/or commitment. Through these forms of religious education a broad spectrum of social, political, and cultural issues is addressed, and educators attempt to bridge the gap between theory and practice.

The best example of a work in this area is Toton's work on Christian education and world hunger (1982). Ground-breaking work is found in the collected writings on *Education for Peace and Justice* (O'Hare, 1983) and in special issues of the journal *Religious Education:* "Unheard Voices and Justice" (1979, 74:5) and "Education and Justice" (1983, 78:4).

It is my hope that this analysis of the relationship of religious educators to various publics may be useful in understanding some of the differences among religious educators of both past and present. This analysis, of course, is limited since it attempts to probe a field from one particular vantage point, that of publicness. Publicness does not account for all differences. Yet it does, I believe, offer both a distinct and a fruitful focus.

CHAPTER 3

THEOLOGICAL TRADITIONS OF CHRISTIAN EDUCATION

INTRODUCTION:
BACKGROUND AND INTENTION

For the past four decades a major debate has taken place in the field of religious education concerning the relationship between theology and religious education. In the earlier years of this debate the participants were mainly Protestant religious educators. In the past two decades Roman Catholics have joined the debate. At the heart of this debate is an unresolved, and perhaps nonresolvable, problem, about the nature of theology, the divisions of theology, and the relationship of theology to related academic disciplines.

A recently published volume (Thompson, 1982) has included a number of different views on this issue. This collection shows that the debate first took place among Protestant religious educators who chose either liberal theology or neo-orthodox theology as the theoretical foundation for religious education. Those who espoused liberal theology usually used the term *religious education* to designate the discipline, while those who were influenced by neo-orthodox theology preferred the term *Christian Education*.

Roman Catholics entered the debate in the 1960s over the role of kerygmatic or proclamation theology as a basis for religious education. Roman Catholic theorists have divided into basically two groups: those who view religious education as a branch of practical or pastoral theology and those who attempt to situate religious education as a separate interdisciplinary field. While the former group usually uses the language of *catechetics* and *catechesis,* the latter speaks of *religious education* and, less frequently, of *religious instruction.*

In the preceding study of this collection, I have attempted to address some of the issues in this debate by taking a somewhat different approach to the controversy. This attempt has led to a definition of the field of religious education in terms of three separate but related subdisciplines.

These disciplines are based on the three publics addressed by religious educators and the three different modes of discourse used in addressing them. *Foundations of Religious Education* addresses the public of the academy in an attempt to establish religious education as a separate academic discipline which draws on a number of other disciplines, including theology. *Systematic or Confessional Religious Education* addresses the public of the church and is a presentation of a particular faith tradition according to an organized theological system. If other disciplines are used, these are subordinated to the theology of the church. *Practical Religious Education* addresses the public of society in an attempt to deal with a broad spectrum of social, cultural, and political issues that religious bodies must face. Theology may or may not be a dominant discipline in this approach, but usually it is subordinated to one or more of the social sciences.

My *first intention* in this study is to examine the relationship that has existed between Christian theology and catechetics or education. These findings may apply to other theologies but my task here is narrowly restricted to Christian theology. To do this requires an historical investigation of the changing meaning of theology and the changing forms of theological education. It is clear that the separation of catechetics from theology is a modern development, for until this century it was considered a part of practical theology. This separation of education from theology has had both advantages and disadvantages for both disciplines. I conclude this first section by arguing for the maintenance of the connection between theology and religious education, especially for church and clergy education, provided a proper view of the theological is assumed.

My *second intention* in this study is to evaluate theories of religious education according to how they promote theological understanding. My contention is that in the history of religious education there have been a number of classic or near-classic works which embody a particular theological perspective. These works may be considered systematic or confessional Christian education. These classic formulations of Christian education have not received the attention of religious educators in recent years, mainly because of the need to establish the legitimacy of religious education as an academic discipline. Yet it is interesting that when religious educators are asked to name books in the field that influenced them greatly, they turn for their responses to theologically oriented classics.

PART ONE:
AN HISTORICAL SURVEY OF
THEOLOGY AND EDUCATION

In Part One I will present a brief historical summary of the relationship which has existed between theology and catechetics or education. At the end of Part One I will propose a theory of theological understanding which I will use in Part Two to examine, classify, and evaluate certain works in religious education. For both my historical survey and analysis I will draw on the works of Edward Farley (1981; 1983) and David Tracy (1975; 1981).

In its long history the word theology has been used in two major senses. Theology is a *saving knowledge* of God and it is a *science or discipline*. Recently, a third meaning has been proposed by liberation and political theologians, theology as *social praxis*. This third meaning is still rather controversial, and I will treat it when looking at contemporary developments.

If Christian history is divided into three main periods, we can trace the changes of meaning in theology over these periods. In the *early Christian centuries* the idea of theology as a saving knowledge of God and the things related to God was essential to the Christian community. This was a lived, preached, and experienced theology. However, in the monasteries of the early Church and the Middle Ages the term theology also referred to a science, i.e., a cognitive or scholarly enterprise using appropriate methods and bringing forth a body of teachings. In this view the theologian was involved in the orderly exposition and interpretation of the sacred texts.

Out of these two forms of Christian theology arose two forms of theological education. All Christians were theologians in the sense that they were to have a knowledge of God which would bring them salvation. Their education took place chiefly through participation in the worship of the community and catechetical activities related to it. In monasteries, however, monks were exposed to a more scholarly exposition of the sacred texts. Thus there was established in the early centuries of Christianity a distinction between the education of ordinary or lay Christians and the education of monks and clergy.

A second period of Christian history extends *from the Middle Ages to the development of the modern university*. At this time the differences between the two forms of theology, and consequently theological education, became even greater. The Augustinian and mystical tradition continued the view of theology as saving knowledge. It viewed theology as a cognitive disposition and orientation of the soul, a knowledge of God and what God reveals. In this view theology was something practical, not theoretical. It had the character of a saving *wisdom*. Though there was some dispute whether or not this knowledge was a divine gift or achievable by human efforts, it is clear that this wisdom was connected with insight into the Scriptures and aided by commentaries on the Scriptures. The difference between theology as knowledge in the first and second periods is that in the second period more attention was given to human study and teaching.

It was in the medieval universities that theology as a science flourished.

Theology became a distinct faculty in the university, along with medicine, law, and arts (including philosophy). Theology in the universities became a deliberate and methodical undertaking which resulted in accepted knowledge. This learning was gathered through the dialectic or rational reasoning. Theology became the domain of the great scholastics: Abelard, Thomas Aquinas, Duns Scotus.

The two types of theology in this period gave rise to two forms of education which are illustrated by the famous distinction between the *lectio* or commentary-exposition and the *disputatio* or rational inquiry, which uncovered what had previously been unknown. The *lectio* promoted theology as saving knowledge and was fostered by participation in the life of the church, involvement in sacramental life, the life of prayer, and meditation upon the Scriptures. It could be enlivened by reading commentaries or, more likely, by listening to a holy person interpret the Scriptures. These forms of education took place in monastic schools, schools under close church auspices, and to a lesser degree in ordinary Christian churches.

The second type of education in theology as an academic discipline took place in the universities, which were not under direct church control. This theology was conceived as a rational inquiry, which was to result in rational knowledge. Authorities were to be respected but also questioned. An attempt was made to reconcile faith with reason. The *disputatio* was the main educational tool. The responses of the master of theology to questions were eventually put into a logical order, the purpose of which was to display the rational order of faith. Thomas Aquinas's *Summa Theologica* is only the best known of the medieval summaries of theological knowledge. This scholastic method of education has been highly influential among church educators in the centuries since the Middle Ages. It has had a pride of place especially in Roman Catholicism.

In the third period of Christian history, *from the Enlightenment to the present time,* some radical changes took place in theology and theological education. Theology now no longer refers to a personal quality, nor to the saving knowledge of God, nor to divine wisdom. These meanings of theology have been subsumed in the idea of faith or described in such terms as spirituality or formation. Though some effort has been made in the Catholic tradition to maintain an ascetical or mystical theology within the theological disciplines, this has not generally been an accepted meaning of theology. Theology as knowledge has become the learning of the skills necessary for church leadership. When theology is taught in denominational colleges, even this dimension of theology has been abandoned because students there are not being prepared for this leadership.

Theology in the university from the Enlightenment on was divided into a group of specializations. This came about from two factors. First, theology needed to justify itself as a universal study suited for all persons. Second, theology needed to relate to the new disciplines that had emerged in the modern university, e.g., history, psychology, and the social sciences. These factors influenced seminaries at a later time than they did the universities.

Theology in both types of institutions began to refer to one of the many specializations taught to seminary students: biblical studies, dogmatic theology, symbolic theology, church history, homiletics, catechetics, etc. As mentioned above, in seminaries what has generally replaced theology as saving knowledge is either spiritual formation or practical know-how for ministerial work. In time the seminary curriculum, especially in Protestant-ism, developed the traditional four-part division: biblical studies, theology, church history, and practical theology. Practical theology in Protestant seminaries stressed homiletics and catechetics, while Catholic seminaries emphasized moral theology and canon law.

During the period of the Enlightenment the oneness of medieval theolo-gy gave way to many theological disciplines. Each discipline within the seminary curriculum attempted to establish itself in connection with a secular discipline: literary studies, historical studies, philosophy, educa-tion, and psychology. In time many of these disciplines lost their contact with theology as they established separate disciplinary identities. Biblical studies utilized the methods of literary criticism. Church history became a division of history and not of theology. This also happened in the area of practical theology which included homiletics, liturgy, and catechetics. Scholars in practical theology attempted to establish disciplines separate from theology. Thus in seminaries and universities specialists emerged who did not consider themselves theologians. *Theologian* was a term restricted to dogmatic or systematic theologians. The medieval unity of theology was thus destroyed.

One attempt to restore the unity of theology came from the Protestant theologian, Frederick Schleiermacher. He argued in opposition to the orthodox theologians who maintained the fourfold division of theology. His task was to justify the teaching of theology in a university, given the criticisms against theology by Enlightenment figures. Schleiermacher justified theology on two grounds. First, it provided clerical education, just as medicine and law provided education for doctors and lawyers. Second, it served to unify the concept of the essence of Christianity. Schleier-macher defined theology as the science of the Christian religion. This essence was determined by a philosophical theology, established through an historical theology, and related to the life of the church through practical theology. Practical theology assessed the activities, procedures, and operations of the church's ministry. Of these two justifications, only the clerical paradigm remained to unify theology in the centuries after Schleiermacher.

The pattern of the fourfold divisions of theology and the unity of theology through the clerical paradigm was adopted in Protestant and Catholic seminaries in the United States. Thus no substantial or material unity was found in the study of theology. This was true in a greater sense in graduate theological education. Thus the rationale for theological education became the mastering of the tasks that the future minister would have to perform. Theology had now moved from a study of divinity and a study of academic disciplines to a study of practical know-how. What emerged was the view of the minister not as theologian but as professional.

Theology and Education Since the Enlightenment

The narrowing of theology to an academic discipline and the breakup of the unity of theology has had repercussions in the area of theological education and catechetics. Theological education became appropriate only for clergy, and catechetics began to lose its connections with theology. Lay Christians thus learned religion while the clergy studied theology. Within the Christian community there developed two forms of Christian education, one for clergy and one for the laity. Clerical theology became more academic and removed from the life of the church. Religious education developed without a strong connection with theology and often became a learning of formulas, rules, and rituals. Religious education also became a matter of techniques for inculcating basics of faith in learners. The upshot of this was the view that lay persons were not to be theologically educated because theology referred to a course of studies for the education of the clergy.

This distinction between two forms of theology and theological education had powerful influences in the field of catechetics and religious education. Religious educators attempted to establish their discipline by aligning themselves with the efforts of educators to legitimize a separate field of education. (Similar alignments took place in other areas of practical theology: pastoral care with counseling, church leadership with organization and administration, moral theology with law.) Thus the religious education movement was born in the United States among Protestants during the first part of this century. This movement had only limited ties to the theologies of the churches, although it was loosely connected with liberal Protestant theology. In the religious education movement Protestant orthodoxy was found an unacceptable theology for informing the theory and practice of religious education.

The religious education movement, with its separation from the dominance of theology and its alliance with nontheological disciplines, has resulted in a number of advantages for education in the churches. Education began to be viewed not merely as the simple handing on of the doctrines of faith but as serious inquiry and study. Teacher education became professionalized, as was education in general. Attention was paid to a variety of methods in teaching religion. Religious education was made relevant both to personal growth and societal problems because of the utilization by religious educators of the psychological and social sciences. Greater attention was paid to the training of administrators for church education programs. It was also in the area of religious education that theology as wisdom and saving knowledge began to reside, as religious education also became concerned with formation and thus maintained some contact with ascetical, mystical, and spiritual theology.

Notwithstanding the many advantages that came from the religious education movement in Protestantism in the 1930s and 1940s, by the 1950s critics within the field of religious education began to question the separation of religious education from theological developments. The same criticisms were heard within the field of pastoral care and counseling. The critics recognized that the discipline of religious education had lost its connection with theology and was suffering as a result of this. It was a noteworthy event when Randolph Miller (1950), a prominent Protestant religious educator, proclaimed that theology was the clue to religious education. The theology that he proposed was the neo-orthodox theology recently developed in Europe and America.

Most of these developments in religious education did not affect Roman Catholicism until the 1960s with the development in Europe of the new theology and the kerygmatic movement in religious education. Some prominent Roman Catholic religious educators studied in Europe and brought these developments to the United States. In a short period of time Roman Catholic religious educators recapitulated developments in Protestantism over the past few decades. It would appear that in Roman Catholicism the religious education movement as known in Protestantism was unknown until the 1960s and 1970s. It was only in these decades that religious education became a matter for study as an academic discipline. This took place, interestingly, not in seminaries where such developments took place in Protestantism, but in Catholic colleges and universities. A number of Catholic theorists in these institutions have developed approaches to religious education which attempt to establish religious education as a discipline separate from theology. (Moran, 1978, Lee, 1978). Thus, criticisms that the movement has a rather loose connection with theology have appeared among Catholic theologians and religious educators.

To summarize, Part One of this study has traced the relationship between theology and education over the three periods of Christian history. It has shown the various meanings of theology over this period and how these understandings have influenced religious education. I have also attempted to indicate both the advantages and disadvantages of the separation of education from theology. The time is now ripe for an attempt to combine a critically formulated theology with sound educational theory. In Part Two I will describe in more detail recent attempts by religious educators to relate to particular Christian theologies.

PART II: THEOLOGICAL MODELS OF CHRISTIAN EDUCATION

In Part Two of this study it is my purpose to present a theory of theological understanding which draws on the work of contemporary theologians. I will then utilize this theory to examine a number of models of religious education.

A Theory of Theological Understanding

Efforts to establish religious education as a discipline with minimal connections with theology do not do justice to the needs of religious communities which have an articulated theology. What needs to be recovered, however, is the unified sense of theology which includes various parts. It is my contention that many professional religious educators have tended more and more to address the public of the academy and less the public of the church. In addressing the public of the academy it is legitimate to use either theology or religious studies to establish the discipline of religious education. But in addressing the public of the church, religious educators should attend more to important theological resources. Religious education has multiple tasks. It needs those who can address and make religious education legitimate for the academy, the churches, and the wider public. Theological understanding is important for all members of a religious body. Thus theological education should take place at various levels: in local churches, in the training of church leadership, as well as in seminaries and institutions of higher education. Most of the criticisms leveled against theology, even by religious educators, are against a narrow view of theology that depends excessively on the force of authority. Theology need not be done in this manner. In the hands of many of its practitioners it is an insightful and thoughtful inquiry. If theology is removed from its clerical paradigm and from its authoritative bias, it can be a powerful force in all forms of religious education.

A helpful model of theological understanding is found in the work of Edward Farley (1981). He criticizes the older *sources-to-application* model: from Scriptures through history and theology to the practice of ministry, including education. Also rejected by Farley is the *praxis model* by which he means the use of field education and case studies as the starting point. He contends that in both of these theory and practice are divided. For him the structure of theology includes these elements: (1) knowledge of the mythos and tradition of the world of faith; (2) the ascertaining of its truth; and (3) the incorporation of both into the contemporary situation. Theological understanding takes place in a particular context and has a number of movements. The *context* or matrix of theological understanding is the individual's or group's total situation: biographical, social, historical, and cultural. To understand a theology one must know about the individuals who fashioned it and the context in which it was fashioned. North American theologians were influenced in the past by European theology, while today greater influences come from Third World theologians. In recent decades an indigenous North American theology has grown in power and influence. This theology should not cut itself off from other influences because such intercultural influences are important. The development of black theology, feminist theology, and native American theology in the United States has also made us aware of the importance of total context on theological understanding.

Theological understanding, following Farley's analysis, includes a number of *movements*. (1) The first movement attends to *the entire world of faith:* essence of Christianity, primary symbols, themes of proclamation, historical events, and dogmas of the tradition. (2) The second movement is an hermeneutics of suspicion about *the claims of the situation to absoluteness.* The situation is subjected to theological criticism in the form of ideology-critique or the uncovering of injustices of the present situation. (3) The third movement is *a criticism of the religious tradition* in order not to give it the status of an idol. It is to recognize that the tradition may foster oppression, false ideology, and the legitimation of privilege. (4) The fourth movement determines *the normativeness of the criticized tradition.* This is an attempt to determine the truth about God and the presence of God in the world today. This final movement attempts to determine "the place, legitimacy, beauty, redemptive possibilities, in short the theonomy of the situation (Farley, 1981, p. 169)."

Farley's analysis of theological understanding in terms of four movements needs to be supplemented by a fifth movement, perhaps implied in his fourth movement. The discovered truth about the criticized tradition needs to be translated into action, activities, life-styles, and spiritualities which address issues in the context in which the theology developed. There is needed a movement from understanding to deliberation, choice, and action to complete this theological method. This insight may be the critical contribution of the theologies of praxis.

Theological understanding is thus existential; it embodies personal wisdom and has a practice-oriented understanding. It is the attempt to deal with self, others, and the world in a religious context. Theology is the effort to interpret the presence of God in the world and to ascertain the call that God makes to individuals in their personal and social lives. In summary, then, theological understanding includes an appraisal of individuals in their relationships to the world and in relation to the sacred, a critical appraisal of the tradition, an appraisal of how religious existence in a faith-community affects choices and patterns of human life, and an appraisal of the connection between ecclesial life and life in the broader public.

Given this view of theological understanding, I now intend to examine a number of works in religious education to determine how they measure up to the criteria expressed in this understanding. What is needed is a critical theology to inform a critical religious education. It is my view that the description of theology presented by theologians such as Farley meet the objections of religious educators about the authoritarian nature of theology and theological imperialism. This does not mean that a theologically based religious education is the only one possible, but rather that for ecclesial communities it is the most suitable form of religious education.

Theological Models of Religious Education

A number of attempts have been made to analyze theological models or theories of religious education. One classification describes traditional theological, contemporary theological, social cultural or liberal theological (Burgess, 1975). Another theological classification has taken the notion of the supernatural as determinative in classifying theorists as transcendist, immanentist, and integrative (Knox, 1975). Other classification schemes have used nontheological or mixed categories of analysis (Elias, 1982; Barker, 1981; Scott, 1984).

For my instrument of analysis in this section I will use David Tracy's (1975) classification of theological models. In this classification scheme there are five models of theology: orthodox, liberal, neo-orthodox, radical, and revisionist. Theological models depend upon how theologians critically correlate the Christian fact with human experience. The five movements of Farley appear congruent with the concept of revisionist theology as proposed by Tracy.

Theological models of religious education attempt to deal with two major realities: (1) a theological world view which includes a view of the religious tradition and a view of contemporary human existence. This reality includes the context of theological understanding and the five theological movements described above; (2) a view of how this tradition is made accessible to or critically appropriated by individuals in the religious community. In the second reality are contained certain implications for determining the aims of religious education and the nature of the teaching-learning process, as well as some implications for the role of the teacher and learner within the model.

Contemporary Models of Christian Education

Orthodox Model

The orthodox model of Christian education allies itself with a theological orthodoxy. Orthodox theologies are based on specific biblical or church traditions. Orthodox theologians look only to the tradition or one part of the tradition in developing their theologies. Examples of orthodox theologies include biblical theologies, patristic theologies, and scholastic theologies. Theology in this model is viewed as an ordered understanding of beliefs within a theological system. Criticism of the tradition is not an acceptable activity for theologians.

In orthodox theologies secular knowledge is not considered as having any internal theological meaning. Secular learning, such as philosophy, psychology, and social sciences, may provide analogies for understanding theological teachings. Human sciences may also provide a system by which theological teachings are to be understood. Another task for secular learning may be assistance in providing a defense of theological truths.

Christian education based on an orthodox theological model is committed to a particular vision of Christian theology. This type of education characterized Roman Catholic religious education before Vatican II with its dependence on Thomism or Neo-Thomism. The kerygmatic movement in Roman Catholic religious education appears, at least in its earlier stages, to have been the replacement of an ecclesiastical orthodoxy with a biblical orthodoxy (Boys, 1980). In Protestantism the break from orthodox theologies began with the beginnings of the religious education movement in the 1920s and the acceptance of many tenets of liberal theology.

An example of an orthodox model of religious education is found in evangelical theories of religious education. K. Gangel (1978, p. 103) has suggested six principles of this education: (1) a commitment to the authority of the Bible; (2) a recognition of the contemporaneity of the Bible and the Holy Spirit; (3) a clear understanding of the nature, source, discovery and dissemination of truth; (4) use of the integrative process in designing a curriculum, based on the centrality of special revelation; (5) a demand for the development of a Christian world and life view; (6) bibliocentric education, which extends to all areas of student life. In this view of religious education teachers do not have to be guided by the research of Piaget, Kohlberg, and Goldman, since the landmark truths of Scripture are revelations of reality and open to persons of all ages. Proponents also argue that educators should not rely on educational philosophy since the Scriptures present all the educational philosophy that needs to be known.

It is clear that in this orthodox model of theological education contemporary understandings of human experience and educational theory have little to offer the religious educator. The dominant religious truths and the dominant educational emphasis come from an understanding of the Scriptures. This theory is committed to a particular understanding of Christian faith and does not make extensive use of scholarly disciplines other than theology. It also takes a rather narrow view of the nature of theology and the task of religious education. The contemporary situation is not appraised in this view. The biblical tradition is absolutized and not criticized. The function of theology as praxis is not adequately considered. According to principles presented above on theological understanding, this approach does not represent true theological understanding nor education.

Liberal Model

Liberal and modernist theologies have arisen in this century in opposition to orthodox theologies. The liberal spirit in theology is deeply committed to modern thought, and especially to modern science. Theological liberals have attempted to reformulate Christian theology in the light of commitments to secular thought. The liberal spirit is more centered on human persons, views God in continuity with creation, emphasizes the ethical and social demands of Jesus' call and mission, sees the church as one of many institutions for doing good, and considers revelation and Scripture as important but not exclusive ways of arriving at truth.

Theological liberalism was dominant in the origins of the religious education movement in Protestantism. The pioneers in this movement, George Coe, Sylvia Fahs, and Harrison Elliot, were greatly influenced by the progressive educational theory of John Dewey. (It is interesting to recall that Dewey addressed the first meeting of the Religious Education Association.) The classic educational work in this tradition remains George Coe's *A Social Theory of Religious Education* (1917). Coe subordinated the traditional goal of individual salvation to the broader aim of social reconstruction (establishing the democracy of God) and recommended social interaction as the dominant method of religious education. The task of teachers and students is the re-creation of Christianity, not its transmission. The Bible and traditional theology are viewed in this model as a powerful body of social literature which is only one means of promoting and reawakening divine life.

The liberal spirit in theology and religious education did not appear in Roman Catholicism until after the Second Vatican Council. This spirit is dominant in a number of works of Gabriel Moran (1970; 1972; 1974). His educational theorizing in these works comes from a broad view of revelation and an attempt to soften the exclusivity of the claims of Christian theology. Out of this theological stance he developed an approach to education which stressed individual and personal experience, lifelong learning, and education for societal change. A major difference between the older liberals and the neo-liberals is less optimism in the latter about the direction of society and less confidence in the power of the schools to bring about societal reconstruction.

The judgment on liberal theologies is that they are strong on their analysis of the cultural context in which theology and education take place. They are also very receptive to the inclusion of secular thought in the development of theological understanding and education. These theologies, however, are rightly criticized for their lack of attention to, or, at least, selective attention to the religious tradition. Their reconstruction of the religious tradition appears to have left out certain elements which do not correspond to their world view. In Farley's terms they have not criticized the absoluteness of the situation. My judgment on this model is that while it may form the basis for a general theory of religious education in society, it is not an adequate theology for religious education within ecclesial communities.

Neo-Orthodox Model of Christian Education

Neo-orthodox theology began as an effort to combine the liberal spirit in theology with an orthodox tradition. The great Protestant theologians

Barth, Bultmann, and Tillich developed a dialectical theology or theology of crisis which attempted to address the issues in Europe between the wars. This theology, through an appeal to biblical revelation, emphasized the transcendence of God, awareness of human sin, and the need for justification by grace through faith. Neo-orthodox theologians recognized the tragic in human existence. At the same time the neo-orthodox theologians accepted certain elements of the liberal spirit: the commitment to scientific and historical methods and the acceptance of a degree of relativism in thinking.

Although neo-orthodoxy is fundamentally a Protestant movement, it is possible to assimilate a number of Catholic thinkers within this mode of theologizing. Tracy (1975) places here the transcendental Thomism of Rahner and Lonergan as well as the systematic theologies of Maurice Blondel, Edward Schillebeeckx, and Gustavo Guttierez. The situation is somewhat different in the two traditions. In Protestantism, neo-orthodoxy was an attempt to combine two spirits, the orthodox and the liberal. Within Roman Catholicism the liberal movement did not have a great influence since it ran into papal condemnation in the form of Catholic modernism. The Catholic neo-orthodox theologians attempted more to counter an older orthodoxy. In a sense they were involved in the liberal enterprise a number of years after this became seriously questioned in Protestantism.

Neo-orthodoxy had its repercussions in the field of religious education. H. Shelton Smith (1941) used this theological approach to offer a critique of the theological liberalism of progressive religious education. He argued that religious educators' dependence upon psychology and social sciences had led them to lose consciousness of the sinful human predicament. He asserted a theocentric side of sin. He reasserted that the kingdom of God was fundamentally a divine or other-worldly reality. Against the social consciousness of liberal religious education, he asserted the meaning of individual selfhood. He urged educators to become more involved in church activities than in educational activities. In this educational model the Bible is to be brought back to the center of education. While philosophy, educational theory, and psychology are considered important, it is clear that they are in a subordinate position to theology.

In the 1950s and 1960s this model of Christian education dominated among Protestant religious educators. For educators such as Randolph Miller, Campbell Wyckoff, James Smart, David Miller, Wayne Rood, C. E. Nelson, and Reuel Howe neo-orthodox theology is the clue, the gospel is the foundation, the church is the context, relationships are the media, and psychology is a description of human growth (Burgess, 1975).

The force of the neo-orthodox model of Christian education did not appear among Roman Catholics until after the Second Vatican Council.

Again it was European theology that became a dominating force. In European catechetical centers educators began to rethink catechetics along the lines of the recent theological developments. Earlier proponents of the new catechetics such as Joseph Jungmann and Johannes Hofinger can only doubtfully be classified as neo-orthodox because of their lack of commitment to liberal values in their educational theories. But the catechetical writings of Alfonso Nebreda, Marcel Van Caster, Joseph Colomb, and Joseph Goldbrunner appear to be closer to the neo-orthodox model.

In the United States a neo-orthodox model of religious education was found in the pioneering work of Gerard Sloyan and in Moran's earliest writings (1966; 1967). Among contemporary Christian educators the work of John Westerhoff and Berard Marthaler can be classified within this category.

The hallmark of the neo-orthodox Christian educator is the attempt to maintain both the orthodox and the liberal spirit. The weakness of neo-orthodox theology has been its failure to allow a more serious re-evaluation or reconstruction of the theological tradition and its symbols. The educational theory is not sufficiently critical of the tradition and does not allow for the full significance of secular thought. The context for theological education has been too narrowly focused on the church community. The very terms to describe education used by the chief theorists—nurture, socialization, and enculturation—do not lend themselves to a theological or educational endeavor that will question the biases found within the religious tradition.

Radical Model of Christian Education

In the 1960s a group of theologians, known as "the death of God theologians" developed a radical model of theology. The consciousness of these theologians is more contemporary than modern in that it attempts to situate theology in a culture which has grown increasingly secular. The major theological thrust of the radical theologians was to negate the central belief of the Christian tradition in God. In a positive manner they affirmed Jesus as the paradigm of a life lived for others and as the decisive incarnation of a liberated humanity. It was the contention of this theology that the traditional doctrine of God alienated persons from one another, from the world, and from their authentic selves. What this theology raised is the critical question of how God has been understood and how the symbol of God has influenced Christians. This position of radical religious atheism is found in the work of the British theologian, Don Cupitt (1980). Cupitt argues against an objective and metaphysical God and in favor of a faith which is understood as expressing an autonomous decision to pursue the religious ideal for its own sake.

Though radical theology is a phenomenon in North America its influence is found in a number of European books. Hubert Halbfas's *Theory of Catechetics* (1971) caused controversy among theologians for its radical criticism of Catholic religious education. Halbfas utilized the criticisms of religion developed by Bonhoeffer to reject the Barthian neo-orthodoxy which he saw as pervasive in religious education. His attempt was to develop a religious education which was authentic in a world of increasing secularization. In a skillful use of language, depending on the hermeneutic theory of Gadamer, he proposed a view of religious education as critical interpretation of a tradition. Halbfas did not want teachers to begin with the assumption that the Bible is the word of God. His criticisms were directed against an easy use of the concept of God and a religious education which depended on an external and infallible revelation. He favored religious education over the catechesis presented in church communities.

Halbfas did not go as far as radical theologians in their rejection of the Christian symbol of God. He did assert, however, that we cannot speak of God in the same way we speak of other realities. He contends that we:

> Can never speak of God, revelation, world, and man separately or objectively since the revelation of God is *eo ipso* the revelation of the world and man; or expressed differently, man in his existence in the world is *eo ipso* man called by God. (1971, p. 25)

Halbfas also contended that talk about God may often be unnecessary in religious education and even harmful since it awakens the suspicion that God is at a great distance from us. For him the content of religious education is God, as expressed by the life revealing language of one's fellow human beings.

The influence of radical theology is also found in a number of British religious educators, notably Ninian Smart's *Secular Education and the Logic of Religion* (1968) and J. W. D. Smith's *Religious Education in a Secular Setting* (1969). Both of these theorists write in the context of religious education in state schools and not in the context of church-based education. Both argue for a religious education in which Christianity is taught not as a self-enclosed self-authenticating system of truth but by discussion and argument, and without prejudice to the final judgment on its truth. Smith deals extensively with the problems of religious language that have been discussed by philosophers for a number of decades. Both of these theorists are sensitive to the problems of teaching religion in schools situated in an increasingly pluralist society. It is not clear how what they propose would affect religious education in a church context.

It would appear that religious educators do not quite approach the radical model of theology which has been presented in recent decades. Yet the cited works are examples of critical theological understanding applied to problems of education. The main question to be raised against radical theologians is whether or not their reconstruction of the fundamental Christian doctrine of God is faithful to the Christian tradition. One thing is clear, however. This mode of theological understanding and educational efforts allied to it have set the stage for new models of theology and religious education that are in the process of development in our time.

Critical Model of Christian Education

A critical or revisionist model of theology has been presented by both Tracy (1981) and Farley (1981). This model is critical in that it includes a contemporary and revisionist notion of the beliefs, values, and faith of an authentic secularity and a revisionist understanding of the beliefs, values, and faith of an authentic Christianity. Of the two approaches to theological understanding by Tracy and Farley, it would appear that Farley's is superior since it includes involvement in the world, at least implicitly, in the basic theological movements. Though Tracy is moving towards a more practical theology, his description of revisionist theology does not have praxis clearly built into it.

When it comes to critical models of religious education, we face a problem. Most works in religious education are written with a view to the religious education of children and youth. Because children are being catechized and socialized into the faith, religious educators do not usually build into their theory of religious education the critical movements that are necessary for true theological understanding. What religious education might do, I believe, is to build a theory of religious education that focuses upon adults, who are deemed capable of full theological understanding.

The work that has the greatest promise of promoting this theological understanding is that of Gabriel Moran (1970; 1972; 1974) since he has long been a major theoretician for adult religious education. Though Moran's work has a critical thrust, he does not now situate it within a particular theological context. Even though some of his criticisms of theology are well founded, these criticisms do not pertain to all types of theology, certainly not the theological methods of Farley and Tracy. A critical approach to Christian education needs to be in more serious dialogue with theologies developed within Christian communities.

The most widely known attempt to develop a critical and theologically oriented religious education has been offered by Thomas Groome (1980). Groome calls for a dialectical relationship between theology and religious education in which there is a mutuality of learning and understanding between theologians and religious education. He comes close to calling religious education a theological activity when he refers to its participants as "doing theology." Groome has some harsh things to say about theology specialists, even though he has made extensive use of their work.

The shared praxis approach to religious education fosters the theological understanding proposed by Farley as the goal of theological education. One weakness in both treatments is an inadequate treatment of praxis as political activity. Praxis does not appear to be well integrated into Farley's concept of *theologia*. In Groome's usage, praxis becomes considerably privatized in the course of his work. For him the *political* is used in a narrow sense to refer to reshaping linguistic patterns and has little to do with the realities of ideologies, power, and concrete issues. His theory contains the framework for a more sophisticated understanding of the contemporary situation and what might be Christian action in it. Yet the theory remains formalistic and abstract in this area.

Groome's five-movement method is revisionist in that it promotes a critical look at both the religious tradition and the individual's interpretation of the meaning of one's life and activity. What needs to be stressed, however, is that neither the religious tradition nor the interpretations of the situation can be absolutized. True theological understanding must also attend to the interconnection among the various spheres of individual existence: personal, interpersonal, and political. People also have to come to some understanding of the normativeness of the tradition for their lives at personal, interpersonal, and political levels.

Conclusion

The purpose of this study has been to examine the relationship between theology and religious education. It has examined the nature of theology and the various meanings theology has had in the three periods of Christian history. I have also looked at a number of classic theological theories of education. The study has attempted to arrive at a notion of theological understanding drawing on recent work by Tracy and Farley. An examination of a number of theological models of religious education was undertaken in light of this notion of theological understanding and revisionist or critical theology.

This study has raised for the author more problems than it has solved. I have not been completely persuaded that there needs to be a unified concept of theology, since I recognize that the division of theology into distinct disciplines has had some beneficial as well as some harmful consequences. I see the point of both views: religious education as theological understanding and religious education as a discipline outside of theology. I recognize that theology must be spiritual wisdom, academic knowledge, and social praxis, but I do not see clearly how it can be this in all contexts. I would hope for one theology and theological education which would accomplish all of this, but I recognize that different contexts call for different goals and objectives. I have become aware that neither theologians nor religious educators have adequately integrated the element of praxis into their concept of theological or religious understanding. I recognize the values contained in all of the models of Christian education.

Notwithstanding these uncertainties, I conclude with the conviction that there is need for theologically oriented Christian instruction in the area of religious education. I am also confident that today a theology is developing that may form the basis for the type of theological education needed in Christian communities.

CHAPTER 4

THE ROLE OF CULTURE IN MORAL EDUCATION

At a symposium on moral education in the 1970s L. Kohlberg made the assertion that only two academic disciplines are able to make scholarly generalizations about moral education: moral philosophy and developmental psychology. He contended that disciplines like theology or religion are not relevant in themselves since they must be ultimately justified on philosophical grounds if their generalizations are to be accepted by nontheologians. He further added that the generalizations that come from the social sciences must also be justified on a philosophical basis, and thus they are not in themselves relevant for moral education (Kohlberg, 1971).

This reduction of the influence of theology, religion, and social sciences in education to the prior question of their philosophical validations, and the concentration solely on the two disciplines of philosophy and psychology, presents an incomplete approach to moral education and makes it difficult to develop an approach to moral education based on religious principles and culture. The purpose of this study is to explore some of the contributions that the neglected disciplines of religion, theology, social sciences, and humanities might make to both the theory and practice of moral education.

LIMITATIONS OF ANALYTIC PHILOSOPHY AND DEVELOPMENTAL PSYCHOLOGY

It is well known that the most recent theory and research in moral education has come from analytic philosophers and developmental psychologists. Philosophical analysts such as J. Wilson (1967) and R. S. Peters (1966) have considerably improved our understanding of the logic of concepts and justifications that are used in discourse on moral education. The work of cognitive development psychologists such as J. Piaget (1922; 1965) and L. Kohlberg (1981) and his associates have presented a fruitful theory for exploring developmental stages of moral reasoning. Yet many who have been informed by these two disciplines have begun to realize the inadequacy of this two-discipline approach. Now that many have begun to recognize the deficiencies and limitations of these approaches, educators, including religious educators, should begin to look to some neglected sources to provide a more adequate understanding of moral development and education.

While philosophy gives criteria for the justification of the moral, and developmental psychology presents theories and research on growth in moral reasoning, our fundamental understanding of how people acquire moral values, attitudes, and behaviors actually comes from social scientists and other scholars who examine the influence of environment, symbols, institutions, myths and ritual, imagination, and mass media. To assert the power of these elements of culture on moral development is not to deny the importance of philosophical and developmental considerations but rather to include other factors which must be considered. Especially in the case of a religiously based moral education, these other dimensions must be taken into account because it is in the sociocultural dimensions that the force of religion in moral education is best assessed. This study presents some considerations for a religiously based moral education drawn from sources outside philosophy and developmental psychology. From these sources it is clear that importance must be given to the transmission and internalization of symbols and participation in religious rituals and activities. This view of moral education goes beyond the rational approach, though not excluding it, to focus on those elements of religious culture which are formative of moral attitudes, values, and behaviors.

INCOMPLETENESS OF COGNITIVE MORAL EDUCATION

It is unfortunate that in recent years some religious educators have accepted too readily the psychological research that contends that religion makes little difference in moral values and behavior. This finding is largely based on studies done by Hartshorne and May in the 1920s on lying and cheating (Hartshorne and May, 1929). Religion in these classic studies was defined not in terms of religious belief or upbringing but rather as current involvement in religious groups. The findings on the relationship between religion and morality have been examined by the psychologist D. Wright (1971), who concluded that little has been definitively established on this topic since the few studies reported allow many possible interpretations. The evidence does show that religious belief and practice influence behavior in the direction of social conformity rather than in the direction of personal moral growth. Yet what is not clearly analyzed in the research is whether or not what is defined as social conformity might be better described as social consciousness, and what is defined as personal moral growth might be better described as an individualistic ethic that lacks a social orientation.

The attention given to cognitive theories of moral education at the expense of other theory and research has prevented some religious educators from exploring the distinctiveness of a religiously oriented moral education that takes into account both philosophical analysis and developmental theory, but places these within a broader context. The focus of inquiry in philosophical analysis and developmental theory has been primarily the school. The public school is certainly better suited to deal with a primarily intellectual approach to moral education. A religiously oriented moral education should not, however, confine itself to cognitive approaches, since it must deal with other institutions and relationships in its approach to moral education. As will be pointed out later in this study, even public school educators have begun to question the almost total reliance on cognitively oriented moral education in the schools.

That cultural factors are of great importance in the development of moral values and behavior is clear from inquiries in many disciplines. Social philosophers such as E. Durkheim (1973 ed.) and J. Dewey (1922) have written classic works on the power of family and school environments to shape moral behaviors. Both of these scholars were sensitive to the problems of reconciling personal freedom with a strong emphasis on the power of cultural forces. Social learning theorists such as A. Bandura (1977) have shown the power of modeling, imitation, internalization, identification, and observational learning in the acquisition of moral values. Among sociologists, both theoretical scholars like P. Berger and T. Luckmann (1966) as well as T. Parsons (1967) and empirical scholars like A. Greeley (1976) have pointed out the importance of the social in the formation of moral and religious values. Foremost anthropologists such as M. Mead (1970), R. Benedict (1934), C. Kluckholn (1962), and C. Geertz (1973) have presented extensive theories and findings on the transmission of moral values in various cultures.

A recognition that there are serious limitations to a cognitively based moral education has also come from religious educators. In his examination of the origins of faith, C. E. Nelson (1967) drew on anthropological theory and research to show how both faith and values were transmitted in religious communities. J. Westerhoff and G. Neville (1972), in their exposition of a socialization or enculturation approach to religious education, have utilized anthropological research in analyzing the transmission of values. A more recent work by C. Dykstra (1981) presents a Christian alternative to Kohlberg and draws heavily on Christian traditions and spiritualities. Yet perhaps the most compelling statement calling for an approach to moral education on a deeper religious basis comes from two educators concerned with public school education. After having attempted to utilize the moral reasoning approach and having found it inadequate, D. Oliver and M. J. Banes (1971) reached the conclusion that moral education needs the power of communication that only ritualistic metaphor can provide. They urged that:

> Educators, philosophers, and psychologists should join with theologians and sensitive youth in a search for the kind of powerful metaphor with which our Christian heritage once provided us. We need somehow to create myths and celebrations by which we can project the common joys, sorrows, and compassion that we share by the fact that we are human. (ch. 9)

From many sources, then, it is clear that cognitively based approaches to moral education are insufficient, particularly for a religiously based moral education. To make the research in moral philosophy and developmental psychology relevant, this work must be seen in a broader sociocultural context, which utilizes ideas drawn from other philosophical schools, theology, social sciences, and humanities. An exploration of symbols and their function in human learning is one way of organizing the findings from these disciplines.

ELEMENTS IN A CULTURAL APPROACH TO MORAL EDUCATION

The approach to moral education rooted in cultural experience recognizes that our values, like our actions and emotions, are at least in part cultural products. Though they come from tendencies, capacities, and dispositions which are innate, they are nonetheless greatly influenced by cultural factors. To say that our moral values are cultural products is to state that they are meanings and viewpoints involved in a system of inherited conceptions which we express in symbolic forms. It is by these inherited and internalized symbols that we communicate, perpetuate, and develop our knowledge about, and our attitudes and behaviors towards, others and towards life.

From anthropological theory it has become clear that religion functions to provide individuals with values, attitudes, and behaviors. Religion provides us through story and ritual with powerful symbols which shape attitudes, values, and behaviors. Religion as a symbol system has been defined by C. Geertz (1973) as:

(1) a system of symbols which acts to (2) establish powerful, pervasive, and long-lasting moods and motivations in men by (3) formulating conceptions of a general order of existence and (4) clothing these conceptions with such an aura of facticity that (5) the moods seem uniquely realistic. (p. 90)

When this view of religion as a symbol or cultural system is applied to the relationship between religion and morality, it brings about a de-emphasis on the importance of purely logical considerations for determining values. Our values come out of direct experience with a symbol system, which includes a view of what is good and what is evil. This emphasis on culture should not replace the need for moral philosophy or psychology but rather provide an empirical basis which can make philosophy and psychology more relevant. Thus a religiously oriented moral education does not appeal exclusively to rational components of morality or developmental stages of reasoning. Religion educates to moral life more through the presentation of symbols or images (in the form of laws, stories, metaphors, analogies, etc.) of what it is to be human and religious in contemporary contexts of life.

The symbolic approach to moral education does not call for the automatic inculcation and internalization of religious symbols. The community lives out its symbols; symbols are presented in stories, rituals, laws, and life. Yet individuals must freely appropriate these religious symbols according to their developing capacities. This approach is similar to the approach espoused by the existentialist philosopher M. Friedman (1967). In his view one educates not by presenting moral principles or moral authorities but by presenting various images or symbols according to which persons might shape their lives. In an examination of modern literature and philosophy Friedman points out both unauthentic images (counterfeiter, wasteland) and authentic images. Authentic images include the social reformer, the vitalist, the mystic, the saint, the gnostic, the psychologically whole person, the pragmatist, and the person in dialogue with absurdity. These images present only some of the many projections that persons utilize in order to establish their moral stance in the world. In Friedman's view the greatest contribution that Plato gave to moral education was not his philosophical analysis of the just society and the virtues necessary for its existence but the moving description of his worthy master, Socrates, who was courageous in living the examined life.

A religiously based moral education is chiefly concerned with presenting symbols of what it means to be a religious person in contemporary society. In this view our moral response does not come from logical reasoning but from our deep-seated attitudes, the results of past situations, and our responsiveness to present situations. It is the image or symbol of the religious person which we wish to be or project that determines our behavior more than any moral principles which have been arrived at on rational grounds.

This cultural approach to moral education has been eloquently described by H. Bergson in his classic *The Two Sources of Morality and Religion* (1935). One source of morality is the sense of obligation which we feel as a result of our participation in society, while the other source is contact with a great moral personality or moral ideal. For Bergson:

> The moral personality takes shape as soon as we adopt a model, the longing to resemble which ideally generates the form, is an incipient resemblance; the word which we shall make our own is the word whose echo we have heard within ourselves. (1935, p. 5)

For Bergson the distinctiveness of a religious morality lies in the opportunity for religious or mystical experience which religions provide for their adherents. He conceded that religious morality was also an instrument for training persons and for providing a philosophical justification for the moral life. The unique potential of religious experience, however, is that through it persons develop the emotions and the power of love. Through such religious experiences persons are motivated to act for the good of others.

What Geertz, Friedman, and Bergson make us appreciate is the important distinction between how morality is analyzed and justified and how persons acquire moral attitudes and behaviors. A similar distinction can be made between faith and theology. Faith and values are acquired and fostered through deeply personal processes—intellectual, affective, and emotional. Moral philosophy and moral psychology take the form of intellectual elaborations, like theology, of values and faith. Although a highly developed rational component may be important for both faith and moral values, it is not the fundamental process by which these are acquired and fostered. The attempt to turn moral education into a purely intellectual enterprise is as fruitless as the attempt to make academic theologians of all believers. Lonergan's (1972, p. 289) discussion of the different levels of human consciousness is helpful here. Christian faith, of itself, does not demand a theoretically differentiated consciousness. A religious experience of the holy coupled with ordinary intellectual consciousness is adequate for both religious faith and moral education.

SYMBOLS AND MORAL EDUCATION

An approach to moral education through religious symbols must take into account both the richness and the ambiguity of religious symbols. S. Freud (1922) showed the importance of religious symbols for individual consciousness but maintained that religious symbols, especially that of God the Father, served to repress moral creativity. G. Hegel (1948 ed.) pointed out that religious symbols can be alienating when they are used to justify false consciousness. He contended, however, that religious symbols from the New Testament which emphasize the power of Jesus' love could motivate persons to authentic moral action. Both K. Marx (1964 ed.) and K. Mannheim (1936) treated religious symbols under the general category of ideology. Marx saw these symbols as fundamentally oppressive of human growth and societal development. Mannheim allowed for both ideological and utopian imagination. Within the latter category—utopian imagination—a more positive and creative view of religious symbols can be developed.

Two sociologists who apparently took different approaches to the study of religious symbols were E. Durkheim (1965 ed.), who emphasized the power of religious symbols in maintaining the social order and M. Weber (1964 ed.), who was more concerned with the potential of religious symbols, especially as embodied in a charismatic leader, to bring about changes in social, political, and economic life. P. Berger and T. Luckmann (1966) have attempted to unite the contrasting views of these sociologists of knowledge in their theory of the unity of objective and subjective elements in legitimating a symbolic universe.

From a theological point of view, G. Baum's (1975) analysis of the different forms of religious symbols is helpful in assessing the power of symbols in moral education. In their *first meaning* symbols are *external signs or images* directed at people's memories to enable them to recall events of their social and personal histories. The symbols used in liturgical rites, sacred objects and action, are examples of this form of symbol. Symbols of this type serve to call forth a subjective response. They are not, however, without their moral significance, for they may serve to call persons to moral action and attitudes in imitation of, or in remembrance of, former commitments. The ambiguity of these symbols lies in the ever-present danger of absolutizing religious symbols and thus using them in some magical or superstitious manner.

The *second meaning* of symbol is a *story or event* which reveals a deeper meaning for persons. Freud (1922) used the Greek myth of Oedipus to explain the workings of the unconscious and contended that this was the story of every person. C. Jung (1961) also explored universal stories which he called archtypes. In a real sense *the* Christian story is the story of Jesus, for this story illustrates for Christians the deeper meaning of their lives. Through contact with this symbolic story, Christians come into contact with God and not only come to know the meaning of human life but are also called to moral commitment. I. Ramsey's (1957) analysis of religious language in terms of discernment and commitment and Bultmann's (1958) interpretation of the gospel as the call to authentic existence are attempts to develop an understanding of the dimensions of the story of Jesus through which Christians are called to moral commitment and action. The ambiguity of this sense of symbol lies in the danger of using the story of Jesus in such a way as to imply that a mere application of the story will resolve all moral dilemmas.

In its *third meaning* symbols are *structures of the imagination* which determine the ways in which we see and respond to the world. In this sense symbols are, as P. Ricoeur (1967) notes, not that by which but that through which we see and act. The task of religious education is to make the great religious stories a part of the structures of the imagination. Through prayer, meditation, worship, study, and religious life, our imaginations become suffused with religious symbols, attitudes, and values. These become the means by which persons discern and respond to moral situations in their lives. This notion of symbol makes it clear that faith is not just a matter of understanding but also a matter of the imagination. Symbols as signs or images and symbols as stories become part of the structure of the imagination. Symbols in this sense are ambiguous in that they might become solidified to the degree that situations are not subject to change and development.

The *fourth meaning* of symbol comes more directly from sociological theory. Symbols are the *reflections of society in* the mind, the effects in the mind of the institutions and structures of society. Marx took the materialist view in which the existing social order appeared necessary because of its determining effects on the mind. Durkheim considered the symbols in the mind as authentic reflections of societal institutions rather than the inverted forms proposed by Marx. This fourth meaning of symbol brings out clearly that people receive symbols not only from the religious institutions in which they are involved but also from general cultural situations. The social order produces a number of symbol systems of which the religious is only one. This fact must be recognized in moral education, for often there will be conflicts between religious symbols and symbols which come from participation in other structures of society. Perhaps the most powerful symbols in our culture are those that come from the mass media. A religiously based moral education must be sensitive to conflicts that exist between religious symbols and the symbols that are powerfully presented in the mass media.

CONCLUSION

A moral education, in order to take advantage of the power of religious symbols, provides opportunities for religious experiences. Prayer and worship are the chief forms that this religious experience takes. It is religious experience that enables persons to come into contact with religious symbols. Experience in religious communities, reflection and study of religious stories and events, participation in rituals, study of the teachings, exposure to the religious heroes—these things develop the internal symbols which enable persons to respond to moral situations in an informed manner. Dealing with moral issues and problems with the power of these symbols in one's consciousness will lead to decisions which are religiously significant. A mystical identification with Jesus, a bond of solidarity with his religious community, contemplation of the teachings and tradition that came from him, the internalized example of many witnesses who have acted on his example—these are more powerful moral forces than casuistic forms of moral reasoning and logical analysis of moral education. This cultural form of moral education is not, I repeat, an alternative to moral philosophy or cognitive reasoning but rather the root of moral education, which might for some persons be supplemented by rational analysis.

It is not to be thought that this religiously based moral education provides individuals with all they need to do in order to resolve moral problems and dilemmas in their lives. What religious and moral symbols reveal are certain moral presumptions which can guide action and provide powerful motivation for action. Persons exposed to the same religious traditions can, and have, come to different moral decisions. What the religious symbols and tradition provide are, rather, presumptive attitudes for moral life. They are similar to the presumptive ethic that P. Wogaman (1976) has developed for Christian ethics. Religious symbols inculcate a number of *positive* moral presumptions about the goodness of created existence, the value of human life, the unity of the human family in God, and the equality of persons before God. They also emphasize certain *negative* moral presumptions about human finitude and human sinfulness. The ambiguity of all religious symbols underlines the tensions which exist in human life and which call for certain *polar* presumptions: between individual needs and societal needs, between freedom and responsibility, between subsidiarity and universality, between conservatism and innovation, and, finally, between optimism and pessimism. Some symbols relate to presumptions about the community of faith itself, the value of its traditions, and the opinions of its theological experts as well as the experts within civil authority.

The approach to a religious moral education sketched in this study is not presented as a new theory but rather as a description of how religion functions to influence moral commitment. Becoming aware of this process will enable educators to draw more on the richness of religious traditions in moral education. Marthaler (1980) has drawn on the Christian tradition in showing how religious education, including education in moral values, can be adequately described as the handing on of religious symbols. Our faith in the power of religious symbols in moral formation needs to be reasserted today in light of criticism and attempts to develop moral educational theory on a nonreligious basis. Criticisms of a religiously based moral education are often well founded, and the attempts to develop a nonreligious basis for moral education have not been completely unsuccessful. But even if a powerful theory of moral education on purely secular grounds were developed, this would be no reason to abandon a religiously oriented approach. An approach to religious moral education based on the handing on of religious symbols finds great support in scholarly theory and research. It is time for religious educators to explore this approach more seriously.

CHAPTER 5

RELIGIOUS EDUCATION IN A TELEVISION CULTURE

A telecommunications revolution is taking place in our culture. To the long accepted radio, phonograph, and television have been added Cable TV, Betamax, Home Video, Videodiscs, and home computers. This revolution is now moving rapidly into schools and homes. In our lives we have already experienced the influences of this revolution in communications. A closer look at the new media will only convince us that the changes are just at the beginning.

Educators have paid increasing attention to the media through past decades. The late 1950s and early 1960s witnessed a great enthusiasm for instructional television and computer-assisted instruction. Although this enthusiasm waned during the 1970s, there is evidence of a renewed interest in educational technology. While television has been proposed by some as a panacea for our educational ills, for others it provides the scapegoat for such educational problems as lower reading scores, increased violence and vandalism in the schools, and greater docility and passivity on the part of students.

Religious educators have given attention to the use of media in religious education. Babin (1970) presented a pointed analysis of the very use of media within religious education. Drawing on the National Catechetical Directory, Sullivan (1980) offered guidelines for developing a critical attitude towards the media in religious education. His examination concerned chiefly the moral values which television attempts to inculcate through its programming and commercials.

Though religious educators have grappled with some of the issues raised by the telecommunications revolution, the most challenging approach to the relationship between education and media is found in Neil Postman's provocative book, *Teaching as a Conservative Activity* (1979). In its own way this book is as radical as the author's previous and well-known work, *Teaching as a Subversive Activity* (1969). The scope of this study is to reflect on religious education in the light of the major arguments of Postman's most recent work.

A THERMOSTATIC THEORY OF EDUCATION

Postman argues that formal education in every culture should provide *the balance* to modes of learning that are dominant in the culture. It should emphasize the forms and contents of learning that a particular culture is in danger of ignoring. In this point of view, education should be conservative of tradition when the culture tends to be innovative; it should be innovative when the predominant thrust of the culture is conservative. Though formal education cannot be the balancing instrument for everything that society is in danger of ignoring, it must attempt to balance those biases that are within its competence and scope.

The information environment in which we live is greatly controlled by television and other forms of telecommunications. These media contain the modes and patterns of communication that control the kind of society in which we live. Most people get a large amount of their information about what is happening in the world and about what is valuable from these media. In light of this, the most important function of formal education in our culture is to provide a needed balance to the information biases of this medium. Postman goes so far as to say that the subject of formal education consists chiefly in "the analysis of different forms of communication, the interpretation of their psychological and social effects, and the development of school environments which supply a balance to such effects. (p. 46)"

The proper way for an educator to analyze television is to focus on it as a curriculum. Postman has utilized this helpful perspective. Postman calls television the First Curriculum in the life of learners. This medium, however, does not stand alone because its effects are constantly reinforced by other media of communication, including records, tapes, radio, photography, and film. In examining these media as educational curricula and not merely as entertainment, we can feel their powerful influence and uncover some of the biases that formal education should attempt to balance. Postman gives the following as the characteristics of the TV curriculum: attention-centered, nonpunitive, affect-centered, present-centered, image-centered, narration-centered, moralistic, nonanalytical, nonhierarchical, authoritarian, contemptuous of authority, continuous in time, isolating in space, discontinuous in content, and immediately and intrinsically satisfying (pp. 60–70). Given this analysis, educators must consider how these biases can be balanced through schooling and other forms of formal education in order to prevent an unchallenged education through mass media.

Postman's analysis uncovers a number of harmful effects of the TV curriculum. It produces persons who are strong on intuition but weak on reflection and analysis. It engenders a short attention span in viewers. Side-involvements during exposure are fostered. TV is inimical to conceptual, segmented, and linear modes of expression, such as speech and writing. The powerful imagery of this medium does not provide grounds for debate or ambiguity. Instancy of information is preferred over constancy. The message of TV commercials directs the search for time-compressed experience, short-term relationships, present-oriented accomplishments, and simple and immediate solutions. TV is biased against scientific and logical thinking, the engendering of a sense of history, the development of language skills, and the advancement of critical thought. Given this situation, it is the school which is the *alternative* curriculum with its subject-matter, word-centered, reason-centered, future-oriented, hierarchical, secular, segmented, and coherent curriculum.

Postman makes some interesting comparisons between the content and structure of TV and religious content and structures. TV uses the parable— a narrative with moral implications. It has something of the power of religious communications; it relies heavily on moral teaching resting on an emotional basis. Commercials are like parables, attempting to teach the means of solving human problems. Postman contends that "the masters of the media have quite simply pre-empted the functions of religious leaders in articulating the moral values by which we ought to live. (p. 98)" Perhaps this analysis helps us to understand the growth and the power of electronic or TV evangelism. God is certainly not dead on TV.

Telecommunications represents the triumph of technique over human purposes. All forms of communication involve a technique, a particular structure or medium. A technique triumphs when human activity is subordinated to the purposes of the technique. For example, testing in schools is a technique that often subordinates other purposes to its ends. It implies that what is valuable is what can be measured in a specific way. Computers, machines, and social institutions are in danger of subordinating human purposes to their own ends. Formal education is a potential force to combat the power of such techniques as TV and other machine forms of learning.

To ask formal education to combat the biases of TV is not to ask it to do anything more than to propose that it do its distinctive work well. Education should be centrally concerned with the topology of education, "its form, its speed, its magnitude, its direction, its accessibility, its continuity, and ultimately with the bias of mind that any information configuration would tend to promote (Postman, p. 113)." In Postman's view schooling should abandon efforts in a number of areas in order to do its distinctive task well. It should not be involved in sex education, teaching the whole child, motivating to learn, teaching ethnic pride, fostering prayer in school, and doing psychotherapy.

What formal education can offer to counter the biases of a fragmented TV education is to provide a sense of purpose, meaning, and interconnectedness in human learning. Postman sees evidence of this in some religious schools but also recognizes that a religious vision as such cannot permeate secular education. Yet formal education does need some transcendent and binding point of view. Postman finds such a vision in Bronowski's *Ascent of Man,* a book filled with optimism and permeated with the transcendent belief that humanity's destiny is the discovery of knowledge. Art and science, past and present, are to be joined in this quest. In studying this quest one is also involved with the religious systems which have developed to provide order and meaning to existence. Formal education includes becoming aware of the growth of knowledge and knowledge systems, as well as becoming familiar with intellectual and creative processes. It includes the study of history, the scientific mode of thinking and the disciplined use of language, and wide-ranging knowledge of arts and comparative religion. These are precisely the forms of knowledge that the TV curriculum ignores and which must be emphasized in formal education.

Postman makes a strong case for teaching religion in formal education. This education should deal with religion as an expression of humanity's creativeness as well as the total and integrated response to fundamental questions about the meaning of existence. He does not feel that we can adequately educate the young unless they study how "different people of different times and places have tried to achieve a sense of transcendence (p. 146)." This includes a study of the metaphors, literature, art, and rituals of religious expression. A study of such sacred texts as Genesis, the New Testament, the Koran, the Bhagavad-Gita, and the Communist Manifesto are suggested as the beginnings of a curriculum suited for these purposes.

Postman argues that within formal education a great emphasis should be given to language education because of its great value in combatting the biases of the TV curriculum. Paulo Freire and others have shown how language education involves the transformation of the personality and even of the culture. Words increase understanding and understanding increases words. Language education involves question-asking according to rules of discourse. Questions have assumptions, limitations, levels of abstraction, and sources of authority to which they appeal. Ability to understand and use metaphor and definition is an essential aspect of language education. These are to be viewed as helpful hypotheses in understanding or expressing a vision of reality. Language education includes attention to such issues as right and wrong, truth and falsehood, facts, inferences, assumption, judgments, and generalizations. To master any subject is to study the language of that subject. Language education, like all education, must take place in a particular social context. Gide has remarked that the only real education is that which goes counter to us. Education involves a hierarchy of values. Education needs to counter and criticize the values contained in the first curriculum of TV and other forms of telecommunications.

The first curriculum of TV is so powerful that it must be brought into formal education not as an aid but as an object of analysis and criticism. Students need to be shown how TV and similar media teach as they entertain. What must be examined in this medium, as in others, are the intellectual, emotional, political, sensory, social, and content biases. Media should not be used in a classroom, according to this analysis, unless the teacher intends to call attention to how the media affect the audience. Questions to be raised are: what attitudes are fostered? who determines what we see? where does the money come from? what political and economic interests are controlled by the media? what methods of persuasion are used in advertising.

It is interesting to learn that Postman, who was identified with the radical movement in education in the 1960s, has discovered new values in the traditional classroom of conventional schools. Although he recognized that schools are a nineteenth century invention, he has also come to the realization that schools are one of the few social organizations in which "sequence, community experience, social order, hierarchy, continuity, and differed pleasure are important (p. 202)." He interprets parents' desires for order and discipline in schools as legitimate ones. Classrooms also imply that there are important distinctions between adults and children and that adults have something to teach children. It even appears that the TV curriculum may bring an end to childhood with its undifferentiated curriculum, notwithstanding some attempts at children's programming.

A THERMOSTATIC VIEW OF RELIGIOUS EDUCATION

A thermostatic view of religious education would *redefine the enterprise* because of the existence and nature of the First Curriculum which is provided through the mass media. We must recognize that religious education in the informal settings of family, church, media, and general culture tends to emphasize present-centeredness, affect, images, and narration. Informal religious education tends to deemphasize reflection and analysis, while stressing the power of intuition and feeling. Furthermore, informal religious education does not usually provide the opportunity to debate ambiguous issues.

A thermostatic view of religious education would make us rethink *the role of the religious school and the religious classroom* as appropriate environment for countering the biases of informal religious and moral education. The values of informal religious education are to be recognized; but its peculiar biases and the potential of the school to remedy these biases also need serious consideration. I realize that these remarks go against much of the modern criticism of the school as a place for providing religious education and the call for more reliance on informal modes of education. But if we are to take up the challenge of Postman's thesis this is precisely what we must examine.

A number of years ago in a critique of Ivan Illich's utopian plans to deschool society I made the point that the school, with all its limitations and weaknesses, may be a necessary institution to prevent the educational indoctrination and manipulation of persons forced to receive education merely through the informal structures which Illich and other educational radicals proposed (Elias, 1976). I believe that the same criticism needs to be made of religious educators who no longer find a role for school and classroom in religious education. Postman's analysis of the media strengthens the case for a critical, academic, and intellectual study of religion to complement and criticize informal and unstructured education in religion.

Since religious education in informal settings is chiefly in the form of the parable, myth, and story, with all their emotional appeal, religious education in formal settings should emphasize *critical rationality and thought*. In this regard as in others, there is a need for a balance between the evangelical proclamation of early Christianity and the practical rationality of the Jewish tradition. Schools need to recover the method of the Talmudic tradition described by Neusner as a method of mutual criticism that emphasized the importance of publicly articulated reasons for moral and religious action. In this Talmudic tradition "what counts is reason, ubiquitous, predominant, penetrating." It was not the authority of the rabbis that counted but the "timeless, impersonal reasons for ruling as they did (Neusner, 1973, p. 224)."

Without formal schooling to provide a serious, critical, and intellectual study of religion, contemporary religious life runs the risk of being taken over by the magicians, mystagogues, shamans, and witch doctors who become the healers, teachers, and counselors of individuals. As Max Weber (1964, p. 23) pointed out in his sociological study of religions, although such persons are always present on the religious scene, their power grows when the element of rationality is weak in religious life. Weber's thesis becomes even more convincing when we see magicians, shamans, and demagogic religious figures presenting their message and conducting their ministry through the medium of TV, which by its very nature highlights affectivity, emotion, and feeling.

Religious education in a telecommunications society which presents fragmented meanings needs to be more concerned with presenting *comprehensive meaning systems*. Geertz (1973) in his study of primitive religion has shown that religions have provided cultures with powerful meaning systems that are able to satisfy human quests and motivate persons for effective action. Postman recognized this as a particularly important and contemporary human need. The attraction of religious schools and religious education for many is precisely the integrated vision of life that religious education can provide. Psychologists are also in agreement on the necessity of such a comprehensive view of life. Allport (1950) considered the possession of such a comprehensive meaning system as one of the chief characteristics of a mature religious sentiment. Yinger (1970) has shown from a sociological perspective the power of religion to establish personal identity and existential stability.

Religious education needs to direct more attention to the *values of history, tradition, and authority in the teaching of religion*. Postman is joined by the cultural historian Christopher Lasch (1979) in decrying the neglect of historical studies and the weakening of respect and regard for authority in contemporary society. The prejudices of a present-oriented mass media are against such values as these. Religious education, however, is in a good position to provide the desirable balance in this area. Turner (1969) in his study of religious rituals has shown how these rites attempt to balance individual and cultural needs for both structured existence and unstructured existence (*communitas* or *liminality*). A dialectical tension necessarily exists between past and present, structure and freedom, world maintenance and world creation. One does not have to embrace the rigid view of schooling espoused by Emile Durkheim to recognize that formal education and, in a special way, religious education have a great potential for teaching the valuable uses of past, tradition, and authority.

Formal religious education is also in a position to educate persons in *religious language*. Those who grow up in a religious tradition learn religious language in the same informal and natural way that they learn other languages of ordinary life, politics, entertainment, and science. The task of formal education in religion, as well as in other areas, is to empower us to better understand the language that we and others use. Religious education can open us to the richness of the written word. It can make us sensitive to the inadequacies and distortions of certain religious metaphors, arguments, definitions, and symbols. Religious educators, I believe, have never taken seriously enough the importance of religious language in religious education that Miller (1970) and Halbfas (1971) argued for. This task is even more important today with the extensive use and misuse of religious language on TV and other news media.

Postman's suggestion of using television in formal education only for purposes of analysis and criticism is a valuable suggestion for religious educators. The religious ministry of TV evangelists and the messages of religious talk shows can provide important areas for critical analysis. More people watch these than watch the more thoughtful and critical religious programs that are aired on Sunday mornings. Though the news media may be helpful in the classroom teaching of religion, their presence in formal religious education can be justified only if they are used to foster a critical understanding of the use of all media.

CONCLUSION:
ANALOGY FOR PHILOSOPHY OF EDUCATION

In the ancient Mishnah there is a wise bit of philosophy of education. It states that there are four kinds of students: the sponge, the funnel, the strainer, and the sieve. The *sponge* absorbs everything, both helpful and harmful. The *funnel* takes in at one end and empties at the other end. The *strainer* lets the wine drain through but retains the useless dregs. The *sieve* is the best of the four because it lets out the flour dust and retains the fine flour.

In my view it is only formal education that is best suited to produce sieves—to produce persons who can distinguish among conflicting claims, visions, and ideologies. It is easy to take in the content and the structure of the mass media uncritically. It is easy to miss the valuable information and helpful values that they do convey. Formal education—by its commitment to critical thought, its emphasis on the powers of reason and imagination, its study of the best minds of the past and present through their writings, its tradition of constant criticism and review, its concern for proper language, and its placing of all things within a critical and comprehensive vision— has greater potential than informal education for enabling students to cherish what is valuable in our culture and to ignore what is worthless. What is true of general education is also true of religious education. This is not to say that formal education has always accomplished the objectives asked of it. Yet it has done so for countless millions in the past. It is imperative that it continue to do so as we move further into the telecommunications society.

PART II: RELIGIOUS EDUCATION OF ADULTS

CHAPTER 6

PARISH ADULT RELIGIOUS EDUCATION; FROM RHETORIC TO REALITY

One of the recent phenomena in Roman Catholicism in the United States and other countries has been a serious effort at adult religious education. The past fifteen years have witnessed the development of adult religious education programs in many parishes and dioceses. Each year more persons are involved in administering and teaching in adult religious education programs. Numerous articles and books have appeared on various aspects of adult religious education: program planning, theory and philosophy, as well as psychological development of adult faith. Impressive statements have been made by church synods and Bishops. Graduate schools of religious education and seminaries now offer specialized programs in this field of study. Persons trained in these institutions have gone on to hold parish and diocesan positions in adult religious education.

This increased activity in Roman Catholicism is paralleled by developments among Protestant and Jewish religious bodies. Stokes (1977) has surveyed Protestant churches and found increased activity at the parish level in programs of faith exploration, action-reflection, and cross-generational or intergenerational education. Cohen (1977) has documented the rise of Jewish adult education as a phenomenon closely related to the search for group identity after the Holocaust and to solidarity with the state of Israel.

The growth of adult education in religious bodies is part of a general trend of increased adult education in many sectors and institutions of United States society. Adult education has become a major concern of colleges and universities, especially community colleges. Business and industry, as well as labor unions, have included adult education and training as essential components of their programs. The federal, state, and local governments each year increase their involvement in adult education, especially in areas of basic literacy, high school completion for adults, health education, and job training. Special programs have been developed for minority groups, displaced homemakers, the unemployed, and the elderly.

Adult education must be seen in this broad social context if we are to appreciate the potential impact that it can have on the lives of individuals in religious bodies, the religious bodies themselves, and the broader society. There is increasing evidence that we are gradually moving toward becoming "the learning society" that Robert Hutchins, the articulate spokesman for liberal education of adults, envisioned in his influential writings. Groups such as UNESCO have promoted in recent years a vision of "lifelong learning." It would appear that only those organizations that are committed to such an ideal will be viable in future decades.

PROMISE AND FULFILLMENT

Although adult education is on the increase in churches and synagogues in the United States, there is still a large gap between the promise and rhetoric of the vision of a learning church and the fulfillment or reality of such a vision. This promise is found in a number of significant Roman Catholic documents, e.g., *The General Catechetical Directory* (1971, n.20), the pastoral letter of the bishops of the United States, *To Teach as Jesus Did* (1972, art. 44), and *Sharing The Light of Faith,* the National Catholic Directory (1979, art. 188). These documents emphasize that catechesis of adults is central to the church's educational mission, that it should take many forms, including small group education, and that attention should be paid to the learning and developmental needs of adults. While the exciting promise of adult religious education is found in these and in documents of other religious bodies, as well as in writings of prominent educators of all denominations, it is also clear that we are at the present time far removed from the fulfillment of this promise.

Although adult religious education has become an important part of the postconciliar church in the United States and other countries, it cannot be said that it is the Church's *central* educational mission at the parish, diocesan, and national levels. Diocesan adult education directors at a national symposium contended that adequate staffing and realistic funding have not been provided for adult religious education at any level of church life. The directors summed up their position briefly when they said that at all levels of church life "rhetoric regarding adult education has been maximal; structural identity, staffing and funding have been minimal (*Position Papers,* 1978)."

Persons involved in adult education in the churches do not naively expect the mere rhetoric of ecclesiastical documents and leaders to bring about a revolution in church structures and attitudes which have developed over the past centuries. The Roman Catholic Church, in the years after the Council of Trent, gradually centered almost all of its educational efforts on children. The Church in the United States continued this practice and decidedly strengthened it through the establishment of the parochial school system. Adult educators recognize that changes in this area are not a matter of years but of decades. But, in the two decades since Vatican II, real progress has been made. We have confidence that each decade will bring us closer to the fulfillment of the promise contained in the theology of adult faith in the secular world recognized in postconciliar documents and theology.

Progress toward the fulfillment of this promise will not be automatic. It entails a serious grappling with theological, cultural, psychological, sociological, and political issues. Progress will necessitate a willingness to examine the *barriers* that prevent adult religious education from moving to the center of the Church's educational mission. It demands an honest look at established practices with their underlying assumptions. Progress toward making adult education the chief form of education in the Church demands a revolution both in our thinking and in our practice. It demands a commitment to a number of ideological shifts that I will attempt to sketch in this study.

A SHIFT FROM SCHOOLING TO A BROAD VIEW OF EDUCATION

The concentration upon schooling as the almost exclusive form of religious education has prevented religious bodies from openness to an expansive view of education. Church educators need to be open to the broad view of education espoused by Cremin (1975) in his history of American education. Cremin describes education as the deliberate transmission, evocation, or development of knowledge, attitudes, values, and sensibilities. In his treatment of American education he includes not only the efforts of schools, colleges, and universities, but also the powerful influences of families, churches, mass media, the world of work, and the general culture of the community. In this view of education it is clear that learning is lifelong and that many institutions besides schools are involved in it.

The effects of this expansive view of education within religious bodies would be to bring about a rethinking of the almost exclusive commitment to schools and school-based forms of religious education as *the* institutions for religious education. A school, where it exists, should be viewed as one among many institutions which are involved in religious education. Religious educators need to give attention to many other forms of education besides schooling.

Rather extensive research has shown that *families* are powerful educating forces, especially in the transmission of religious knowledge and values (Greeley, 1976). The practical implication of this fact is that religious educators should be more deeply involved in parental education than they have been in the past. Programs such as Family Learning Teams, Family Clustering, and Family Religious Education deserve more support in parishes. Family education provides the opportunity for intergenerational education where two or three generations are involved in educational experiences. This type of educational pattern gives the support that families need for fulfilling their roles and responsibilities in religious education.

The increasing power of the *mass media* in the education of the public and its implications for other forms of education is the major thrust of analysis of certain educational theorists, especially Postman (1979). In his writings he argues persuasively that the mass media comprise the first formal curriculum for the child. From the informal education within the family and the formal education of the mass media children move to the formal curriculum of the schools. Throughout adult life the media remain a powerful curriculum for developing ideas, shaping values, informing sensibilities, and affecting behavior. It is Postman's major contention that the schools must redefine their educational task because of the increasing power of the mass media, especially television. Since this position of Postman's was discussed in an earlier study, it will suffice to note at this time that this revolution in our culture has important implications for religious education. Programs are needed to promote an intelligent and critical approach to the modeling presented by the media. The values and the world views presented through the mass media need to be examined according to sound educational and religious principles. Perhaps the most valuable adult religious education program within a parish might be a serious evaluation of these powerful media.

The world of *work* as an educative institution has been largely ignored by educators, including religious educators. Most adult men and an increasing number of adult women spend a large portion of their adult lives in institutions of work. These institutions shape many of our fundamental values: competitiveness and cooperation, motivation for self-fulfillment and profit, attitudes towards the consumption of goods, subordination of our wants, needs, and values to those of others, and our fundamental attitudes towards what is important in life. The world of work also presents many areas where difficult moral decisions must be made. Unfortunately, religious bodies have rarely involved themselves in the world of work beyond preaching a work ethic, establishing a few industrial chaplaincies, and experimenting with a worker-priest movement in Europe. The United States Catholic Bishops designated the 1980s as the decade of the family. Is it inconceivable for a religious body to have a decade dedicated to a consideration of work? Could not the solemnity of St. Joseph the Worker on May 1 be an occasion to reflect on the meaning and value of work as creative activity? The positioning of this solemnity was not an accident: May 1 is celebrated as Labor Day in most European countries.

I have given only three examples of the broadened view of education that would place the education of adults at the center of the Church's educational activity. Other examples could be given. Family education needs to be balanced by educational opportunities offered to adults in general and to adults in particular groupings, e.g., single young adults, divorced and separated adults, and elderly adults. The analysis of the mass media must be complemented by an analysis of contemporary books and literature. Education for the world of work must be balanced by education for leisure and retirement. A narrow view of education that equates education with schooling prevents us from realizing the importance of these other powerful forms of education.

A SHIFT FROM CHRISTIAN INITIATION TO CHRISTIAN LIFELONG LEARNING

Partly because of the strong sacramental tradition in Roman Catholicism and some other Christian bodies, parish religious education is largely concerned with educating persons for sacraments of Christian initiation: baptism, confirmation, and eucharist. A great percentage of the time of parish directors of religious education focuses around preparation for participation in rites of initiation. One positive aspect of this type of education is that in recent years parents and other members of the community have been involved in education for participation in these rites.

Education for Christian initiation is certainly important but it should not be overemphasized at the expense of lifelong learning in the faith. I interpret the great interest among Christians in such conversion and experience-centered renewals as Cursillo, the charismatic movement, marriage encounter, and Bible study and prayer groups as an indication of the attention that should be given to the life of faith after initiation has been completed. A friend of mine once remarked that Jesus would have done religious educators a great favor if he had instituted a sacrament for each year of life so that people would be constrained to be involved in lifelong learning.

Deeper concern with Christian life beyond initiation is necessitated by a theology of faith. Faith is a free act of the individual in response to God's revelation. The life of faith in adulthood must include, as the Vatican II document on *The Church in the Modern World* noted, "the critical ability to distinguish religion from a magical view of the world and from the superstitions which still circulate (Abbot, 1966, art. 7)." The Council also recognized that many, especially young adults, abandon religion because they become committed to new ideologies through philosophy, literature, the arts, the humanities, and history.

One of the major findings of recent theory and research in adult developmental psychology is that growth and development is lifelong. Whether one accepts the neo-Freudian position of psychologists such as Erikson, Gould, or Levinson, the cognitive developmental approach of Kohlberg and Fowler, or the social psychological theory of Neugarten and Havighurst, it is clear that significant development takes place throughout the adult years until the very end of life. In the light of this new understanding of adulthood, it is clear that no initiation into religious faith in the early years of life, no matter how thorough or deep, will be adequate for the entire span of adult life.

The implications of this research for adult religious education are numerous. Religious education must be brought to bear on young adults struggling with self-identity and intimacy. The role of religious faith in establishing a marriage covenant and in child rearing should be a major focus for religious education. Problems and challenges which single adults experience in their lives call for greater attention by church educators. Adults in the middle years have numerous needs that touch on religious faith: a search for a new meaning system or life-structure, the tendency to turn to inner spiritual desires in the second half of life, problems within marriage and family, and changed situations in work and career. Adults in advanced age have spiritual and religious needs that are often neglected in parish adult education. The psychologist Carl Jung wrote of the great world religions as schools for the elderly, which prepare them for the challenges of later life, including suffering, bereavement, and death. Psychologists have also described other needs: a sense of self-worth and integrity, a realization that there is meaningful life after retirement, and a need to belong to a caring family and community.

It is not my contention that the answer to all religious needs in adult life are found in formal adult education. Liturgical life, preaching, pastoral care, counseling, and social ministry also attend to adult needs. But education, broadly conceived, is integral to all these forms of ministry.

This is true because the first step in bringing about personal and social change, as Paulo Freire, the Brazilian educator, has noted, is to raise people's consciousness about themselves and about the world in which they live. Education affords persons the opportunity to see new possibilities and to transcend their present mode of existence. Religious education should provide adults the opportunity to see in each crisis, problem, and developmental task the potential for spiritual growth.

The practical effects of this shift from initiation to lifelong learning in religious faith are numerous. Preparation for marriage, parenthood, work, retirement, suffering, and death become as important as preparation for baptism, confirmation, and communion. The mid-life crisis of adults would receive as much attention as the adolescent crisis of faith. Parishes would be as interested in developing ways for adults in mid-life to manifest loving care as they are in providing service programs for the young. The family of the sick and dying adult would receive as much care and instruction as the family of the child to be baptized.

The obvious response to all of this might be to ask, how can we further burden overworked religious educators with these added adult educational responsibilities? My response is at least threefold. First of all, parish adult education must be seen not as the exclusive task of a pastoral team or director and staff. It must be seen as the effort of the entire community to educate all members of the community. All members of the parish community can participate as teachers and students. My second response to the problem of the overburdened educator is to point out how ineffective the education of the young is when it is not supported by the efforts of parents and the entire adult community. This ineffectiveness is not a reason to neglect the education of the young but rather a reason to direct more attention to the education of adults. A third response concerns a view of pastoral ministry, the third shift needed at the parish level.

FROM A NARROW TO A COMPREHENSIVE VIEW OF PASTORAL MINISTRY

A quiet revolution is taking place in many parishes in the United States and elsewhere. This revolution is indicated by the extension of the term "minister" to a larger group of people within the churches. Parishes now call and hire pastoral associates and pastoral assistants who are not ordained priests. One of the results of this development is a broadened view of parish ministry. When parish ministry was totally the responsibility of parish priests, this ministry was viewed almost exclusively in liturgical and sacramental terms. The education of ordained clergy has been predominantly directed toward this form of ministry. The training of the new pastoral associates and assistants is most often in the areas of education, counseling, or social work. Many of these ministers are deeply involved in the work of adult religious education. Through their efforts many parishes have become sensitized to the need for lifelong religious education.

A comprehensive view of pastoral ministry includes the tasks of leadership and administration, education, pastoral care and counseling, social action, and liturgical life. While education can be viewed as a specialized function, it is also an integral element of all parish ministries. In the local church where I have been volunteer director of adult religious education, our entire program has been considerably strengthened by the adoption of the principle of involving all members of the parish staff as well as many ordinary parishioners in the work of adult religious education. The ordained priests have discovered teaching abilities within themselves and learning desires within parishioners that they were scarcely aware of in their previous work. The religious sister who directs religious education in the parish has become an effective teacher of adults as well as of children. Lay persons whose secular work is education, counseling, or social work have felt more a part of the church's ministry by utilizing their talents in a religious setting.

Adult religious education, and for that matter any ministry in the local church, will never become a dominant force unless many people share in this work. Fortunately, in many of our parishes there are enough persons who, through natural gifts and training, are prepared and motivated to become involved as educators of adults. This involvement will be accomplished only if there is some person or persons who will take on the responsibility of coordinating and enabling adult religious education to take place. Ideally, this person would be a member of the parish staff; but, in many places, volunteers can perform this task on a part-time basis, provided they are asked to concentrate on this one area and are not expected to be involved in many other parish activities.

FROM RHETORIC TO REALITY

Thus far in this study I have dealt chiefly with changing assumptions and to a lesser degree with changing practices in adult religious education. In the concluding section of this study I should like to make a number of practical suggestions that might move the practice of adult religious education more decisively from the rhetoric stage closer to the reality stage. These suggestions come from my experience both in teaching about and conducting programs in adult education at the parish and diocesan levels. I have developed these suggestions more fully in another work (Elias, 1982).

Leadership in Adult Religious Education

As in all areas of practice, leadership is an extremely important factor in developing an effective program in adult religious education. Leadership may be vested in one person or in a committee of persons. Adult religious educators usually stress the importance of a committee or council at the local level. I am not enthusiastic about this form of leadership as appropriate to all situations. Too often I have found group leadership to be an obstacle rather than an aid to the development of an effective program. Leaders in this area need advice from others and accountability to others, but this need can often be met in less formal ways than established councils and committees. Also, where the local church group is rather small, a single person as leader might be more appropriate.

All types of persons can be tapped as leaders of parish programs. Those who have had experience in education, counseling, business, social work, and government service have done remarkably well in this area. I personally know of men and women, young and old, both professionally trained and naturally gifted individuals, who are effective leaders in adult education programs. Many such persons do not require specific training for these positions. In other cases, it is essential that training programs be provided by dioceses or educational institutions. One can learn the tasks of leadership by serving a type of apprenticeship with an effective director.

Involvement of Parish Staff

I have already mentioned the importance of the clergy and parish staff in developing a strong adult education program. Their involvement gives priority status to adult religious education and makes such matters as recruitment of educators and participants an easier task. Adult religious education, however, must never become exclusively the function of the clergy or parish staff, if it is to accomplish the goal of the entire community educating the entire community.

Often I have been asked to address clergy on the topic of the priest or minister as adult educator. My first advice to them is to get a qualified person to do it, unless they feel that it is their particular gift. Besides this type of leadership, clergy and staff can be involved by preaching about the church as a learning community, supporting the programs, teaching courses in the programs, and manifesting in their own ministry the importance of continued learning.

Assessment of Needs and Establishment of Goals

There is need in a parish for a periodic assessment of needs of adult members that can be met through educational programs. This effort should be a cooperative one which involves many persons and all sectors of the parish. Strong programs have the flexibility to remain relevant and topical as well as the stability that comes from continual treatment of essential religious issues of beliefs, morals, rituals, and doctrines of religious bodies. They have a place for both prayer and study groups, serious study of theology, action-reflection on contemporary problems, and humanistically oriented sharing and growth groups.

A parish should utilize various methods in assessing needs and setting objectives. Methods that I have found helpful are questionnaires, phone interviews, and open parish meetings. At open parish meetings a wide number of issues are brought up by parishioners. Many of these are helpful in giving a sense of particular needs of the community. It is also beneficial to attempt to meet the needs of a different group within the community each year and to experiment yearly with a different educational design.

Flexibility in Programming

Successful adult education programs in a parish are characterized by flexible programming. They provide educational experiences for both small groups and large groups. One-day programs and year-long programs are held, with many forms of programs in between. I learned an important principle of good programming at CIDOC, Ivan Illich's center in Cuernavaca, Mexico. Only one session of a program should be scheduled which people can attend free of charge. The decision to continue the program for a longer period of time should be made depending upon whether a sufficient number of persons make a commitment to attend for a specified period of time.

Flexible programming demands that a program of education for the year should not be so rigidly drawn that extremely topical issues cannot be introduced rather easily into the program. In one parish the tradition of Sunday Morning Adult Forums has been established, where current topics can be aired. If there is sufficient interest, more attention can be devoted at other times to the particular issue.

Climate for Adult Learning

One of the essential ingredients of a successful parish adult education program is the establishment of a friendly and caring atmosphere. Adults come voluntarily to programs and are very often attracted as much by the need for human contact and companionship as they are by the educational content. A friendly and caring atmosphere translates into many small but important things: knowing one another's name; respecting the opinions of all, no matter how they differ from one's own; allowing adequate time for small talk and refreshment; encouraging a lively sense of humor; missing one's group and being missed by them; manifesting a sensitivity to particular problems that persons feel free to reveal; and enjoying an opportunity for shared prayer and insight.

I often judge the atmosphere of an adult education program by what happens after the day's or evening's program has ended. If people stay around and speak with one another, it is usually a sign of a healthy atmosphere. I recall incidences where programs ended abruptly, and I had to depart from a group of people who obviously wanted to spend more time discussing the evening's program.

Ongoing Evaluation of the Program

Successful programs are programs which subject themselves to constant criticism and evaluation. They are willing to accept both failures and successes. The most successful adult education programs are those that eliminate failures, repeat successes, and take chances with new programs. The directors of these programs consider the opinions of those who attend, listen to the views of those who drop out, and seek out the reasons why persons do not involve themselves in educational programs. Evaluation should include an honest assessment of the types of people who attend in comparison with the types of persons who do not attend. Judging from my experience, it is often the young adults and the elderly who are poorly represented in adult education programs.

The time to evaluate programs is in the middle, to receive suggestions for changing a program in mid-stream, and at the end, to utilize the information in planning future programs. Evaluation is a difficult matter because it affects our judgments of individuals. Very often evaluations cancel each other out when opposing opinions are formed about a given program. Judgments have to be weighed carefully, and decisions based on them have to be made with a bit of tentativeness.

CONCLUSION

I began this study by reviewing some of the rhetoric that is found in church documents about the importance of adult religious education in the local church. It is my contention that this rhetoric can be translated into reality, first of all, by changing our view on three important issues: the nature of education, an exploration of lifelong learning in religion, and a broadened view of pastoral ministry. Second, a number of practical suggestions have been given for the conduct of parish adult education.

There are a number of indications that we are entering into a new educational era which might appropriately be called the "century of the adult." One sees more and more attention devoted to adults in educational circles. The hope of this era will not pass religious bodies by if they take up the challenge of adult religious education. The thrust of this study is that history, culture, and faith make the meeting of this challenge possible and necessary.

CHAPTER 7

ECCLESIAL MODELS OF ADULT RELIGIOUS EDUCATION

The enterprise of adult religious education in the churches and synagogues is a growing one. This judgment is attested to by a number of factors. There is an increasing awareness that religious bodies have considerably broadened the scope of their educational programs beyond the needs of children and youth. Documents of religious bodies in the past two decades have highlighted the importance of adult religious education. Published books and articles have increased in the past decade. Some publishers have begun to pay more attention to the expanding market of adults interested in continuing education in religion. Graduate programs have added courses and even developed concentrations in this field. A number of prominent religious educators have devoted their attention to establishing a field of adult religious education.

Accompanying this growth in adult religious education are many forms or models of adult education. From my personal experience with adult education in Roman Catholic parishes and dioceses, I have been impressed with the rich variety of ways in which this education takes place. Creative models, developed at both grass roots and leadership levels, have emerged in many places. Programs developed by publishers have presented additional models of adult education.

The rich diversity of models being used in adult religious education calls for, I believe, some clarification and analysis. My intent in this study is to describe models of adult religious education that are presently in use and to explore their appropriateness. This attempt will be made from the theoretical side, utilizing the models of the church proposed by Avery Dulles (1977; 1982). I believe that it is most helpful to use these models for understanding religious education of adults within Christian communities. These understandings might also be applicable to other religious bodies.

This attempt at describing ecclesial models of adult education is not the only way to analyze adult religious education. In earlier works (Elias and Merriam, 1980; Elias, 1982), I classified and analyzed six adult religious education models by using educational categories, drawn from philosophy, psychology, and the social sciences. The theories I considered were liberal education, progressive education, humanistic education, behaviorist education, radical (or sociopolitical) education, and conceptual analysis of educational concepts. This theoretical analysis was more appropriate for establishing in the academic community the theoretical foundations of adult religious education.

Since my intention in this study is to analyze the religious education of adults in Christian communities, I intend to utilize theological models. My basic contention in this study is that *forms and formats of adult religious education are shaped by the particular model or models of church that are operative in the leadership and membership of a church community*. In other words there exists a congruence between models of the church, explicit or implicit, and the objectives and designs of adult religious education. This study is based both on reflections upon theological models of the church and my own experience as an adult educator in religion. Since this experience comes from work in a Roman Catholic parish, my examples will pertain chiefly to this community. To fully establish the relationships that I draw would demand controlled empirical study.

My procedure in this study is to describe each model of the church, indicate its strengths and limitations, then apply the model to adult religious education. The sketch of the models will be done briefly since my major concern is with the application of the model to adult religious education. Also, since the community of disciples model is a more recent one I shall devote more attention to it in this study.

INSTITUTIONAL MODEL OF ADULT RELIGIOUS EDUCATION

The institutional model of the church has been a prominent one in official church documents of the past. In this model the church is primarily a structured organization which has rules, members, leaders, and some form of hierarchical authority. The powers of the church are generally divided into teaching, sanctifying, and governing. Clear-cut distinctions are made between those who exercise these powers and those who are at the receiving end: between the teachers and the taught, the sanctifiers and the sanctified, the governors and the governed. Ultimate authority in all of these three functions rests in the hands of a hierarchy.

In this model of the church the authority to teach comes from above, from those in authority. The distinction between those who teach and those who are taught is maintained, perhaps even to the extent of a required license for teaching. The role of theologians in this model is usually that of loyal but critical defenders of present teaching of the church. This model takes little account of charisms and ministries of teaching that might arise outside official structures.

The institutional model of the church has not generally been supportive of the religious education of adults. In fact, it may be said that the prevalence of this model in Roman Catholicism and in other religious bodies has led to the positive avoidance of serious efforts at educating adults in the faith. The spirit of obedience, docility, and acceptance of authority that the model fosters actually presumes that adults are to be considered more like immature children. It is easy in this model to avoid the painful encounters that occur when critically thinking adults are given the opportunity to openly react to official teaching. The 1976 Call to Action Conference in Detroit where adults spoke out on many issues indicated to the hierarchy and to the church at large that Catholic adults both think and act independently and do not automatically accept the established rules of an organization.

Though the institutional model of the church has been rightly criticized by Dulles and others, there are a number of values in the model that might well inform adult religious education. The importance that this model gives to continuity in the Christian tradition is valuable since adult education in religion always entails dealing with the tradition and wisdom of the past. Institutional structures often embody and maintain important dimensions of religious life that might not spontaneously emerge from community life. Structures also entail elements that provide corporate identity for adults in the church.

Adult education in the Catholic community must always deal with the Catholic tradition and the contemporary attempts of the institution to restate this tradition. Papal Encyclicals, Conciliar and Synodal Teachings, Pastoral Letters of individual bishops or conferences of bishops both maintain and foster Catholic identity and continuity. These forms of institutional teaching are especially valuable when they have resulted from a broad consultative process as was the case with the Bishops' Pastoral on Peace and Nuclear Disarmament. It has always been important in the Catholic tradition to give an intelligent and critical hearing to teachings of the institutional church.

Adult education might well benefit from a correctly conceived institutional model for adult education. In this model respectful attention is given to authoritative teaching. What must be avoided, however, is an authoritarian manner of presenting this teaching which attempts to impose doctrines on others and does not allow for critical reflection and even dissent. It must be recognized that teachings of the church vary in the authoritativeness with which they are presented.

Though institutional teaching is usually associated with didactic methods of education, it is possible to utilize different formats in dealing with official teachings. To lectures, courses, and forums might be added group discussions and other more participative forms of learning. A learning group in which I have been involved for a number of years has with great profit devoted attention to institutional teachings.

Though the teaching of theologians might also be considered within the institutional model—since theologians attempt to offer interpretations of official church teachings—it is preferable to consider theologians within the herald model of the church since their work is best viewed as primarily reinterpreting, revising, and re-presenting the faith of the tradition and the faith of the community (Gilkey, 1979; Tracy, 1981).

COMMUNAL MODEL OF ADULT RELIGIOUS EDUCATION

In the past two decades both church documents and theologians have focused upon the church as a mystical communion, a community, and a fellowship. Dulles speaks of the church as "a communion of men [sic], primarily interior but also expressed by external bonds of creed, worship, and ecclesiastical fellowship (1977, 59)." The Scriptural images that correspond with this model are the Church as the People of God and as the Body of Christ. Both of these images find expression in the documents of the Second Vatican Council and have corresponded to the needs of many people for a view of the church which addresses the various needs of persons in community.

The advantages of this model of the church are the emphasis placed on interior gifts and graces of the Spirit which are found not only in the leadership of the church but also in all of its members. The vision is the Pauline description of a church with many gifts, charisms, and ministries which are shared among the members of the community in their efforts to build up the Body of Christ. Thus this model focuses on equality among members, on the community of faith, a communion of brothers and sisters united in spiritual life. Reformers in the churches have often appealed to this vision to criticize objectionable aspects of the institutional church.

Experience with this model of the church has brought out some of the weaknesses and limitations of the vision of church as communion. This model leaves unclear the relationship between the inner life of the community and the visible organization. Can communal life be sustained without some connections with institutional structures? Emphasis on the communal dimensions may lead to a vision of two churches and two types of Christian: the institutional and the communal. Such a model may also tend to exaggerate the holiness of the church and not take account of human failings and weaknesses.

Despite all its strengths and weaknesses the communal model of the church has greatly informed recent developments of adult education in the churches. Some of the most widely used programs take the model of church as sharing communion as a primary focal point. *Genesis II, Ashes to Easter, Romans VIII,* and *Renew* all attempt to form small Christian communities which share spiritual gifts and visions. Anyone who has participated in these programs recognizes that the dynamics of such programs foster a sharing of spiritual gifts. The focus of such programs is not on official institutional teaching as expounded by an authoritative teacher but rather on shared faith, i.e., the sharing of particular insights and experiences of individual Christians. Often such programs proceed without significant input from pastors and teachers within the community.

The adult education that takes place where the model of mystical communion prevails manifests the same strengths and weaknesses of the ecclesial model upon which it is based. Personal faith sharing is good so long as people are growing in religious knowledge and insight. Such small groups must make strong efforts to avoid self- and group-centeredness as well as other-worldliness. Personal and interpersonal development in faith requires that persons be connected with broader ecclesial and societal concerns. Such religious groups are also not immune from the dangers of cliqueishness and navel-gazing that social psychologists have found in their analysis of some small groups.

Notwithstanding these problems, it is my view that the proliferation of communal models of adult education is a significant development in contemporary Roman Catholic communities and in other religious groups. Such groups counter the clericalism that once dominated religious education and allow all members of the church to participate in its life. This communal model recognizes the spiritual maturity of adults and the charisms through which adults express their searching faith. It is hard to imagine a Christian adult education that does not include dimensions of communal sharing of faith.

SACRAMENTAL MODEL OF ADULT RELIGIOUS EDUCATION

The liturgical revival in Roman Catholicism and other Christian churches with strong liturgical elements has resulted in a model of the church that places stress on the church as sacrament. This model attempts to combine the best elements of the institutional and communal models. It views the church as of both divine institution and human origin. It presents a vision of the church as the sign of God's presence and activity in the world. The interior life of the church is the activity of the grace of God. The visible activities of the church are signs of God's graceful activity.

In his comments on this model Dulles indicates his belief that the view of the church as sacrament has been couched in technical theological language that renders the model inaccessible to preaching and ordinary teaching. Though this may be true, it is also clear that the sacramental mentality is so strong in Catholic life and consciousness that it influences many forms of activity including education. Perhaps the problem is with the word "sacrament" which has too long been associated with distinct ritual actions and has not been used to describe the very nature of the church and all of its activities. The reality of sacrament—that God is present in, and that we encounter God in, visible and external action—is deeply rooted in Catholic piety.

The power of the sacramental model of adult religious education was dramatized for me by the creative pastoral ministry of William Bausch described in his excellent book, *The Christian Parish* (1980). When Father Bausch assumed leadership of St. Mary's Church in Colts Neck, New Jersey, he announced that his two priorities would be liturgical life and adult religious education. Recognizing the educational value of good liturgy and the liturgical possibilities of sound education, Bill Bausch has formed a community where worship and education unite in a dynamic and fruitful relationship. The liturgical renewal at St. Mary's has even included the introduction of the Divine Office or official liturgical prayer of the church. Many different types of educational opportunities are offered.

A sacramental model of adult education utilizes the educational possibilities of both formal and informal worship. The reform of the rites of the church has given ministers many opportunities for explaining the meaning of these rites. The increase in Bible and prayer study groups has resulted in part from the more extensive and creative use of the Scriptures in the church's liturgical life. The restoration of the homily as an integral part of the liturgy of the word has served to increase the importance of education within a liturgical context.

In recent years religious educators have devoted more and more time to sacramental preparation of adults for entrance into the church through the adult catechumenate. As an educator I confess that I had many reservations about the adult catechumenate as proposed in the RCIA. Through the experience of two years' involvement as a director of a parish catechumenate, I have been able to overcome these objections and to recognize the great potential of this particular form of liturgical education. My feeling is that liturgists have tended to underestimate the educational components of the catechumenate, and educators (like myself) have slighted the liturgical dimensions. My present view is that this rite incorporates many sound educational principles that can be used in different contexts, e.g., marriage preparation and faith renewal programs.

The sacramental model of adult religious education is not restricted to education and participation in the rites of the church. The purpose of formal worship is to call us to find God's presence and activity in all of human experience. This model puts the mystery of God at the very center of human life. It challenges us to think about the usual distinction that we make between the sacred and the secular. Our meeting with God in visible sacraments and symbolic activities must alert us to the presence of God in nature, persons, communities, societies, and all other dimensions of individual and social reality.

HERALD MODEL OF ADULT RELIGIOUS EDUCATION

The biblical-liturgical revival within the Christian churches has brought to the fore a view of the church as herald or proclaimer of the Word of God. In this model the church is seen as the place and assembly where the Word of God is proclaimed and where members respond to this Word in faith. The preaching of the word is a concrete event which makes God present and calls forth a response in faith. This view of the church has its roots in Scriptural accounts of preaching the message of salvation to prospective believers. The proclamation theology of Karl Barth and other Neo-Orthodox Protestant theologians gave this perspective on the church a twentieth century orientation. Catholic theologians and the documents of Vatican II have given prominence to the church as herald of the Word of God.

This model of the church is strongly evangelical and kerygmatic. It places emphasis on the process of evangelization, the announcement of the death and resurrection of Jesus and the calling of persons to repentance, salvation, and conversion. The sovereignty of God over history and human life is highlighted in this model. It contends that the power of God's Word is stronger than human words. One can get some indication of the strength of this model of the church by reading and meditating upon the powerful sermons of Barth, Bultmann, and Tillich.

In Dulles's analysis this model, as all the other models, has its strengths and weaknesses. The strength of the model lies in its power for proclaiming salvation, calling persons to conversion, and making judgments on individual lives and societal structures. The weaknesses of the model include a deemphasis on the institutional dimension of the church and a tendency to emphasize witness at the expense of action. To be effective as a model of the church in the contemporary situation, the proclamation of the Word must be accompanied by a deepened understanding of the Word of God as it was originally preached and a corresponding penetration into the cultural contexts in which this Word is preached. It is not enough to merely restate the Christian message using the very words of Scripture. This message must respond to the human situation in different cultures.

A herald model of adult religious education is found in many Christian parishes today. The biblical-liturgical revival has led to a greater emphasis on the proclamation of the Word in many forms. The first attempt to incorporate these theological ideas into religious education resulted in the kerygmatic approach to religious education. The seminal work of James Schaefer (1972) was influential in extending this model to adult Christian education. Schaefer showed how, in planning adult Christian education, attention had to be paid to a sophisticated and modern understanding of the Scriptures and contemporary theology.

The Scriptures have increasingly become an open book for many Christians. Surveys of existing programs and assessment of needs of adults usually find prayer groups and study groups in the Scriptures at the top of the list. All the major forms for parish renewal have a strong scriptural component. Pope Paul VI's encyclical letter on evangelization has to be seen within this herald approach to religious education. The regional conferences held by Alvin Ilig's Office of Evangelization attest to the power of this model in contemporary Roman Catholicism. The well-designed program *Sharing the Word,* developed by his office, has brought a sound knowledge of contemporary biblical scholarship to countless Christians. In addition to this program there are many other fine programs for use in fostering a prayerful study of the Scriptures.

The limitations of this model for adult religious education must also be recognized. In dealing with the Scriptures there is always the danger of falling into an ahistorical biblicism or fundamentalism. Just as one may approach the sacraments of the church in a magical manner, so the written Word of God can be distorted into magic formulas. Though the meaning of some parts of the Scriptures is clear, many important parts cannot be understood properly without interpretation and commentary. Also, since particular issues that many contemporary Christians face are not directly dealt with in the Scriptures, there is a need for biblical scholars, theologians, and educators to make the meaning of the Scriptures accessible to Christians.

In adult religious education there is a great need for introducing adults to the work of theologians. I can give two examples of the fruitfulness of this from my own experience. In my involvement in the adult catechumenate I underestimated the need for bringing contemporary theological understandings to the attention of the members. After the first few sessions we asked the candidates to evaluate the catechesis they had been given. The chief objection was that we were not giving them anything solid, theologically speaking. We had purposely taken a more formational and inspirational approach and had decided against an intellectual and substantive presentation of Christian theology. In revising the catechumenate I decided to give many of the same lectures in theology that I had prepared for graduate students in religious education. The priest who became the backbone of the catechumenate was the one who was most up-to-date in his theology. There were no major issues in contemporary theology that did not become the focus of discussion. At times we moved far into the realm of speculative theology.

My second example of the importance of theology in adult education comes from my experience in my primary learning group, a parish book-discussion group. For the past four years this group has met almost monthly to read and discuss a book or article in contemporary theology. Most of these people had been involved in such adult education programs as Bible groups, *Genesis II,* and short courses. What they desired was a deeper study of theology. Interestingly enough, one of the first books we discussed at an early session was Dulles's *Models of the Church.* Members of the group still refer back to this book and its framework for understanding the church in which we live and work. Other authors studied by the group include Monica Hellwig, Tad Guzie, John Dunne, Hans Kung, John Shea, and Thomas Merton. Recently the group has begun to examine Christian classics. The group has also discussed institutional teaching in the form of Papal Encyclicals, bishops' pastoral letters, and other official documents.

Lest one think that conversations on these books began and ended at a discussion level, I hasten to mention that this group has in the past year become deeply involved in sponsoring adult forums on social issues and has developed a deep concern and commitment in the area of social justice. Beginning from an adult education model that stresses theological exposition of the Word, one moves rather quickly to the doing of God's Word in the world.

SERVANT MODEL OF ADULT RELIGIOUS EDUCATION

The movement from hearing the Word to doing the Word is what characterizes the model of church as servant to the world. The Christian Church began as a movement which defined itself in opposition to the existing culture and attempted to avoid contamination by the culture of that world. It then passed through a long period of history when it was intimately identified with the dominant culture. Today the church again has a minority status, but with a difference. The church in the servant model views itself as a conscious minority group in service to the majority. It can exercise this service in a number of ways.

Within Roman Catholicism, the view of the church as servant was one of the achievements of the Vatican II Pastoral Constitution on the Church and the Modern World and the Declaration on Religious Freedom. The theology in these conciliar documents was first developed by such theologians as Yves Congar, Hans Kung, John Courtney Murray, Karl Rahner, and Cardinal Suhard. This model of the church is also in continuity with the notable papal encyclicals of Leo XIII, Pius XI, John XXIII, and Paul VI. The bishops of Latin America gave expression to this view in their conferences at Medellin and Puebla. Recent documents from other episcopal conferences have also stressed this dimension of Christian teaching. Similar statements have been issued by other Christian religious bodies and by the World Council of Churches' Faith and Order Commission.

The strengths of the servant model of the church are clear. The model provides an image of the church which is both active and dynamic in the world. It gives the church new life, a sense of modernity and a spirit of relevant mission to the world. The model breaks down the excessive other-worldliness that is often associated with religious bodies. The model of church as servant has borne fruit in the lives of many Christians who struggle for justice and peace in all parts of the world.

Some of the problems with this model have come to the fore in the debates over liberation and political theologies in the past decade. The Scriptural basis is not as strong for the servant model as for other models since the early church took such a negative attitude towards the world and viewed service as action directed only to members of the community. It is significant that political and liberation theologians have repeatedly turned to the Jewish experience of the Exodus and the Hebrew prophetic tradition as chief sources for developing a theology of liberation. Another problem with the servant model is the danger of tying the Christian gospel too closely to particular political ideologies, positions, and parties.

A servant model for adult religious education has emerged in Christian churches. As Christian communities grapple with such complex issues as nuclear disarmament, world hunger, abortion, corporate responsibility, unemployment, racial justice, and poverty, the educational tasks relating to these issues have received attention. Though many of these issues are found in the curricula for children and youth, it is more important that such issues become central focuses for adult religious education. It is adults who are deeply involved in the social, economic, and political structures of society. It is they who are more able to exercise leadership in these areas.

Education for peace and justice with adult groups is a difficult venture. For a number of years I have been involved with adult forums and action groups on social issues. These issues are potentially very divisive for Christian communities. Many do not even want anything that borders on the political, social, and economic discussed in church contexts. The Catholic Bishops' Pastoral on Peace and Nuclear Disarmament has anticipated both non-acceptance and resistance on the part of many in the Catholic community.

A number of religious educators in recent years have developed models of education which are consonant with a servant model of the church. Brian Wren, a British Protestant, has utilized Paulo Freire's conscientization method for raising consciousness about sociopolitical issues (Wren, 1977). Wren deals carefully with issues of ideology and political strategy. Thomas Groome's (1980) method of shared praxis can be utilized to provide an opportunity for theological reflection and action on issues that Christians face in the public order. Perhaps the most promising educational approach to making a religious community conscious of its servant role has been developed by Suzanne Toton (1982) in her treatment of world hunger from the perspective of the Christian educator. Toton utilizes the methodology of liberation theology by beginning with an analysis of the political, social, and economic contexts, correlates this with church teaching and theology of liberation, and develops both a theory and a practice. Her approach can easily be extended to other areas of societal concern.

Adult education in the action-reflection mode needs to utilize educational formats that allow for serious study, present contrasting viewpoints, and point to concrete actions which persons might take up in their individual and social lives. Study and discussion groups, forums, symposiums, and panel discussion groups are the best formats for this type of education. With regard to the taking of individual action, excellent suggestions are found in material developed by the organization *Bread for the World*.

THE CHURCH AS COMMUNITY OF DISCIPLES

Those who have found Dulles's earlier description of five models of the church fruitful for understanding the nature and mission of the church have now been challenged by him to explore the implications of the biblical concept of discipleship for understanding the nature and mission of the church (Dulles, 1982). Dulles has presented this model as an image of the church for the 1980s.

The strengths of this model are easily indicated. It establishes a continuity of life and belief with Jesus and the early Christian church. The model is a constant reminder that all Christians are disciples and that discipleship takes place in a community context. This model has potential for minimizing the differences between liberals and conservatives in the church by stressing unity in discipleship. An emphasis on discipleship can soften the bureaucratic image of the church, give specificity and direction to the community, provide a view of sacraments as growth in discipleship, establish what it is that is proclaimed by the community, and, we hope, help to motivate Christian service to the world.

Before drawing implications from this model for adult religious education, I should first like to indicate a number of limitations of the model for understanding the church. First of all, the search for one master model that might incorporate all others may be a form of monistic or essentialist thinking that runs the risk of oversimplifying the complexity of church life. Secondly, a stress on the discipleship model may foster a sectarian or elitist view of church membership. There are manifest limitations to the master-disciple model, as is clear from Dulles's attempt to give a community dimension to his model of discipleship.

The major weakness of the model, I believe, is in what it implies about the relationship of disciples to the world. Dulles describes discipleship as entailing a "radical break from the world and its values, a total renunciation of family, property, income, worldly ambition, and even personal safety." There is no doubt that these elements are found in the gospel tradition. But from an examination of the entire Christian tradition it is clear that there are other ways of being a disciple of Jesus while relating to the broader culture of the world. Richard Niebuhr in his classic work *Christ and Culture* (1951) identified this discipleship approach as fundamentally sectarian. He also showed that followers of Christ have at times identified discipleship with affirming worldly values, establishing syntheses between Christian and worldly values, attempting to live out the paradoxical tension of accepting both Christian and worldly values, and working for the religious transformation of cultural values.

The limitations of this model must be indicated before one attempts to utilize the model to examine or propose models of adult education shaped by it. The model of community of disciples has power to inform adult education, provided it is rightly qualified and modified by some of the aspects of the other models. I do not believe, however, that it is the best model for imaging the task of the church in the 1980s and beyond, which will become clear as this study proceeds. Before developing this point, I should first like to indicate some of the implications of this model for adult religious education.

DISCIPLESHIP MODEL OF ADULT RELIGIOUS EDUCATION

The model of the church as a community of disciples puts *lifelong discipleship or learning* (the Latin word *discere* means to learn) at the center of church life. This parallels the secular and religious educational emphasis on lifelong learning. One's learning from Jesus and about him—as well as about the implications of the gospel and religious traditions for one's life—never ends. No matter how old or learned people become, they must still have the humility to learn from others and be willing to have their views corrected by this learning.

The model stresses that adult religious education must be centered on *learning from and about Jesus*. It is easy for educational programs to lose this dimension as they proceed to the practical issues of family, child rearing, church, and world. The discipleship model stresses the importance of a personal spiritual relationship to Jesus in prayer, worship, and other aspects of community life. Above all, it entails a serious study of the Gospels and the theological applications of the gospel to contemporary issues.

The concept of discipleship, with its emphasis on the importance of *hearing a personal call* and responding in a free and self-conscious manner, makes clear the risk that is involved in all learning. This model is consonant with the view of the adult learner as a free and autonomous learner. To learn is to take the risk that our most cherished and deeply rooted notions will be found wanting. To learn is to be involved in a risky adventure that may entail radical changes in our lives. To reflect on the cost of discipleship that many disciples of Jesus have paid in previous eras and also in our time makes us realize the risky adventure that some forms of religious learning may be.

Discipleship takes place in *a community context*. Though religious learning on a one-to-one basis is not minimized in the Christian tradition, with its emphasis on spiritual direction and private confession of sins, the normal mode of religious learning and formation is active participation in the life of a Christian community. Persons need support in the challenging task of learning what Jesus means for them in the concrete situations of their lives. Christians would not be able to undergo the high cost of discipleship unless they had strong community support. This emphasis on the community of disciples parallels the notion of the learning society, a society that keeps in touch with its history and traditions by attempting to bring these to bear on contemporary life.

The model of discipleship puts great emphasis on the importance of *the ministry of teaching adults* within the church. This office has great responsibilities and can no longer be exercised in an authoritarian manner.

The model strongly implies that official teachers in the church have a special responsibility to remain lifelong disciples. All ministers of the church should be involved in this teaching ministry to adults at some time. Clergy who are brought into a teaching relationship to members of the community find themselves in a role where they have to offer fuller explanations, make necessary qualifications, and respond to concrete questions and criticisms. The teaching function most often leads to a genuine discipleship encounter.

Though one cannot underestimate the importance of official teachers in the church, the discipleship model implies that the church is a teaching community as well as a learning community. This results from the awareness that although all are disciples all can be in some sense teachers of others. Dulles's attempt to soften the distinction between ministers and those ministered to is significant in this regard. His point can be extended to the distinction between teachers and students. The value of "the sense of the faithful" in influencing church doctrine has long been recognized. Adults are teachers in many contexts: family, friendship, community, work, and church life.

Though I believe that the discipleship model of the church is a fruitful way of understanding the church in our times and the task of adult religious education, I feel that Dulles overstates his case for this model when he contends that it resonates well with the situation and needs of the church in our day. My disagreement with him is with his particular theological approach to ecclesiology, and, in an indirect way, with the implications of this approach for adult religious education. Though this study is too short for an extended treatment of this issue, I think that the issue is important enough for at least a brief treatment.

CONCLUSION: IMAGING THE CHURCH FOR THE FUTURE

Dulles draws his models of the church primarily from scriptural and theological sources. His theology is basically an exercise in creative biblical and historical theology. Dulles's approach to theology is not, however, in serious dialogue with the social sciences. Given that the church is a social reality and can be studied as such, any theological understanding of the church must include both theory and research on the church as a social organization. No one expects the ecclesiologist to become a sociologist. But the value of understanding the church through a creative use of theology and social theory is demonstrated by Gregory Baum in his work *Religion and Alienation* (1975). Baum, a Canadian theologian, spent two years at the New School of Social Research in New

York City to ground himself in the classical social theories of Hegel, Marx, Durkheim, Mannheim, Weber, and others. Baum also draws on empirically oriented sociologists of religion who have investigated the church as a social organization. He then correlates these theories with a critical theology to provide an understanding of the social reality of the church.

Social theory and research bring to our understanding of the church a touch of realism and a powerful corrective to idealistic ways of imaging the church. Ecclesial models tend to be abstract and spiritualistic. These models need to be correlated with social models which speak to such issues as power, authority, conflict, dissent, consensus, compromise, and accommodation—involving human relations as well as other social and social-psychological categories. An approach to the church that would focus only on these issues would dangerously reduce the church to a social organization and ignore the spiritual reality of the church. But equally dangerous is any approach to understanding the church that remains exclusively within the models presented in Scripture and the religious tradition.

In reading a study of the church based solely on biblical models, I often feel I am hearing about what the church can and might be. In reading social theory and research on the church I get the feeling of what the church is. Both views are necessary in order to move the church from its present reality to a future and better one. Social research also has the added advantage of indicating what the problems are that prevent the realization of the ideals presented in ecclesial models. Furthermore, there is a danger in constantly using religious or sacral language in describing our life in the church. This language may serve to cover over conflicts that need resolution and problems that need attention. The debunking tendency of the social sciences puts us on guard against such dangers. On the other hand, the message of the Scriptures and the religious tradition can utter judgments on the best social theory and research.

My purpose in these comments is not to pit social theory and research against theology in understanding the church but rather to argue that any relevant theology of the church must be in creative and corrective dialogue with the social sciences. The implications of this position spill over into religious education. My view of religious education is that it is an interdisciplinary field which draws on theology, philosophy, the behavioral and social sciences, and the humanities. The only type of theology I find relevant in the enterprise of religious education is one that is in serious dialogue with all these fields and disciplines. It is this dialogue which makes education contemporary and relevant to religious needs and issues.

I believe that there is value in imaging adult education in the church from the perspective of ecclesial models. If I did not, I would not have authored this study. However, I also consider it worthwhile to develop models from philosophy, the human sciences, and the social sciences, as I have done in other works. The more challenging task for imaging the church and its educational task for the future may be in the creation of theological models which are faithful to biblical and traditional sources but which also deeply explore contemporary individual and social experience.

It is my view that the discipleship model is too limited a model for imaging the church or its educational task for the future, despite its potential for incorporating some aspects of other models. The model focuses too narrowly on the inner life of the church and not broadly enough on what the church must do in present social, economic, and political contexts. The community of disciples is important but it must be placed in a broader context of world responsibility. Of the ecclesial models presented by Dulles, only the servant model appears to have this potential, though the word *servant* may have some undesirable connotations for this task.

Any imaging of the church for the future must be powerful enough to dramatize the task of the church in the face of multiple oppressions (sexual, racial, social, economic, and political) that threaten people's individual lives and the possibility of nuclear warfare and holocaust that threaten human existence. It may be that no one model can image this uncertain and fearful future. The limitations of all images in this regard may serve to remind us that the creation of a future reality is far more complex and difficult than our feeble images of it. It is no easy task to image the future of justice and peace that we desire and to which we as Christians are committed. Interestingly, the only images that come to my mind are those that have currency in both biblical tradition and in contemporary world society: "Blessed are the peacemakers." "Blessed are those who hunger and thirst after justice." The future beckons Christian communities to become Peace and Justice Churches. The educational task of the future is best seen within this perspective.

CHAPTER 8

THE ADULT'S JOURNEY IN FAITH

We portray human life with many different images. It is described in biological terms as growth and development. Psychologists use various interpretative schemes. According to some theorists, persons pass through a predictable life cycle or have a life span. In psychoanalytic terms, human growth and development is a search for integrity, a quest for meaning, a process of individuation, the striving for personal power, or the lifelong struggle to deny mortality and death. For humanistic psychologists, human life is growth towards self-actualization, fully functioning existence, autonomy and independence, or universalizing faith.

Social scientists suggest such images as lifelong conditioning, socialization, acculturation, or symbolization. Philosophers have traditionally used more rational images: the unceasing quest for wisdom, love, truth, and beauty; a lifelong obedience to an inner sense of duty; the gradual task of becoming a self-made person; or continuous development towards a socially functioning self. It is clear, then, that attempts to explain and capture the complexity of human life have produced a myriad of interpretative schemes.

Images of human life are also found in religious traditions. Religious writers often portray human life as a *journey* that a person takes. Human life is a way—the story of a journey, a passage, or an adventure. Themes of travel and journey abound in the Hebrew Scriptures. Abraham, Sarah, Joseph, Rachel, Moses, and the entire Israelite people are pilgrims on a journey. Jesus' life is one of journeying from place to place, from Bethlehem to Nazareth to Jerusalem. Luke's Gospel in a particular way has this travel theme, which is then continued in the Acts of the Apostles. In a more profound sense, according to the Gospel of John, Jesus' journey is a passage from the Father to the world and then back to the Father again. Journeying and traveling are found in the accounts of Paul's missionary activity. His journeys have inspired the religious practice of pilgrimage. One classical image of Christian life is the "pilgrim's progress." Christians are beckoned to follow and imitate Christ. In Lent there is the practice of following in the footsteps of Jesus in the *Via Crucis,* the Way of the

Cross. Religious processions and pilgrimages are symbolic manifestations of inner journeys.

Since similar images of journey are found in all world religions, one can conclude that the journey, pilgrimage, or way is a primary symbol of religious life. The Moslem sees life as a sacred pilgrimage in imitation of the flight of Muhammad. The Buddhist journeys like the Buddha in search of true wisdom. The follower of Confucius travels the *tao* or way of the master in order to find his or her own way. These physical movements of the journey are nothing less than symbols of a spiritual journey which persons undertake.

Recent attempts to describe the life of faith of religious persons have made use of biological, psychological, and social science constructs or images. Adult faith development has become an area of serious theoretical and empirical research (Fowler, 1981; Stokes, 1983). Recent studies also report data on the process of adult faith socialization. These research efforts are valuable in showing how the growing life of faith is closely related to all aspects of human development. This research, which is just at the beginning stage, can be helpful for those involved in religious ministry, especially counseling, pastoral care, and religious education.

What is also needed, I believe, is an attempt to understand adult faith and religious development from the perspective of more explicit religious images. Religious images shed a light on faith that is not usually found in other theories. They make more explicit the full meaning of life's journey, the companions on the way, and the ultimate destination of the journey.

My attempt to look at faith development through the journey image comes from a dissatisfaction with present work on faith development by psychologists, especially cognitive developmentalists. This approach most often uses the rational models of Piaget and Kohlberg, which have proved so fruitful in many areas of human understanding. Rational structures are important but they do not capture the core of religious faith. Faith is more in the realm of affective and dynamic life. It is better located in the realm of paradox, mystery, enigma, and encounter in the depths of one's being. Faith is not essentially a rational construing of the world. It must deal more with the realities of the spirit than with the realities of the mind. From the perspective of a sociologist like Wuthnow (1983) the cognitive model of faith development is tied too closely to the rational culture within which the research was done.

My dissatisfaction with cognitive developmentalism does not extend to the approach of psychoanalytic psychologists like Erik Erikson, Carl Jung, Ernest Becker, and Otto Rank. I believe that the psychoanalytic approach, in the hands of those who take a sympathetic understanding of religious experience, can deal in a better manner with religious experience, since it focuses more on dynamic and affective elements of the person. Even the less sympathetic work of Freud opens to us an understanding of important religious pathologies. An understanding of religious journey from the perspective of Erikson's developmental theory has been developed by the Whiteheads (Whitehead and Whitehead, 1979).

My main sources for understanding adult faith as a religious journey are reflections on the religious tradition, work with persons involved in the adult catechumenate, and analysis of faith biographies developed by graduate students at Fordham University. The chief scholarly source for my understanding of religious journey is the profoundly penetrating work of John Dunne (1978). In a number of works he has probed his own religious journey and that of a number of significant historical persons. I have utilized Dunne's work in two settings to probe the religious journey: in my courses in adult religious development and in a parish book-discussion group. Dunne's works had such an effect on members of the discussion group that, after reading one of them, the group decided to spend an extended period of time on his works.

FAITH AS A JOURNEY

All of us, on approaching adult life, realize that we are on a journey through life which is strangely familiar to us but which we are sure we have not travelled before. Often we had more certainty in childhood about the journey. We know the destination of the journey only dimly. We are searching for something or someone, but we are not sure what or who it is. What we know for sure is that on this journey we need guidance, encouragement, and companions. We move along on this journey in an atmosphere of faith and trust.

The image of faith as a journey has, like all metaphors, certain limitations. There is a sense in which we can not find faith by searching for it, nor can we reach it by any journey, no matter how long. In a mysterious way, faith is present both at the beginning and at the end of the journey. It takes us a long time to come to this realization.

The very notion of faith is a complex one in religious traditions. Numerous interpretations are often found in the same religious community. In some traditions it is an active search on the part of the individual. In others, it is viewed as a passive and unmerited acceptance of divine life. In this latter viewpoint God is the one who searches after us, like Francis Thompson's "The Hound of Heaven," as we attempt to escape from God down darkened ways. Faith can also be viewed as a personal desire to walk more closely or faithfully with God. Religious faith for some is the dramatic experience of meeting God after being delivered from danger or sin. It must also be highlighted that faith is a daily journey which we must take; its life is first lived and experienced. Only secondarily is faith the rational reflection on this actual experience.

In approaching religious faith we must be aware of both negative and positive images. Faith can be an escape from the terrors of life (Freud), an opium that drugs us against all forms of oppression (Marx), or a joyless denial of humanity (Nietzsche). In positive terms faith is the experience of trust and love, the finding of the meaning or truth in life, a commitment to what is truly valuable, and an appreciation of what is beautiful and attractive. In our time we have become more aware of faith as commitment to work to bring justice, peace, and love into our world. Though the symbol of God is the most powerful one in religious faith traditions, other helpful images and symbols are also found in the life of faith.

JOURNEY'S BEGINNINGS

Though the adult's journey in faith begins in the twenties, the first steps of the faith journey in pre-adult years are critical for later parts of the journey. The basic features of this part of the journey have long been known from religious and psychological writings. This journey takes place in the context of family, neighborhood, church, school, and community. In the years of *childhood,* one generally tags along in the journey of others: parents, sisters and brothers, teachers, and church leaders. As children develop, parents and teachers often get the bittersweet intuition that their children want to set out on their own journey. They travel where parents and teachers have not gone and might not want their children to go. They often give glimpses that they have been in mind and imagination to some places on their own. They meet God, make religious friends, confront the terror of death, and have a personal life of prayer.

The faith journey in childhood has a number of important aspects. It is a search for trusting persons and atmosphere in which to journey through life. It is a journey in which children must have the opportunity to develop a personal self that can freely exercise will and power. The child's faith journey is one that is imaged in stories, myths, fantasies, and playful rituals. Children begin to realize that they must live and work in a number of different contexts.

Adolescents take a more painful step in the faith journey. They begin to sense the aloneness as well as the inner and outer conflicts and struggles that often mark the journey of faith. Sexuality, power, faith crisis, alienation, and disillusionment are met for the first time. Some adolescents begin to wonder about the journey, whether or not it is worthwhile. Other journeys, more immediate, concrete experiences, and interesting new traveling companions appear more satisfying. Adolescents often change their minds about the religious journey; they have false starts; they set out on entirely different journeys. They may cease religious journeying altogether. Often they are in tension between the journey that they began with their parents in childhood and the new journey upon which they want to embark. The journeys of adolescents are not all of one kind. Many types of cries and pleas are heard during this painful part of the journey, as has been perceptively described by Strommen (1979).

Many adults can look back to adolescence as the time when they made definite progress in their journey of faith. For many it is a time of faith crisis, in which the search for self and love totally eclipses the search for God. Often this is the time for genuine religious conversion and commitment. It is at this time that the young are most susceptible to influences and examples of others in their lives. Many young persons are living out a drama in their own lives, and they find in the lives of faithful people around them inspiration and guidance. Very often young people are strengthened in their religious faith by their own peers. Churches which present challenges to the faith of the young through programs of service often find that the young respond to such challenges.

YOUNG ADULTHOOD: BEGINNING THE JOURNEY ON ONE'S OWN

For the Christian, the paradigm for the faith journey of young adults is found in the life of Jesus. The Gospels tell us of his break with his family and his journey to seek his own identity and mission. Christian piety has tended to minimize the impact of this parting from his parents, but the gospel tradition indicates that this separation had both misunderstanding and pain. The gospel tradition also tells us that Jesus' journey brought him to places and situations of temptation and self-doubt in which he is portrayed as searching for identity, intimacy, and mission. He gained some support from the close friends whom he called to accompany him on his journey.

The classical description of the identity crisis can be used to interpret the early stages of Jesus' journey. According to Erikson (1964), self-identity entails a separation from family and others, a stage of moratorium where different identities are attempted, and the resolution of the identity crisis through a commitment to an ideology which is of one's own choosing. Jesus precipitated the separation from his parents, and, in a way, he distanced himself from the old order of religious beliefs and practices. He endured in the moratorium of the desert, for forty days and forty nights, a period of testing out certain possibilities for his mission in the world. Finally, at his baptism by John, he became committed to do the will of his Father. At the very end of his life we still see him struggling, in the garden of Gethsemane, with his identity and mission. In essence, this is the journey of faith of young religious persons.

The first part of life's faith journey in the twenties is a journey in search of self. By this stage in the journey we have developed an awareness of personal existence, individual mission, and personal power. We also experience in young adulthood the beginning awareness of our own mortality. With this awareness we set out on a quest for life. The great Gilgamesh epic describes the inner dimensions of this journey. Gilgamesh's best friend has died and so he begins a journey in search of the meaning of life. Instead of finding life, he finds wisdom. The young adult's journey of faith begins at the moment when, on recognizing that we must die, we ask how we should live our lives.

While psychologists rightly describe the journey of early adulthood in terms of an often painful struggle for identity and mission, religious traditions describe the journey more often as a search for the true self, a response to an inner call, the seeking of a mission, or the search for God. Conversations with young adults who are dealing with such issues as career, friendship, marriage, and community reveal that a religious dimension is often a part of their thinking and probing at this time of life. When young adults first become aware that their journey is limited and that there are important decisions to be made, they often recognize the need for the power of God and faith for their lives.

While many young adults journey with a conscious awareness of God as a companion in their journey, many others lose this awareness and belief. Their focus is so much on what they must see and do on their journey that they become unaware of the seemingly silent companion on their journey. Very often they become reawakened to this awareness by the sudden presence of a loved person in their lives. Our research at Fordham has shown that this is especially true of young men who are reawakened to the presence of God through a love relationship.

The religious journeys of young adults have been described by Manno (1979) as the distancing of themselves from the religious journeys of childhood and adolescence. This distancing can take a number of forms. Young adults may become alienated from their earlier selves and prefer to move out on their own. They often sever connections with the religious bodies in which they were nurtured. They may experience dissatisfaction with the religious faith of their parents. This often leads to a disidentification from their churches or synagogues. Such young adults move in one of two directions. They may move away from all religious practice, maintaining remembrances of a former journey, or they may move into one of the recently developed religious groups or cults.

The other side of the distancing of the young adult is the search for meaning and certainty in life. The awareness of mortality opens up a life to be lived, an exciting journey to be pursued. In this uncertainty of the meaning of both life and death, it is helpful, as Dunne does, to look at the lives of others, and their stories. The stories of Jesus, Augustine, Paul, and Pascal are valuable examples used by Dunne. The young adults whom I have worked with are especially interested in the young adulthood of such people as Dorothy Day and Thomas Merton. The novels of the young Catholic novelist, Mary Gordon, reveal the searching and journeying of a contemporary young Catholic looking for a spiritual life in the modern world. In her writings there is a struggle between the older journeys of Catholics in times past and newer journeys. What fascinates young adults in these stories is the realization of the characters that the search for life is the search for God. To search for God, as Dunne insightfully notes, often means to give up the quest for something which is certain and true in favor of the quest for something which is only understandable.

Faith journey in young adulthood is often an implicit one. Engaged as many young adults are in forming a family, beginning a career, and establishing themselves in a community, they often do not connect themselves to religious communities. One has to see in these important aspects of their lives the attempt to deal with real issues of meaning, commitment, and mission. Many young persons find in action for justice or peace in the world the arena for religious commitments and energies.

THE MIDDLE OF THE JOURNEY: RELIGIOUS ODYSSEY AND ADVENTURE

No one knows exactly when he reaches the middle of life's journey. One thing is certain, the journey takes a turn with the awareness that one is at the middle point, with more yesterdays than tomorrows. The journey of faith at this time becomes an odyssey and an adventure. This is so because of a heightened sense of mortality and limits that arise in mid-life. The journey of mid-life is interpreted in various ways: the struggle for individuation or wholeness, the attempt to remain generative and caring, and the time to build a new life structure. For many religious persons, this part of the journey can best be described as passing through the dark night of the soul, the experience of existential loneliness.

Mid-life is often a time of religious stock-taking. One psychologist speaks of mid-life as a time for leaving the compulsive, unreflective busywork of occupational apprenticeship and becoming explorers of the world within (Vaillant, 1977). In another description it is a time for *de-illusionment,* i.e., the task of reconciling ourselves with the idealistic dreams of young adulthood (Levinson, 1976). For the religious person, these experiences provide the opportunity of looking again at one's religious faith and the opportunities it presents for development and growth.

The religious journey of many adults in mid-life can be described as an odyssey. It entails the passing over into the lives of others. We are able to pass over into the lives of people in times other than our own. We do this because of the realization that we are not all that we thought we could be. We may experience a lack of wholeness, in that we have not developed certain aspects of our personalities. In studying the religious journey of adults, we often find a growing interest in other faiths and standpoints. It is in mid-life that we become aware of the capacity for dealing with the paradoxes, dialectics, and contradictions of life. We accept the value and importance of our particular journey but also recognize that there are many equally valuable roads to take.

The faith journey in mid-life includes a number of difficult obstacles to be overcome, as has been described by Whitehead and Whitehead (1979). We must accept the fact of aging by neither clinging too tenaciously to youth nor becoming prematurely aged. Faith demands a certain acceptance of the changes that take place in our journey. The experience of aging, with the weakening of physical powers that it entails, is an opportunity to reflect upon the spiritual dimensions of life. With increase in pain and suffering, even in small ways, one is challenged to find meaning in a realm beyond the purely physical and material. With increasing age we grow in both dependence and independence. We must accept the new roles that increased age in life brings. We must learn to accept and utilize the advantages that various types of experience afford.

In mid-life we can deal on religious terms with the dark side of our personalities, with the destructiveness that is present in all of us. This darkness exists in connection with a creative and generative potential. The perfectionist or idealist attitudes of younger years often give way to more realistic and accepting attitudes. An acceptance of the self that we are can lead to an acceptance of others and to the possibility of a greater union with God. In a Lenten group that I participated in recently, I was amazed at how candidly people spoke of their strengths and weaknesses, their successes and failures. A mature attitude toward God has developed in the lives of these people, in which they recognize God's help but do not blame God for their failings.

A third obstacle to be faced in the mid-life journey of faith is the problem of integrating contrasting characteristics into our personality. Jung described this issue as the need to deal with the feminine and masculine poles of existence. The faith life of men and women can be seriously diminished if they maintain rigid stereotypes of what is proper for men and women in personal, interpersonal, and religious expression. In mid-life one can integrate toughness, achievement-orientation, ambition, power, and thinking with tenderness, cooperation, nurture, and feeling. Men and women in mid-life learn from their companions on the journey how to integrate these. We assimilate the qualities of those whom we love and appreciate. Mid-life is also a time for rethinking images of God, prayer, and worship along this masculine-feminine continuum.

The fourth obstacle in the mid-life faith journey is the struggle between the need for attachment and the need for separation. This tension, like the others, exists during one's entire life to some degree, but becomes especially acute at this time. One must be attached to parents, family, friends, and work, but also have some distance from all of these concerns. We must be prepared for the death of parents, the parting of children and friends, and retirement from work. In a paradoxical sense these can be viewed not as losses but as freeing opportunities for growth. Persons need not feel guilty about a newfound sense of freedom and excitement that comes after a painful separation. Correspondingly, in our religious lives we need both attachment to older forms of faith in which we were socialized and a separation from these in order to develop new forms of religious expression. Neither total separation nor total attachment to past and present are helpful as we attempt to move into an uncertain future. We need to move along ways that are both new and old.

In religious terms the dealing with tensions and failings in life is termed reconciliation. Religious bodies, through their formal and informal worship, pastoral care, and counseling, provide opportunities in which persons can reconcile the fourfold tensions in their lives. Though religious reconciliation is often subsumed under the headings of sin, repentance, confession, and forgiveness, we should recognize the connection of these notions with psychological obstacles to growth. Through reconciliation we are not returned to a former self but are able to pass to new selves. A religious community needs to have both formal and informal support groups for individuals who are in need of reconciliation: divorced and separated, bereaved, parents of problem children, etc.

Just as Jesus was a paradigm for understanding the faith journey of young adults, so he can be an example for the faith journey in mid-life. One can find in him the tensions that I have just described: the dealing with suffering, the acceptance of limitations and failures, the expression of a tender and caring person, as well as the polarity of separation and attachment. He is a model for adults both in his conduct under these tensions and in the type of generative leadership he provided for his disciples and followers. He sent out others, empowering them to preach and to continue his work.

It is important for religious communities to recognize the need for persons in mid-life to be leaders and teachers of others. On the religious journey we need to sense that we are helping others. Religious bodies need to be so organized that leadership is shared among as many persons as possible, both men and women, young and old. Adults need to become ministers, stewards, and mentors in the religious communities in which they live. One parish has developed a marriage preparation program in which prospective couples spend four sessions with a married couple discussing important aspects of married life, including the importance of building on a spiritual basis.

Persons in mid-life also have opportunities to make a positive contribution to the secular community in which they live and work. They have the challenge of making the values of religious faith relevant to the world of work, neighborhood, and nation. Persons in mid-life hold responsible positions in the community and in the industrial world. Faith challenges them to look carefully at the values which infuse their communities and to attempt to find ways to make their small worlds more livable.

Since I am at a mid-point in my own religious journey, paradoxically I know this part of the journey both best and least. These are the tensions of my life and who can know them better? But, in another sense, we need perspective on our present experiences. I may have a better understanding of earlier parts of the journey from my present vantage point. In trying to understand the next part of the journey, however, I can draw little on personal experience and must look more to what others have said and done.

THE CONCLUDING PART OF THE JOURNEY:
THE JOURNEY WITH GOD

It appears that the latter part of the journey is more clearly a journey with God. One learns to live with lack of engagement, with loneliness and solitude. This does not mean that there are not people in one's life to the end, but rather that we are more aware of ourselves and God as we are left with more time to ourselves. The pattern of our lives, according to Dunne, is that we are first drawn by the mystery of life that we see in others and the glimpse of hope, peace, and friendship that this appears to hold out. Then we all go through a time when we are deprived and bereft of these gifts. Finally, we recover this hope, peace, friendship, and understanding when we realize that God is the mysterious life that provides these good gifts.

The human journey at its latter stages is both into a new solitude and into deeper friendships with others. At this time in life we have the capacity to follow the desires of our heart. While I still raise the question "Is there a God?," my elderly friends experience God, walk with God, wonder at who God is. There is an elderly couple in my learning group—a three-generational learning group—who speak rather easily and authentically about God, prayer, problems, and sufferings. They are at peace on their journey with God. At one time I thought they did not feel deeply enough the problems of human life and the paradoxes of religious faith. Now I realize that where they are on their faith journey provides them with a trusting and hopeful perspective on life.

I recognize that the last part of the journey is not the same for all older adults. The last stages of the journey for some are days of disgust, despair, and destitution. There are different endings. My belief is that, deep down, those at the latter stage of the journey are searching for someone who will make them new persons. To become new persons we need to let go of everything and everybody. Only if we are willing to adopt again the dependence of the little child can we become new persons. Perhaps this is the only way we can finally acknowledge that our journey at its deepest level is a journey with God.

The latter part of the journey in many religious traditions is portrayed as a search for true wisdom, a wisdom that enables us to live despite physical suffering and fear of death. This wisdom consists in accepting what one's life has been, a gesture of forgiveness for others, and the struggle to continue to find meaning in each day of life. This wisdom is achieved through attempts to transcend bodily ailments, diminished existence, and even our personal selves.

Religious communities need to explore ways to utilize the wisdom and witness of the elderly to build up the community of faith. The elderly are not meant just to be ministered to; they also have a ministry to exercise in the church. They need to be reminded of the powerful witness value of their lives, for as Erikson has noted, "Healthy children will not fear life if their elders have integrity not to fear death." They are the examples of how one grows old in the faith. The religious memory of the elderly needs to be preserved for future generations as an example and inspiration. But they can also aid others in present trials and bereavement. On the death of my father, my mother was considerably supported by other widows in her church community.

As Jesus is, for both young and middle-aged adults, an example of how one passes through a journey of faith, so he is a model at the journey's end for the aged. Though Christian tradition presents his death as that of a young man, the quality of his life at the end speaks to the situation of the elderly Christian. He had to go through the painful letting-go that is the experience of every person at the end of life. He was alone with his Father at the end, having been left by many of his closest disciples. His final hours were a struggle. Yet he remained faithful in his acceptance of his need to continue to do God's will.

COMPANIONS ON THE JOURNEY OF FAITH

Most persons in their faith journey have and need companions. There are people who help us on our faith journey in many ways. It might be helpful to conclude this study on the faith journey by reflecting on the various types of companionship that are possible in the journey of faith. This section has been inspired by the thoughtful reflections of Alistair Campbell in his book *Rediscovering Pastoral Care* (1981).

We must recognize that we are greatly limited in what we can do for another in his or her faith journey. We cannot know the right path that others should follow on their journey. We cannot create for other persons the conditions for their growth in faith. In a real sense we cannot be teachers, guides, or directors for others in their faith journey. What we can do is to be companions to them. We can go along with them, share the twists and turns of the journey with them, and help them as best we can with our own limited vision and the support of our love.

There are different ways of being a *companion* to others on their faith journey. The word *companion* literally means "to share bread." We are companions when we share bread with others or share what bread symbolizes. At one level we share bread by sharing a common humanity with others. We share the equality of companionship. This level of companionship is most appropriate in young adulthood when we first move out alone into the human circle. We can share with others the bread we have found in our lives. We recognize that human beings do not live by bread alone. People need to find the living bread which came down from heaven to give everlasting life. We know God will give us bread if we ask for it. We can break bread for others in love for them. As Campbell strikingly notes, religious faith is no more than one starving person telling others where the bread is to be found.

The second level of companionship goes beyond sharing a common humanity to a *communion* with others. We can also enter the life of another and stay for a while. We can become more than chance acquaintances; we can give to them something of ourselves. In this form of companionship we do more than show where the bread of life is. We become present to others in both body and spirit. In entering into communion with another we are willing to expose more of self and talk about what is really important to us.

Communion with others becomes a real possibility in adulthood. We need to enter into communion with others as we begin to experience the limits of our being. We gain strength from our union with others, from holding them and joining with them in common efforts. This communion, in a mysterious way, opens up the way for the presence of God. "Where two or three are gathered in my name, I am there in the midst of them." Jesus was present to the disciples on the road to Emmaus. Though they did not fully recognize him until he broke bread with them, they recognized that they had had communion or sharing with him in the journey to Emmaus. This story also reminds us that true companions often begin as strangers in our lives.

This type of companionship is the essence of friendship. It is the sharing of both activity and repose. The heart of friendship is not any particular activity or intimacy. It is a way of being with, and being present to, others. Repose can be an important dimension of this friendship. We need companions who do not take our anxious striving too seriously, friends with whom we can waste time.

The third level of companionship is the most difficult but also the most necessary. In later adulthood and especially at the journey's end we want not just a companion or a confidant but a *comrade*. The comrade is the person who accompanies us when we are in battle. The comrade is needed when mortal danger looms, when we face the uncertainties surrounding life and death. We do not want to face the end—death—alone. We need someone to face the darkness with us. Comradeship is essential when the reality of life and death are too much for us. Two of my close friends who died in recent years wanted their wives with them at all times of night and day when they faced death from cancer.

It is clear that the fear of death presents religious faith with its greatest challenge because it suggests that there is nothing to hope for, nothing to gain in journeying, that in the end there may be only loss, blankness, and final extinction. Companionship in battle may be the most appropriate stance in the face of death.

My belief is that when we reach the end of the journey of faith we will recognize that the end or goal of the journey has been with us in some mysterious way through the entire journey. In our life—in our bodies and spirits, struggling to find peace in the world, in our wanderings, searchings, and journeyings—it is God who has been present. What has been hidden shall be revealed.

It is only in the end of our journey that we learn to recognize that the human journey is not linear but circular. The world, after all, is actually a globe. After we travel a certain distance we begin to return home to ourselves. Our journeyings in the end become homecomings. But we get there by a different route. As the poet T. S. Eliot (1963, p. 208) tells us:

> With the drawing of this love
> And the voice of this calling,
> We shall not cease from exploration
> And the end of all our exploring
> Will be to arrive where we started
> And know the place for the first time.

CHAPTER 9

PAULO FREIRE: ADULT RELIGIOUS EDUCATOR

A reader of Paulo Freire's *Pedagogy of the Oppressed* (1970a) may easily miss an important aspect of the social and educational thought of this significant and contemporary educator. This aspect is the deeply religious nature of Freire's view of person, society, culture, politics, and education. This dimension of Freire's thought comes to the fore in this work in an explicit manner only in a couple of instances, though a closer examination of the work will reveal this dimension in clearer terms. Freire himself tells us that he downplayed explicit religious themes since he wanted to reach both Christians and Marxists in this work. However, if other writings of Freire are examined, works written both before and after *Pedagogy of the Oppressed*, the classification of Freire as a religious educator is seen to be a most accurate one. This study will attempt to bring into perspective the religious dimension of the social and educational philosophy of Paulo Freire. This chapter is only a brief treatment of this topic, since I have written on Freire's religious thought at greater length (Elias, 1976).

A CHRISTIAN HUMANIST

Freire can with justification be called a Christian humanist. He calls himself a humanist and refers to his philosophy as humanistic. He constantly refers throughout his writings to the vision of man, which is the basis of his thought. Humanization is for Freire the goal of every enterprise in which persons are involved. It is opposed to the process of dehumanization, which describes for Freire every action which is destructive of true human nature and dignity. Freire's clearest description of his pedagogical theory is presented in these words:

> Our pedagogy cannot do without a vision of man and of this world. It formulates a scientific humanist conception which finds its expression in a dialogical praxis in which teachers and learners, together, in the act of

analyzing a dehumanizing reality, denounce it while announcing its transformation in the name of the liberation of man (Freire, 1970b, p. 20).

The roots of Freire's humanism are religious, or more specifically, Christian and Catholic. Though he utilizes various traditions in developing his vision of man, the controlling concepts are religious. The central religious problem is that of man's relationship to a transcendent Being. Freire affirms a transcendent Being, God, and speaks of man's relationship to this being as central to his view of man and the world. The relationship that man should have with others and the relationships that should exist in society are determined and modeled after the relationship that man has to his Creator. Domination and oppression should not exist among persons in human society because this would not be true to what persons are in light of their relationship to their Creator. Freire describes the relationship in this manner:

His [God's] transcendence over us is based on the fact of our knowledge of this finitude. For man is an incomplete being, and the completion of his incompleteness is encountered in his relationship with his Creator, a relationship which, by its very nature, can never be a relationship of domination or domestication, but is always a relationship of liberation. Thus religion (*religare*—to bind) which incarnates this transcendent relationship among men should never be an instrument of alienation. Precisely because he is a finite and indigent being, in this transcendence through love, man has his return to his source who liberates him (Freire, 1969, p. 15).

The vision of man which Freire espouses is a vision which sees man as a reflective and free person who has been created by God to extend continually the potentialities of his being by living out relationships with God and other persons. Man is essentially distinct from animals in his power of consciousness and freedom. The fact that some persons are oppressed by others is a sin not only against man but also against God. There should exist among men and women a spirit of fraternity characterized by loving relationships.

The sources of Freire's religious humanism are varied. He relies on some of the concepts of scholastic philosophy and existential phenomenology in describing human consciousness as opposed to animal consciousness. When he speaks of the dialogue that should take place among persons at every level, he echoes the ideas of Martin Buber and Gabriel Marcel. He takes a key concept, "limit situation," from the religious existentialist Karl Jaspers.

More recent theological trends in Latin America are even more influential in Freire's vision of humanity. He has connected himself with the Latin American theology of liberation which has attempted to cast religion in the role of liberating men and women as well as societal institutions from oppressive elements. Theologians of this persuasion are keenly aware of the role that religion has played in Latin American countries in maintaining existing oppressive political and social institutions. They have drawn on certain elements in the Hebrew and Christian tradition which point to a more liberating and prophetic role for religion. This liberating view of religion has as one of its central ingredients a view of the human person as essentially free and active in combatting all forms of domination and oppression.

A final source of Freire's vision of man is in Marxist thought of a humanist persuasion. Within this tradition persons are viewed as unfinished and with an inborn disposition to act in shaping themselves and the world. Within persons there is also a utopian capacity to image new possibilities and to struggle for their realization. From Marxist thought Freire drew the view of the dialectical tension in which persons are situated: they are shaped by cultural forces but also have the responsibility of changing these forces through their own personal action.

A CHRISTIAN SOCIAL CRITIC

The social criticism in which Freire engages is partly based, as was his vision of man, upon a religious and theological vision and his experience as a member of the Roman Catholic church in Brazil and Chile. This particular perspective is also that of the Latin American theology of liberation developed by such theologians as Rubem Alves and Gustavo Guttierez.

Freire's social criticism includes a criticism of the Christian church as an institution. In earlier writings Freire did not explicitly include the church among the objects of his societal criticism. Later writings found him concerned with the oppressive nature of church institutions. Freire's position as an educational consultant with the World Council of Churches in Geneva afforded him an opportunity for closer analysis of the role of the church as an institution in Third World countries.

In two important articles Freire (1972; 1973b) criticized the churches for failing to exercise the true prophetic function which is theirs. He urged the churches to work more actively against oppression, in whatever form it existed. The churches, he contended, should not be neutral because neutrality means supporting the status quo. Examples of such oppression are class-determined societies, oppressive power elites, and capitalism.

The true gospel for Freire is prophetic, utopian, and revolutionary. It calls for believers to work for change, revolution, and liberation. Jesus is presented by Freire as a person who worked for radical change. The religious revolutionary engages in living out the Passover or Easter through denouncing oppression and announcing liberation. Redemption is interpreted as the Christian's willingness to undergo death by struggling for new life and freedom for oppressed people.

In these articles Freire expressed his belief that he is calling the churches back to the true message of the gospel. His critique of the church was both clear and radical. In attempting to remain neutral for so long in the Latin American struggles of liberation, the churches actually supported the existing oppressive regimes in those countries. The churches preferred to involve themselves in bureaucratic paper-shuffling. They were dying of cold in the warm bosom of the bourgeoisies.

Freire was not even satisfied with the efforts of the churches which were attempting to reform themselves. These reforms were not radical enough. He criticized the churches for merely talking about humanizing capitalism and doing nothing about it. He wanted the churches to work to remove the capitalist systems which were oppressive. He viewed the modernizing efforts of the churches as basically a conservative action, reforming only to maintain the status quo.

Freire's view of God is influential in his social criticism. The symbol of God presented by him is not the Unmoved Mover of Aristotle or the Subsistent Being of Aquinas. It is rather the active and dynamic God of the Hebrews plus the human person of Jesus. God is One who acts to save mankind. God creates human beings and governs the world with human cooperation. The divine Being delivers a people from bondage. Jesus is presented as the radical critic of oppressive institutions. In this view, the symbol of God as Saviour refers not so much to individual salvation but to the process of bringing persons and societies to true freedom. The task of the Christian is not to save his soul but to work with God in saving the world by combatting all forms of oppression. Original Sin is given a social interpretation as referring to all forces of evil against which God and mankind struggle and which prevent true freedom. The Resurrection and Future Life with God are concrete symbols of the new life which exists in the Utopian Future.

A look at Freire's writings shows how this symbol of God is operative in Freire's thinking. God is one who stands not for the domination of humans but for their liberation. Freire asserts that our transcendent relationship with God is an integral part of human nature, and it is a relationship in which our freedom is guaranteed (Freire, 1967, p. 15). He attacks "the false view of God which fosters fatalism in oppressed peoples (Freire,

1970a, p. 162).'' This false view of God is based on the myth that rebellion is a sin against God (1970a, p. 136). In his famous ''A Letter to a Theology Student'' Freire gives expression to the dynamic nature of the God symbol which underlies his social criticism:

> The Word of God is inviting me to recreate the world, not for my brother's domination but for his liberation. . . . The Word of God is not some content to be poured into us as if we were mere static recipients for it. And because it [the Word of God] saves, the Word liberates, but men have to accept it historically. They must make themselves subjects, agents of their salvation and liberation (Freire, 1967, p. 15).

Freire's social philosophy is clearly based on Christian principles. The democratic society that Freire proposes in *Education for Critical Consciousness* (1973b) is clearly to be founded on Christian principles of freedom, justice, equality, and charity. References to Christian sources in this particular work are not numerous, but they are significant. Man's awareness, and his living out, of his existence is one of the important ingredients of the critical consciousness that is essential for the development of the New Man and the New Society. (1973b, pp. 17–8). The education that Freire proposes is described in religious terms borrowed from Jaspers and Buber. Educational dialogue, for Freire, is:

> nourished by love, humility, hope and trust. When the two poles of the dialogue are thus linked by love and mutual trust they can join in a critical search for something (1973b, p. 45).

The basic principles of a Christian social democratic philosophy are also found in *Pedagogy of the Oppressed*. Freire addressed his book to both Christians and Marxists, though he expected disagreements from both. He was sensitive to the idea that revolutionaries might dismiss him because of certain concepts in his writings. These concepts are those that obviously come from his religious vision: ontological vocation of man, transcendent relationship with God, love, dialogue, hope, humility, and sympathy. When he wrote of the necessity of violence or rebellion these acts were termed acts of love (1970a, pp. 41, 77).

The fatalism of oppressed people was attributed to a false concept of God. He rejected the concept that oppressors are the defenders of Western civilization. Although elements of the Marxist critique were introduced into *Pedagogy of the Oppressed* and this represented a change from the earlier social criticism of Freire, these Marxist elements were integrated with the principles that underlay his Christian view of society.

The religious element in Freire's social philosophy became increasingly more explicit in his later writings and speeches. Freire saw the Christian gospel as proclaiming the radical reordering of society in which persons are oppressed. He appealed not only to the gospel but also to the social encyclicals of Pope John XXII and Paul VI. At a talk in Rome he made these remarks:

> I am not yet completely a Catholic; I must keep on trying to be one more completely, day after day. . . . I just feel passionately, corporately, physically, with all my being that my stance is a Christian one because it is 100 percent revolutionary and human and liberating, and hence committed and utopian (Freire in Donohoe, 1972, p. 170).

While Freire expressed praise for democratic principles, he made it clear that he was not praising Western democracies. Rather, he saw these democratic principles best in places like Cuba, and in Chile before the fall of the Allende government. For Freire, these countries were not merely modernizing but were developing in the true sense of the word (1973a, p. 42).

THE CHRISTIAN REVOLUTIONARY

Pedagogy of the Oppressed is a veritable handbook for revolutionary education. Freire contended in it that a liberating education is a necessary condition for bringing about a social or political revolution. His book is a description of the type of education that must take place in order to initiate a revolution among oppressed peoples. What is not generally known about Freire is that he himself has never participated in the type of revolutionary activity which he propounded in his book. He made this statement in the preface of the book:

> It is possible that some may question my right to discuss revolutionary action, a subject of which I have no concrete experience. However, the fact that I have not personally participated in revolutionary action does not negate the possibility of my reflecting on this theme (1970a, p. 24).

Freire contended that through his experience as an educator he "accumulated a comparative wealth of material which challenged [him] to run the risk of making the affirmations contained in this work (1970a, p. 24)."

Freire has been an advocate of political revolutions for oppressed peoples in the Third World. In proposing revolution he has been particularly sensitive to the question of whether or not political revolution, especially violent revolution, can be justified according to Christian principles. This question has long been discussed in Catholic Leftist circles in Latin America. Freire placed himself in league with radical Christians who argued for the justification of revolution, even violent revolution.

In speaking of the myths which the oppressor society imposes upon the oppressed, he pointed to two particular myths that bear on this issue: the myth of the heroism of the oppressor classes as defenders of Western Christian civilization and the myth that rebellion is a sin against God. The implication here, which is supported by other statements of Freire, is that rebellion and revolution are actions that can be in accordance with Christian and religious principles. Furthermore, Freire described revolutionary violence in terms which have, at least, religious connotations surrounding them:

I am more and more convinced that true revolutionaries must perceive the revolution, because of its creative and liberating nature, as an act of love. For me, the revolution which is not possible without a theory of revolution—and therefore science—is not irreconcilable with love (1970a, p. 77).

Freire has argued in an even more explicit manner for the justification of Christian participation in revolutionary action. He asserted in his letter to the theology student that:

We as Christians have an enormous task to perform presuming that we are capable of setting aside our idealistic myths and in that way, sharing in the revolutionary transformation of society, instead of stubbornly denying the important contribution of Marx (1973b, p. 7).

The most explicit treatment that Freire has given to the religious justification for revolutionary action is found in his article, "The Educational Role of the Churches in Latin America," (1972b). Freire repeated the treatment of this topic in "Education, Liberation and the Church." (Freire, 1973b). The church, he contends, cannot remain opposed to transformation in social structures. He criticized conservatives in the churches for "castrating the church's prophetic dimension and fearing the radical transformation of the unjust world (p. 3)." He praised the developing political theology of liberation which says something about the revolutionary transformation of the world. Within this prophetic theology there is room for those who recognize "revolution as the road to liberation for the oppressed classes, and the military coup as a revolutionary option (p. 12)."

Two other religious motivations are used by Freire in urging Christians to become involved in revolutionary activity. He referred a number of times to the revolution of the oppressed as a Passover or Easter. These events entailed struggles of life and death. Redemption or liberation from oppression was achieved through active resistance and violent death. Christians who involve themselves in revolutionary action against oppression involve themselves in a New Passover, a New Easter. The revolutionaries' "setting out is really a sort of Passover in which they will have to die as an oppressed class, in order to be reborn as a class that liberates itself (1972b, p. 4)."

Another motivation which Freire utilized in urging Latin American Christians into revolutionary action lay in the example of Christ. The image of Christ is of one who is a radical, not satisfied with the status quo, anxious to move on, willing to die in order to bring out a continuous rebirth. Freire put these words in the mouth of those who would counsel conservative activity on the part of Latin American Christians: "They say to Christ, Master, why push on, if everything is so beautiful here (1972b, p. 12)?"

A RELIGIOUS EDUCATOR

Freire is an educational theorist who draws upon religion for some of his basic views on education. His most complete treatment of the relationship between religion and education is found in two articles (1972b, 1973b). In these articles he developed three views of religion and compared them with the types of education that each view of religion engendered. The *traditionalist* view of religion stresses life in the world to come. It is a view that urges people to reach transcendence without passing through worldliness. This type of religion fosters the closed society and is instrumental in maintaining the status quo even if it is a state of oppression. This religious view has concepts of the world, religion, human beings, and human destiny which promote an education which will inevitably be quietistic, alienated, and alienating.

The second view of religion, of which Freire was also critical, is the *modernizing* perspective. Freire believes that religion in Latin America has manifested this tendency. It has changed some of its practices, restated some of its doctrinal positions, and gotten more involved in problems of a social, economic, and political nature. But the measures taken go only half-way and do not bring about the truly radical changes that are necessary. Modernizing religion has its own perspective on education. It speaks of a liberating education, but in doing this it stresses a change in technique, a change in individuals rather than the drastic changes in society that are needed. The form of education fostered by this type of religion:

> means no more than liberating the pupils from their blackboards, from passive classes and bookish curricula; it means just providing slide projectors and other visual aids, dynamic class plans, and technico-professional instruction (1972b, p. 11).

Freire's view of religion is the *prophetic* one. It commits itself to the dominated classes and seeks to transform society radically. It refuses to separate concerns for this world from concerns about transcendence. It defines salvation in more worldly terms. For many, this view means the recognition of the necessity of violent political revolution. Education according to this religious view "will always . . . be a mode of action meant to change things, a political program for the permanent liberation of man (1972b, p. 18)." Freire made this statement about the nature of the prophetic view of education:

> From the prophetic point of view, the specific subject matter of education is of little importance: whatever the subject matter, education is always an effort to understand better something that is concrete. As they focus on it together, the educator-educatee and the educatee-educator will be joined in creative, active presence, in a clarifying praxis that, as it unveils the reality of awareness, will help to unveil the reality of reality, too (1972b, p. 19).

Freire was careful to point out that this type of education must include a political program for bringing about objective and radical changes in the structures of society.

Freire's position with the World Council of Churches afforded him the opportunity to develop more carefully the relationships that existed between his theological and educational views. In an interview held in 1973 he spoke of his desire to work with theologians to explore the relationship between a theology for liberation and an education for liberation. In Freire's writings this education includes a focusing on the three traditional cries of all revolutionaries: liberty, equality, and fraternity.

Freire's call to revolution is made in the name of *freedom*. For Freire human freedom is a gift of God; it is God who empowers men and women to liberate themselves. Freire criticized the education which he termed "banking education" for its failure to respect true human freedom. In this form of education teachers make deposits of information into the minds of students, who are viewed as passive recipients of information. To counter this banking education Freire proposed a liberating education. In his type of education, students are to be on equal terms with their teachers in developing the problems which are to be discussed, and they are to be free during the entire educational process.

Cultural action for freedom is the expression which Freire uses to designate the educational process itself. This action is one in which a group of people, through dialogue, come to realize the concrete problems which they face in their particular situations, analyze the reasons for these problems, and consider the possible solutions to them. In order for this to be authentic action, the participants must be free to pose problems and arrive at solutions along with the teacher.

Freire's call to revolution was also made in the name of *equality*. He proposed an egalitarian ideal for society and was extremely critical of the great disparities that exist in modern societies in the areas of wealth, power, and status. For Freire, it is the domesticating nature of most forms of education that prevents people from seeing the true social reality of their lives and thus forces them to accept the inegalitarian society in which they live. The school as presently constituted is the institution of society which prevents the emergence of the classless society which Freire envisions. Freire proposed his liberating pedagogy as an instrument for achieving the revolution that would bring about the classless society. His position can be assimilated to the view of social reconstructionists in education. His views differ from these thinkers in that his major focus is not on the schools but more properly upon adult or community education.

Finally, Freire's call to revolution was made in the name of *fraternity*. Fraternity implies the quality of relationship that should exist among persons in society. It is held to represent a certain quality of social esteem, the absence of manners of deference and servility, a sense of civic friendship and social solidarity (Rawls, 1971, p. 105). The ideal of fraternity involves bonds of sentiments and feelings. True fraternity exists in society when the institutions of society enrich the personal and social lives of its citizens. Freire saw contemporary arrangements as militating against the existence of true fraternity in society.

For Freire the concept of fraternity has obvious religious roots and overtones. He often speaks of the "communion" which should exist among persons in society. For him fraternal solidarity is essential for religious, political, and educational solidarity or education. He made the parallel himself:

Men free themselves only in concert, in communion, collaborating on something wrong which they want to correct. There is an interesting theological parallel to this: no one saves another, no one saves himself all alone, because only in communion can we save ourselves or not save ourselves (1972c, p. 8).

Freire's criticism of banking education is controlled by the ideal of fraternity which he espoused. Banking education offends true fraternity because, according to Freire, the teacher is the only subject in the learning process while the students are mere objects. It is the teacher who teaches, knows everything, disciplines, chooses, and has authority. The pupil is in a position of subservience and must pay deference to the teacher. The student is not admitted to true partnership in learning according to this form of education. No solidarity exists between teacher and pupils where there is not true communication upon which solidarity is based. This type of education: "stimulates the credulity of students, with ideological intent (often not perceived by educators) of indoctrinating them to adapt to the world of oppression (Freire, 1970a, p. 59)." To the banking form of education, Freire opposes his problem-solving education which is based on respect, communication, and solidarity. This type of education promotes that spirit of fraternity which is essential for truly democratic education in a democratic society.

EDUCATION AS CONSCIENTIZATION

In the past decade and a half Freire has been associated with the term "conscientization." Although he did not coin the term, he has used it as the key concept in his educational philosophy. Freire writes of conscientization as the development of critical awareness, achieved through dialogical educational programs associated with social and political responsibility (1973a, p. 19). The aim in this process is to bring about critical attitudes in people. Freire also calls his educational theory one of democratic education, for it is founded on faith in humans—on the belief that persons cannot only discuss the problems of their society but also have the power to solve these problems. Conscientization includes the exchange of ideas, debates, and discussions; it means working *with* students and not *on* them (1973a, p. 28).

Freire's religious philosophy is implicit in his description of conscientization. This process is the only type of educational process that respects human nature. Man's God-given freedom is respected in a situation where particular ideas are not imposed on students but rather result from the open discussion of many ideas. This type of education respects the basic equality that should exist among persons in society. The fraternity or community of persons is fostered by a type of education in which students and teachers face one other on an equal basis. The prophetic religion which Freire espouses finds its logical focus in a process in which the ultimate purpose of education is a radical transformation of oppressive social, political, and economic structures.

Crucial to an understanding of Freire's concept of conscientization is his theory of the various levels of human consciousness (1973a, pp. 16–22). He uses an analogy from grammar and linguistics to illustrate these levels. The lowest level of consciousness he calls *intransitive consciousness*. People at this level are preoccupied with meeting their most elementary needs. They are characterized by the near absence of historical consciousness. Such persons are almost impervious to problems beyond the biological and physical sphere. They are immersed in a time which is experienced as a one-dimensional oppressive present. The relationships into which they have entered have shaped their sociocultural situation and can barely be comprehended by them.

Semi-intransitivity or *magical consciousness* is the second level of consciousness in Freire's theory. Freire contended that this type of consciousness was prevalent in the emerging societies of the Third World. It is the prevailing consciousness of closed societies, the culture of silence. Persons at this level take the facts of their sociological situation as "givens." This form of consciousness is characterized by a fatalistic mentality which views all of life as related to destiny or fortune, forces beyond human control. Self-depreciation is a most common attribute of this level, for people at this level have internalized the negative values that the dominant culture has ascribed to them. This level of consciousness is also marked by excessive emotional dependence. To be is to be under someone, to depend on him or her. This type of consciousness often expresses itself in defensive and therapeutic magic.

Semi-transitive or *naive consciousness* is Freire's third level of consciousness. Freire also calls this level *popular or populist consciousness*. Silence is not the characteristic of persons at this level. People at this level can engage in a serious questioning of the situation, but in a naive and primitive manner. This form of consciousness is more likely to see the cultural situation as determined by other persons. People can be seduced by strong populist leaders who seem to give persons a sense of the strength and power they have over their own lives. The great danger of this form of consciousness is that people can be manipulated by exploitive and populist leaders.

The highest level of consciousness for Freire is *critical consciousness*. This level is achieved through the process of conscientization and is marked by depth in the interpretation of problems, self-confidence in discussions, receptiveness, and refusal to shirk responsibilities. The quality of discourse here is dialogical. At this level the person scrutinizes his own thoughts and sees the proper causal and circumstantial correlations among events. For Freire, conscientization essentially means a radical denunciation of dehumanizing structures, accompanied by the announcing of a new reality to be created by the persons themselves. It demands a rigorous and rational critique of the ideology that supports these structures. Critical consciousness is brought about not solely through intellectual efforts but also through praxis, the authentic union of action and reflection.

After this discussion of Freire's analysis of the levels of human consciousness, it is possible to understand what his theory of human learning is. Learning, for Freire, is the process by which one moves from one level of consciousness to another. The content of this consciousness is the view that one has of one's existence in the social world and the power that one has to determine one's destiny. Learning begins with the present level of consciousness as this is manifested in the language, self-concept, world view, and present living situations. Learning is becoming aware of the contingency of social reality. Its basis is the idea that there is an essential difference between the givenness of the natural world and the contingency of the social world. The contingent world lies within the power of persons to change. Learning is thus the process of challenging and being challenged by the givenness of one's life situation and of the sociocultural world.

IMPLICATIONS FOR RELIGIOUS EDUCATION

Freire has provided, in the first place, *a new theological basis for religious education* by wedding his educational philosophy to the theology of liberation which has been developed primarily by Latin American theologians. This theological basis brings to the fore the social and political dimensions of religious education. It also requires an emphasis on the dynamic aspects of great religious symbols. Change rather than stability is clearly seen to be the primary aspect of human life. Involvement in the world rather than flight from it is a dominant element in this form of education.

Theologies of liberation and political theologies have begun to engage the attention of religious educators who seek a theological basis for religious education. In recent years Wren (1977), Groome (1980), Toton (1982), and others have appealed to both Freire and liberation theology in developing an approach to religious education. In another study in this collection, I will present an approach for dealing with power and liberation which appeals to both of these strands of thought.

Philosophical Influence

Freire's pedagogy of the oppressed can give to religious education a broader *philosophical basis* for its educational theorizing. Freire is clearly an eclectic in his theoretical approach to education. One finds in his work elements from existential phenomenology: the analyses of dialogue and encounter, the description of human consciousness and knowledge, and the notion of the limit-situation. Pragmatic thought is found in his description of democratic education through inquiry and problem solving. The Marxist elements in his thinking have become more pronounced in his writings: the analysis of oppression, the description of society in terms of infrastructure and suprastructure, the analysis of the influence of class in society, and the reliance on revolutionary praxis and social change. Though it can be questioned whether Freire has organized these various strands of thought into a consistent whole, his eclecticism is a valuable contribution to the discipline of philosophy of education which has traditionally broken itself down into opposing schools.

Freire's growing importance in philosophy of education is seen in recent developments in sociology of knowledge as applied to school learning and adult education. This approach to education stresses how all learning is conditioned by the social context in which it takes place. It examines the roles that power, ideology, and class play in the determination of what counts as knowledge. Education in these terms is not merely passing on absolute truths but questioning, defining, observing, classifying, generalizing, verifying, applying, valuing, and deciding upon what criteria are to be applied to knowledge (Young, 1971; Apple, 1979). I will treat this aspect of his work in my study on ideology and religious education.

Aims of Religious Education

Freire's educational philosophy contributes to the discussion of the *aims of religious education*. His emphasis is on the social and political dimensions of education. Though he sees freedom as a primary concern in education, he tends to place more emphasis on the task of education in changing social structures which are dehumanizing and oppressive. His thinking here parallels what Gabriel Moran has written about the role of education:

I would maintain that the starting point for an educational anthropology is the question of freedom and social organization. I will take up this issue first. Only then will I try to analyze the human capacities for learning. They are to be understood in relation to changing the social structure for the increase of freedom. Thus, I move from the social to the individual and back to the social (Moran, 1970, p. 52).

It is clear that Freire's work has made educators in many areas think seriously about the social and political dimension of education. This is also true of religious educators. Action-reflection modes of education, education for peace and justice—praxis forms of education have developed which all have reference to Freire's educational philosophy.

Content of Religious Education

In Freire's writings one can find many implications bearing on the *content of religious education*. The content is to be drawn primarily from the life of the people: their concerns, problems, fears, myths. The educator must be careful not to impose ideas on the learners. The content of education is less often found in books than in the real-life problems of people. Freire used no primers in his adult literacy program because he felt that such books would impose a world view on the students. Such a practice applied to religious education would certainly place students and teachers alike on their own resources.

Freire's approach to educational content raises questions about the role of the received tradition in religious education. I believe that Freire would be more interested in how this tradition is handled than in whether or not it plays an important part in religious education. His approach would be to handle it in a critical manner and in such a way as to be open to the ideological elements of this tradition. Handing on the tradition, in this approach, means to enter it critically. It results in:

re-entering the world through the entering into of the previous understandings which may have been arrived at naively because reality was not examined as a whole. In entering into their own world, people become aware of their manner of acquiring knowledge and then realize the need to know even more (Freire, 1973a, p. 155).

Methods in Religious Education

Freire obviously has an important contribution to make to the use of *methods in religious education*. Though there is little in Freire's methods that cannot be found in other educators, his obvious success in using these methods both in Brazil and Chile has commended him to educators the world over. His method includes a number of stages: (1) a thorough search into the life situation of the students; (2) the choice of themes of cultural and political significance for discussion, from the life situation of people; (3) a graphic codification, problemizing, or representation of these themes; (4) decodification or open and critical discussion by all concerned on these themes; (5) a commitment to action on the part of both students and teachers following the discussion.

Role of Teacher

Discussion on the *role of the teacher in religious education* can benefit from reflection on Freire's description of the coordinators of the culture circles. This person is to have the greatest respect for all individuals in the group. He or she is to be deeply committed to dialogic learning. The coordinator is to view the teacher as one who brings clarity to the confused ideas which students hold. The relationship between teachers and students is one of equality. There is to be no imposition of ideas. If religious education is to be true education and not a form of indoctrination, the role of the teacher must be thought out in terms similar to those described by Freire in his description of the coordinator of culture circles.

Subjects of Religious Education

The final implication of Freire's pedagogy bears on the *subjects of religious education*. Freire is totally committed to the education of adults. There is little in his writings bearing directly on the education of children, though many of his basic principles can be applied to the education of children and youth. Freire saw the hope for change in society as resting in the education of adult members of the community. His thinking and practice in this area go contrary to the common practices in religious education in this country. Although there has been an upsurge in adult religious education in recent years in many denominations, this educational effort is still considerably less than the effort directed at children and adolescents.

CONCLUSION

One would do a great disservice to the pedagogy of Paulo Freire and to the field of religious education if one were to think that his method is some kind of magical formula for solving our problems. Freire's greatest value for religious educators lies in his example of how an educator should go about his task. We should look to what he has done for himself and for the people with whom he worked. He was obviously in touch with himself and with his people. The task of the religious educator in trying to find benefit in Freire's pedagogy does not lie in a slavish imitation of his methods. It lies, rather, in the attempt to come to grips with one's own experience and with the experience of other people, in order to work out ways to better understand these experiences and to work for the transformation of structures which impede true humanization.

CHAPTER 10

RELIGION AND ADULT EDUCATION IN BRITAIN

When I first took on the task of preparing a study of religion and adult education in Britain, I was unaware of the monumental work of Basil Yeaxlee in this field. In 1925 he published his doctoral dissertation, *Spiritual Values in Adult Education,* a magisterial two-volume work. After reading this work I was humbled to realize that I have proposed to do at this time something to which he devoted 600 pages of text. Thus, I have taken up this task with a bit more humility and a great debt of gratitude to this truly remarkable pioneer in the field of adult religious education. Yeaxlee later published a shorter work with a rather contemporary title, *Lifelong Education: A Sketch of the Range and Significance of the Adult Education Movement* (1929).

If one examines the early history of adult education in both England and the United States, one is struck by the fact that in its beginnings the enterprise was a highly religious one. The two standard histories, that of Kelly (1970) on Britain and that of Knowles (1977) on the United States, show that movement after movement in adult education was inspired by religious ideals. This appears to be true at least until the First World War. After that time adult education came increasingly under the influence of secular forces. Consequently, when the discipline of adult education emerged in the period after the First World War, religious studies was not one of the major fields that was utilized in establishing this new discipline. The new field of adult education looked especially to philosophy, history, sociology, administration, and psychology for its intellectual grounding.

It is my purpose in this study to attempt to do three things. Firstly, I will detail briefly the influence of religion on the adult education movement in the past. Secondly, I will speculate about some of the reasons for the decline of religious influence in adult education as a practice and as a discipline. Thirdly, I will attempt to indicate what resources religious studies might provide today for the theory and practice of adult education.

In this study I am using the term *adult education* to include both informal and formal means of adult learning. I use the term in the broad sense that Lawrence Cremin, a historian at Teachers College, Columbia, gives to the term. Thus, adult education is the "deliberate, systematic, sustained effort to transmit, evolve, or acquire knowledge, attitudes, values, skills or sensibilities, as well as any outcomes of that effort (1975, p. viii)." Thus, adult education includes not only the work of formal institutions such as schools but also of churches, self-education, industry, family, etc.

RELIGION AND ADULT EDUCATION: HISTORICAL PERSPECTIVE

Pre–Eighteenth Century Developments

The earliest motivation for adult education was religious. Conversion efforts in Anglo-Saxon times were efforts to educate and convert persons to the Christian religion. Thus, the first adult educators were the clergy, who used pulpit, confessional, and special classes to convert persons to Christianity and then to confirm them in the Christian faith. Education also took place through miracle and morality plays as well as through the frescoes and carvings of churches.

It was the work of the friars that made the pulpit a popular form of church education. Their work gave rise to manuals for preaching to the people. Advice was given for speaking slowly, modulating the voice, making clear the division of the sermon and its principal links. Preachers were urged not to crowd in too much, or make the sermon long, for excessive prolixity would induce sleep. Gestures were to be natural; preachers were not to stand like statues, nor to indulge in exaggerated hand motions. Beginning preachers were advised to practice in some far-off place where there would be no one to laugh at them (Kelly, 1970, p. 4).

In the sixteenth century there emerged a familiar theme in the early adult education movement, the connection of adult education with religiously inspired nonconformist movements. John Wycliffe and the Lollards insisted that the common person should be able to read the New Testament. The religious motivation of opening the Scriptures to the common people played a very important role in fostering adult education from this time well into the nineteenth century. This movement to bring the Bible to common people had a great influence on the adult education movement, for the desire to read the Scriptures became, for centuries, one of the main motives for making persons literate (Kelly, 1970, p. 9).

During this early period, adult education was clearly for purposes of salvation. Such was the extent of this mode of education that historians find very little trace of adult education applied for secular purposes in the fifteenth century (Kelly, 1970, p. 4). Such traces are found in the traditional lore of wandering bards and minstrels and the civic training provided by the guilds.

During the Reformation and Renaissance period, adult education advanced considerably through the printing of the Bible and the importance given to preaching and expounding its message. In this vein, a significant development took place in Scotland, where clergy and people met for prophesying, whereby every person had the liberty to declare his mind and knowledge to the comfort and edification of the church (Kelly, 1970, p. 17). The Puritans were especially committed to this form of learning. The established church through Elizabeth I forbade this practice in 1577. What the established church fostered was preaching lectureships, supplementary to the regular services of the church.

Puritans continued in these meetings even after they were forbidden. When sermons were preached, people would take notes and later meet at a private house, with or without a preacher, to discuss the sermon (Kelly, p. 39). Once nonconformity was tolerated these practices became even more widespread. In this same period dissenting academies and charity schools also expanded. In addition, the religious impulse was found in the continuing movement to make persons literate in order that they might read the Bible.

In the seventeenth century the adult education movement was greatly affected by the development of modern science. This development was important for the rise of a secular adult education. For some educators, however, there was no conflict between religion and the developing science. For example, George Winstanley attempted in 1672 to develop a comprehensive view of adult education in which the humanistic and scientific are placed within the religious. God was viewed as the spirit of reason which exists in all persons and in nature. The main function for the clergy was adult education—the exposition of the Word of God. The Boyle lectures established in 1691 had as their purpose to prove the truth of the Christian religion.

Eighteenth Century Developments

The eighteenth century witnessed the continuation of the religious impulse in adult education, though it also included the further development of a secular adult education. *The Society for Promoting Christian Knowledge* (S.P.C.K.) was a major effort by the Established Church of England to promote, among other things, the religious education of adults. Some adult schools were established but their full flourishing had to await the

Sunday School movement at the end of the century. S.P.C.K. distributed religious literature and set up libraries for adults, even though its principal impetus was for the education of children. The society had more success in night schools for adults, which operated in Wales and Scotland.

The Methodist movement of the Wesleys made a valuable contribution to adult education in its internal organization of class meetings. This format also provided a model for working-class political organization. A weekly meeting was held for self-examination and encouragement in Christian living. Any member could aspire to be a class leader, even a woman (in the early days but not later). Methodist preachers were drawn from the middle and lower classes. Methodists were also interested in enabling their members to become literate.

Within the established Church, the Sunday School movement at the end of the eighteenth century, though primarily a children's movement, did become involved in the education of adults, especially in Wales. Eventually, separate schools were set up for adults. Adult religious education was also a primary motivation for the work of Hannah and Martha More and the Birmingham Sunday Society, which took a special interest in the work of literacy. A school for women was established at Nottingham to supply the needs of women workers in factories. This was an adult Sunday School for Bible reading and instruction in basic literacy and numeracy.

Religion was also the motivation for debating societies and political reform societies at the end of the eighteenth century. David Williams formed a club for the study of rational religion, of which Benjamin Franklin was a member. The Society of Friends became involved in political reform. Societies were formed in London with such names as The Moral and Political Society, and the Friends of Morality. Literary and Philosophical Societies were also formed and eventually developed into dissenting academies. Kelly notes the strong strain of nonconformity, both religious and political, in adult education. At this time many Unitarians were deeply involved in these academies—Joseph Priestly, Thomas Percival, Thomas Barnes, and William Turner. The Quaker John Dalton was also involved in this movement. In Keliy's view it was the Unitarians who were most involved in adult education in both the eighteenth and nineteenth centuries (Kelly, 1970, p. 108).

It must be recognized that these early forms of adult education were not fully developed, but rather in an embryonic stage. It is also clear that religious education included the education of the adult illiterate. Kelly sees two strains of adult education during these early years, a religious one and a secular one. Religious groups took the lead in the education of illiterates. When religious groups began to develop an education for middle and upper classes and secular adult education showed more concern with the education of the working classes, the two strains of adult education began to converge (Kelly, 1970, p. 81).

Nineteenth Century Developments

The nineteenth century witnessed the development of a number of important adult education institutions, some of which have passed from the scene, others which still remain to this day. Here again we see the same pattern of religious motivation playing a prominent part in each of these new developments.

Many groups were involved in the founding of Mechanics Institutes, and thus the motivation was mixed, both religious and secular. Among the main motives were industrial education, political education in self-government, social alleviation of the poverty and misery of working persons, social control and obedience to the laws of the state, and general cultural education. In religious contexts the Mechanics Institutes were of special interest to nonconformists, especially the Unitarians. The Established Church was at best neutral and at worst hostile to these institutions (Kelly, 1970, p. 123).

The religious motivation is decidedly clearer in the formation of the Young Men's Christian Association (Y.M.C.A.). Founded in 1844 by George Williams, the organization had as its purpose the improvement of the spiritual life of young working men. This organization has had an impressive history in religious education and social improvement in the nineteenth and twentieth centuries.

Working-class movements of the early nineteenth century were often organized into Hampden Clubs. These radical clubs had a strong connection with Methodism, for this religion provided a high percentage of the leaders of the independent working-class movements of this period. These clubs also adopted for their own purposes the Methodist plan of the weekly class meeting and the small weekly subscription (Kelly, 1970, p. 135).

The radical Chartist movement among workers included a strong educational effort under religious impulses. Scotland was the center of Christian Chartism, a movement which united Chartism with a primitive Christianity. A Christian Chartist church was founded in Birmingham, where democratic principles were studied and efforts were made to foster temperance, morality, and knowledge (Kelly, 1970, pp. 141–42). In some areas of Scotland there were nightly meetings. A remarkable effort in adult education was developed by the Leicester Chartist Thomas Cooper, who educated himself extensively and sought to bring learning to others. As a Methodist minister and later as a Baptist, he edited journals and established adult Sunday schools to study the work of political and literary radicals (Kelly, 1970, pp. 142–44).

The Owenite utopian socialist movement was interested in providing a sound education for workers. This movement took on the character of a religious sect, preaching a secular ethic and holding services which were similar to those of the Established Church. This movement, however, was rather negative towards the form of religion found in organized religious bodies.

The adult school movement became increasingly strong in the nineteenth century. A great number of schools were established in Wales under the influence of Rev. Thomas Charles of Bala. This expansion led to an increased demand for Welsh Bibles. The movement also spread to Bristol under the influence of two Methodists, Thomas Martin and Stephen Prust. By 1816 in Bristol twenty-four schools for men and thirty-one for women were established (Kelly, 1970, p. 150). The movement spread throughout the Midlands and to the Berkshires, where the Church of England established fifty-seven schools. Kelly estimates that between 200 and 300 schools were established in the early nineteenth century (p. 191).

In a number of places, e.g., Bristol, Leeds, York, and Yarmouth, Quakers were very active in the work of the adult schools. Most of the schools of this period held nondenominational Bible classes. Some of the schools ventured to teach writing as well as reading but others questioned the propriety of this activity for the Sabbath. Besides these religiously oriented schools, there were many night schools in England and Wales where secular subjects formed the exclusive curriculum. This movement knew both decline and recovery, as many adult education movements have.

Churches were involved in the nineteenth century in the development of libraries, with supplies often coming from the Religious Tract Society, which distributed in England and Wales over 4,000 libraries of about 100 volumes each. Many clergy supported libraries throughout the country (Kelly, pp. 174–75).

Religious influences were also prevalent in the founding of working men's colleges and institutes in the middle of the nineteenth century. The Reverend R. S. Bayley established the Sheffield People's College for men and women, with a broad curriculum in the humane arts. Because of his troubles with his church, the college lasted only till 1846.

The Sheffield experiment inspired the founding of the London Working Men's College in 1854, a venture associated with the Christian Socialism of Frederick Maurice. The avowed purpose of this socialism was to raise all individuals to full personhood and unite all classes in the pursuit of high spiritual ideals. The Christian socialists were involved in adult education, social work, and publications. It was their view that education was the heart of the solution to social problems and that the curriculum should center in the humane arts. Many distinguished persons taught at the college in its early days: Charles Kingsley, J. Ludlow, Thomas Hughes, John Ruskin, and D. G. Rossetti.

The weakness of the college lay in finances and the disconnection of the curriculum from the interests of the ordinary working man. This experiment, however, is credited with differentiating between technical education and liberal studies, for Maurice made a clear distinction between the means of livelihood and the means of life. He was convinced that social reconstruction demanded a more spiritual analysis than earlier movements had included (Kelly, 1970, p. 189). Out of this movement came a classic in British adult education, Maurice's *Learning and Working* (1855, 1969).

By mid-nineteenth century the evening school for adults became a major focus of adult education. Many of these schools were now connected with the Church of England. The schedule of many rural parsons was taken up with education and social activities. Quakers such as George Cadbury, Joseph Rountree and J. S. Fry were deeply involved in a revival of the adult schools. These men were both organizers and teachers in the schools. These schools provided both religious instruction and elementary education for adults. The efforts of the Y.M.C.A. were greatly increased at this time.

The nineteenth century also saw the development of university extension adult education. James Stuart of Cambridge is recognized as one of the pioneers in this area. Religious motivation is found in the ideals of Christian Socialism that inspired many in this movement. It was also present in the extension summer schools where the American Chautauqua was imitated at Oxford and elsewhere. The Chautauqua movement in western New York was first concerned with the education of Sunday School teachers of the Methodist religion. The term "chautauqua" became synonymous with summer school. The real significance of the University extension was its emphasis on the liberal or humane tradition, which included the study of religion.

Of greater religious significance at this time was the emergence of university settlements, the involvement of the universities in the attempt to better the social and educational well-being of persons living in the vicinity of the universities. Maurice was also very influential in this movement. University extension and university settlements might be considered the twin offspring of Christian socialism, the one in the direction of education and the other in the direction of social work (Kelly, p. 239). The educational effort of the settlements was extensive: popular lectures, discussion groups, Sunday afternoon concerts, and many other activities.

Twentieth Century Developments

The immediate past and the present are most difficult to analyze because of the lack of vantage point. History is the movement forward, and it is rather difficult to see what has moved forward at a particular time until that time is past.

The twentieth century has seen the continuation of previous efforts in adult education and the development of a number of important new movements. It is clear that religious influence in adult education has lessened as has the general degree of religious influence in society. It is first important, however, to recognize the religious influences that have been present in the adult education movement in this century, before assessing the reasons for the decline of this influence and the meaning and opportunities that this decline affords for the future development of adult education.

Although founded in the latter part of the nineteenth century, the Workers Education Movement is better situated among twentieth century developments. The founder of the movement was Albert Mansbridge, considered one of the great figures in British adult education. His vision of workers' education is a religious one. He started as a lay preacher in the Church of England and attempted to rally the forces of church and university to provide education for workers. Mansbridge's principles of Christian democracy which infused the movement were continued in the writing and work of the theologian William Temple, who became the first elected president of the movement in 1908.

The adult school movement was also a powerful force in the years before the First World War. Bible study continued to be a major focus in this movement. The schools, however, became increasingly interested in social problems. A connection was forged between biblical teaching and current social problems.

When the adult school concept was combined with the work of the Quakers there emerged, in the early years of the century, the educational settlement. This was the attempt to bring religion to bear on social problems. The most enduring institution from this period is Woodbrooke, a Quaker educational settlement in Birmingham. John Rowntree transformed the Quaker summer school into a residential settlement or "a wayside Inn, a place where the dusty traveller, stepping aside for a moment from the thronged highway, shall find refreshment and repose (in Kelly, 1970, p. 262)." Persons of all religious denominations have been welcomed from its beginning. Both short and long courses are provided. Tutors also travel throughout the country and abroad to bring a religious message which is closely related to contemporary issues, especially war and peace.

Another college from this period, still in existence, is Fircroft, a college in Birmingham modeled on the Danish Folk High School, which from the beginning included religious studies in its curriculum and attempted to provide for the education of the working class. Peace studies have long been an important part of the curriculum of this institution.

During this period churches also carried on a considerable amount of education and social service. Groups involved include Congregationalists, Wesleyan Methodists, and Unitarians. The Catholic Social Guild, founded in 1909, had 100 study clubs by 1914. The Church of England organized tutorial classes (Yeaxlee, 1925, Vol. II).

The thrust for liberal adult education received a major impetus from the *Final Report of the Reconstruction Committee* published in 1919. This report recommended a larger expenditure of public funds on adult education through extramural departments of universities, extension programs, local educational authorities, and other bodies. The fulfillment of these recommendations between the world wars was a strong force in the development of adult education. Although Mansbridge and Tawney were on this committee, there does not appear to be a strong religious or spiritual motivation in the recommendations. Religion, however, was not excluded. The emphasis was upon citizenship studies, as well as science, music and languages, literature and drama, and craftsmanship (Kelly, p. 267).

One of the indications that religion was playing a smaller part in the adult education movement between the wars was the decline in adult schools, from 1,900 before the war to 1,096 by 1937 (Kelly, 1970, p. 284). The reason given for this decline is that "in an increasingly secular age the religious atmosphere of the schools and their emphasis on Bible study were no longer congenial (Kelly, 1970, p. 284)." One deeply involved in the movement commented that:

> The modern tendency to broaden our religious ideas has been associated with a decrease of conviction, while the reaction from this attitude has been in the direction of a Fundamentalism, which it is difficult to harmonise with Adult School ideals of free inquiry (E. Champness, 1941, in Kelly, pp. 284–85).

Although the Sunday School movement declined there was an increase in Church Tutorial Classes of the Church of England and in the Catholic Social Guild. Perhaps what this indicates is not a general decline in religious influence but a decline in a certain type of religious adult education.

In assessing the adult education movement of this period a number of themes have been indicated. With the increase of state aid, a uniformity

among forms of adult education developed. The previous pattern—
extension courses, W.E.A. tutorial classes, adult schools, educational and
social settlements, residential colleges, and working men's colleges—was
notable for its diverse forms.

The more significant trend concerns motivation. The motivation of the
earlier period was mixed. People were motivated by personal culture and
personal advancement. But strong social and religious motivation was also
found in the residential colleges' concerns with social emancipation, as
well as in the adult school, college, and Y.M.C.A. concern for religious
fellowship and service.

What happened in the twenties and thirties was a lessening in the driving
forces of social reform and religious service and an increase in the motive
of personal culture. What developed was a general trend toward ''a broad,
undifferentiated form of adult education, inspired mainly by the desire for
personal culture, and dominated by the humane tradition of the universities
(Kelly, 1970, p. 286).''

During the Second World War, the only mention by Kelly of religious
involvement is in regard to the work of the Y.M.C.A. Basil Yeaxlee
served as secretary for the Central Advisory Council for Education in H.M.
Forces.

In the postwar pattern the amount of adult education increased at a slow
rate, dipping during periods of recession. Extramural departments increased, and W.E.A. educated more students. Adult education moved into
broadcasting, especially with the Open University.

The present situation is accurately viewed as a partnership of the central
government with the universities, the voluntary bodies, and the local
education authorities. Religion no longer appears a major motivating force
in the adult education movement, either as a motive in establishing new
forms as a subject which is seen to be valuable in itself, or as a discipline
from which the field of adult education might draw for its theory and
practice.

DECLINE OF RELIGION IN THE ADULT EDUCATION MOVEMENT

In the historical survey just completed a number of reasons have been
offered to explain the decline of the influence of religion in the adult
education movement in Britain. It may be helpful now to expatiate a bit on
these reasons in order to present another backdrop for dealing with the role
that religion might play in an adult education of the future.

The influence of religion as such in adult education changed as society
moved from an undifferentiated society to a differentiated one. From the

medieval period to the present we have seen the emergence of institutions with specific functions. Before this time there were no clear differentiations among politics, social work, education, church, and industry. With the emergence of modern society, institutions developed with specific and differentiated purposes. The close connection between religion and education gave way to two separate but related institutions, with their respective tasks. This had both good and bad repercussions. The development of education separate from church influences led to the increase of freedom and autonomy in educational institutions. The harmful side effect is that education developed without the historic values of religious traditions to inform its theory and practice.

This separation between religion and education is not complete in society for religion is a mandated subject in state schools. Perhaps the very existence of this mandated education in religion has been one of the reasons for giving less attention to it in adult education endeavors. It would appear that religion as a subject in adult education does not, today, face the many political, religious, and educational problems that its teaching faces in the state schools.

Connected with the division of labor among modern institutions is the development of the modern state and its increasing role in education. Beginning in the nineteenth century and increasing in the twentieth century, the state has taken over more and more the function of education in society. This interest in, and control of, education has extended into the area of adult education. Many religious and social reformers realized that adult education would become an extensive movement only if the state took a greater role in its development. The increasing secularity of the modern state dictated that religion would have little role to play in the shaping of educational policy. This was partly in response to the nature of the secular state and partly in response to the reality of religious diversity in society. Even such institutions as the W.E.A. forbade the teaching of religion in courses, though this was done with some qualifications. Furthermore, key educational developments in adult education took place precisely at times when denominational rivalries were strongest in society.

Another major influence in the decrease of the force of religion in adult education proceeds from the former two realities; it is the increasing privatization of religion. As institutional purposes were differentiated, religious bodies gradually took on the task of looking to the personal spiritual, religious, and moral needs of their members. Some of the social aims of the churches of previous periods were achieved, and the achievement of other goals was often accomplished by newer institutions. The churches turned more and more to the spiritual needs of their members and less to the world and its problems. This privatization of the churches lessened their impact in society and decreased the attention which persons would give to the teachings and guidance of religion outside a purely personal sphere.

Education as an academic discipline developed with the emergence of philosophy as well as the human and social sciences. Though religion played a major part in educational theory of the past, present educational-ists pay little attention to religious studies in developing a theory and practice of education. This is less true in school education than in adult education, because of the teaching of religion in the schools. I believe that it is time to reconsider a modest role that religion might play in the theory and practice of adult education.

RELIGION IN ADULT EDUCATION THEORY AND PRACTICE

I should like to propose that the theory and practice of adult education would be improved if more attention were paid to contemporary de-velopments in religious studies. It is not my contention that adult education needs to include religious studies in any essential sense. But I believe that the field would be fuller and more adequate to the human situation if this dimension were included. I shall give a number of examples of how religion might be of benefit to the field of adult education.

History of Adult Education

No one who is unaware of the role that religion has played in this history can understand the history of adult education in this country. I believe that this point has been made in the first part of this study. Again and again we must recognize the influence of religious motivation and institutions on the adult education movement. Many of the present forms of adult education evolved out of previous religious movements and institutions. Understand-ing the historic connection of adult education with religious and political nonconformity may shed light on present conflicts and help to explain the minority status of the enterprise. The nonestablished religions are often in a position to offer radical and prophetic proposals to the existing institutions of society. The radical thrust today comes often from Marxists and feminists.

Ideals of Adulthood

Adult educators devote a great deal of attention to analyzing concepts or ideals of adulthood. Usually these are drawn from historical, legal, philosophical, and psychological analyses. What is not usually considered is that religious traditions have also contended with these issues. A symposium in California in the late 1970s, inspired by the work of Erik Erikson, explored adulthood in religious traditions (Erikson, 1978). It examined adulthood in the Judaeo-Christian, Islamic, Indian, Japanese, and Confucian traditions. The studies make the point that these ideals have a formative power in the socialization of many people in present society. I can give an example of only a few of the ideals presented in this literature.

The Jewish ideal emphasizes membership in a people, a covenant relationship with God, and a fidelity to God's law and God's people. This tradition emphasizes that one is not truly mature or just unless one exercises care and love for poor and destitute members of society. Thus the maturity of love manifested in action is the highest spiritual ideal. An entire group of writings delves into the question, Who is the wise person? This person is one who has achieved insight into the deeper meaning of life, in its practical and theoretical aspects. The book of Job dramatically argues that maturity is to be judged only in the light of a person's attitude in the face of sickness, suffering, and fear of death.

Within Christianity there have been two ideals of adulthood (Bouwsma, 1978). A historic concept accepts the Greek distinction between mind as higher and body as lower and has produced an ethics of repression, chiefly of sexuality. This concept associates adulthood with asceticism, self-discipline, and control. A normative Christian concept goes counter to this ideal. It associates maturity with personal stability as well as with loving solidarity within a community. Maturity is seen as growth in a lifelong process whose goal is a transcendent one. In this concept there is a close distinction between sin and refusal to grow or develop. Maturity is the proper balancing of the active, engaged life with the contemplative or withdrawn, reflective life.

In *Islam* adult maturity entails the integration of the individual with the norms of religion and culture. It is personal reconciliation to the reality of the world and one's place in the world as Allah has willed it. Through a life of faith one is relieved from false maturity and from the anxiety of self-sufficiency to face the inadequacy of all that is merely human. "In Islam trust in God and humility open the way to the inward healing and outward responsibility which is on the way to adulthood (Lapidus, 1978, p. 111)."

One final example of a religious ideal of adulthood is found in the rather secular Confucian tradition. Adulthood is becoming, being on the way. A person becomes an adult through an inner direction and a knowledge of established social norms. Adulthood requires creative adaptations to the inevitable process of aging. Rather interestingly, Confucius recognized stages of adulthood:

In his youth, before his blood and vital humors have settled down, he is on guard against lust. Having reached his prime, when the blood and humors have finally hardened, he is on guard against strife. Having reached old age, when the blood and vital humors are already decaying, he is on guard against avarice (In Wei-Ming, 1978, p. 117).

Confucius was not without suggestions for handling these age-related problems. To young adults troubled with lustfulness, he recommended poetry as a force for harmonizing the emotions. For middle-aged adults in the midst of strife, he suggested ritual for harmonizing human emotions to accord with cultural values. For the aged, beset with clinging avarice, he recommended music for achieving peace and directing oneself to transcending interests.

Development in Faith or Meaning Systems

In the past two decades adult educators have paid increasing attention to the work of developmental psychologists and their description of adult stages of development. This research has been thoroughly reviewed by the British researchers Osborn, Charnley, and Allman (1982). Much of this research has been done in North America. Building on the seminal work of Erikson (1962), such researchers as Vaillant (1977), Levinson (1978), Loevinger (1976), and Gould (1978) have given us a description of the various stages through which persons pass in their adult life. In examining these works, it is apparent that little attention has been given to an explicit religious dimension, although Erikson's work, with its biographies of Luther and Gandhi, paid explicit attention to the religious dimension of development.

The work of James Fowler (1981) of Emory University, Atlanta, Georgia goes a long way toward filling in this gap. Fowler is a theologian-psychologist who, in the past ten years, has done research on the development of faith or meaning systems in individuals. Faith is given a highly personal meaning as a way of knowing, construing, or interpreting experience. It expresses the universal tendency to make meaning of experience and to give coherence to life. It is a relational reality, bringing persons into contact with others—with a community and with the ultimate environment of reality. This faith can be theistic or nontheistic, religious or nonreligious.

Fowler has described the growth in faith in six stages which are built upon the theoretical work of Piaget and Kohlberg. In early life, faith is undifferentiated from other dimensions of life. In early childhood, faith is of an intuitive nature—not a matter of conceptual understanding but rather a process of projecting the faith of those most significant in one's life. From this stage persons pass to a faith which depends upon the literal interpretation of myths and stories. Meaning is found in symbols, myths, rituals, music, and heroic figures, that sustain children as they confront the dark side of life. From the age of twelve children are capable of building a preliminary synthesis of meaning, according to the conventions of the group with which they are associated.

Three stages of faith are characteristic of the adult years. In young adulthood one seeks to develop reflectively a faith that is individuative, i.e., of one's own making and judgment. Faith in middle adulthood is paradoxical, in the sense that one can accept the truth of one's position and still respect the truth of another's faith or meaning system. In late adulthood there is the possibility of holding a universal faith which sees the oneness of all reality.

Fowler's work is not the only work in the area of faith or meaning system development, but it is probably the most important paradigm in the field. In North America and Canada an extensive research project has been underway for a few years to test a number of hypotheses drawn from this literature and other research in developmental psychology (Stokes, 1983). I believe that this research should be of interest to adult educators. The research probes an essential dimension of many persons, their basic faith position or life stances—the growth and development that take place in it, and the interrelationship between faith and other dimensions of the person.

Theoretical Approaches to Adult Education

In the area of theories of adult education, there have been some significant theories that have been built upon, or include, a religious perspective. In two works I have examined theories of adult education and adult religious education (Elias, 1980; 1982). The liberal education tradition in religion includes the educational theories of Thomas Aquinas and Jacques Maritain. Basil Yeaxlee's religious idealism fits into this tradition (Yeaxlee, 1925). The concept of the person underlying this theory places emphasis upon the intellectual, moral, and spiritual development. Classic works, including great religious classics, are an essential part of the curriculum. The liberal education of adults need not include an explicit treatment of the religious, for the theory is also proposed on purely humanist bases. Yet, the inclusion of the religious does provide a breadth and a vision which many find enlightening and uplifting.

Progressive theories of education developed in reaction to the formalism and rigidity of certain forms of religious education. In the progressivist's extolling of science, psychology, and sociology there was often included a deemphasis on the humanities, including religion. However, from the very beginnings of the movement there were religious educators such as George Coe (1917) who attempted to restructure religious education along progressive lines. Yet, as the years have passed, certain educators have been able to develop a progressive form of adult education which combines the humanistic and the scientific. The concerns of neo-progressives such as John Westerhoff (1976) and Gabriel Moran (1979) are with personal growth, the totality of human experience, and social change. Religious traditions are respected but their particular elements are subjected to ongoing revision and reinterpretation, not only from revised understandings from within these traditions but also in the light of new knowledge from secular understandings of human life and culture.

Humanistic theories of adult education have become increasingly prevalent in the past decades. These theories owe a great deal to the progressives, but they are more closely related to existential philosophies and humanistic psychologies. These theories have developed partially to combat the pervasive behaviorism that has dominated educational thinking and practice. While not all humanistic theories include a religious dimension, many do; those that do not are often open to this dimension. Carl Rogers's approach to education is humanistic. He focuses upon personal and interpersonal growth. One sees in his writings traces of the liberal theology that he imbibed when he began studies for the Protestant ministry at Union Theological Seminary in New York. In a number of works Leon McKenzie has developed a religious philosophy of adult education based upon existential philosophy and phenomenology (1978; 1982).

Political theories of adult education have become prevalent since the work of Freire in the early 1970s. What is not always recognized about Freire (and also Illich) is the powerful religious dimension included in his work (Elias, 1976). Freire is an adult educator who attempted to combine humanistic Marxism with a radical Christianity. His view of the human person, the goals of education, and the institutions of society are suffused with religious themes and ideals. In Latin America his method of conscientization forms the basis of a Latin American-style liberation theology that attempts to unite Christian belief with radical political action. In Britain Brian Wren, in his *Education for Justice* (1977), has extended Freire's ideas into this cultural situation and deals with such issues as power and its abuses, conflict, and political and educational strategies.

I have reviewed some of these theories to indicate how the religious dimension forms an integral part of many contemporary theories of adult education. My attempt has been to show that the religious need not be identified with the otherworldly, the dogmatic or the narrowly personal. The failings of the religious point of view are well known. Not adequately known are the efforts of religious persons to develop theories and practices that are truly relevant to contemporary human and societal development. A review of these theories shows that religion can be connected with liberal learning, progressive views of education and societal change, personal growth, and political action.

Religious Modes of Learning

The practices of religious tradition might well be explored by adult educators for insights into how adults learn. A number of common learning practices in adult learning began as practices of religious groups.

Within the Quaker tradition there is an emphasis on learning through silence and the inner light. All religions, of both East and West, have forms of meditation and contemplation. The monastic practice of *lectio divina,* the slow meditative reading of the Scriptures, can be utilized in the reading of works that demand a great deal of contemplation. We have put such an emphasis on speed-reading that we are in danger of losing the value of slow, reflective, and meditative reading.

Thousands of people have utilized such highly directive forms of learning and discernment as the Spiritual Exercises of St. Ignatius to aid them in arriving at important decisions in their lives. Spiritual retreats have been formative experiences for many people. In adult education we need to pay attention to the values of contemplation, retreat, and leisure as well as the values of activity, engagement, and work.

Some religions have made extensive use of revivals for the revitalization of their members. The Wesleyan movement in this country was a powerful religious and social movement. In the United States there have been three great revival periods which have affected the lives of many individuals and led to the permanent establishment of churches, schools, and other educational institutions. Recently, Mission Britain was preached by Billy Graham and other Protestant ministers in this country. It is interesting to compare such movements with the past efforts of adult educators to mobilize large numbers of people in adult education activities, e.g., the lyceum movement.

The ritual and worship of religious bodies show the power of symbols, drama, music, and environment in bringing about learning. Participation in such activities is a powerful learning experience for many people. It is fruitful to reflect on the fact that for centuries it was the liturgy, rituals, and environment of church buildings which provided a great deal of adult education.

The capacity of some religious groups to ritualize events in the life of individuals should make adult educators reflect on the potential of education to affect individuals at significant times. Psychologists have studied the power of transitions and of turning points in the lives of individuals. Birth, coming to adulthood, marriage, parenthood, assuming leadership in the community, sickness, and retirement are universal experiences which religious groups have attempted to ritualize in order to bring a religious dimension into people's lives.

Recently psychologists have rediscovered a relationship long recognized in religious groups, that of the mentor or sponsor. Within some religious traditions great emphasis is placed on the spiritual guide, guru, or mentor in helping a person through the spiritual life. The Protestant tradition has seen dangers in these practices because of the risks of clerical and authoritarian direction. It has usually favored more personal and group forms of direction. This divergence sheds some light on the ambiguities of the mentor-pupil relationship.

CONCLUSION: RELIGION AND EDUCATION

It is the thesis of this study that the relationship between religion and adult education needs to be rethought and refashioned in our time. Adult education needs religion; religion needs adult education. Adult education needs religion for its questions, answers, values, myths, stories, rituals, and traditions. Through contact with religion it becomes open to an important aspect of human persons and communities.

On the other hand, religion needs adult education. It needs to learn to focus more attention on adults at various times in their lives. It needs the sound principles of education to avoid attempts to indoctrinate or manipulate persons into belief and conformity. Religion needs adult education's methodological and institutional analyses.

PART III: THEOLOGY, JUSTICE, AND PEACE

CHAPTER 11

IDEOLOGY AND RELIGIOUS EDUCATION

A number of years ago I offered a critique of two educators who had clearly articulated political ideologies. My study of the two radical educators, Paulo Freire and Ivan Illich (Elias, 1976), brought me face-to-face for the first time with the relationship between political ideology and education. This study, done in the context of a resurgence of ideological conflicts in the United States and elsewhere, was a critique of radical ideologies from a liberal-reformist perspective. It was only in the course of the study that I gained the awareness that a criticism of an ideology entails the taking up of an ideological position. This insight went contrary to the value neutrality of the philosophical and social analysis that I attempted to employ in that work.

The relationship between political ideology and education is one that still interests me greatly. This is an area that has been examined in a number of important books and articles. Of immediate concern to me in this study, however, is the relationship between ideology and education in religion and religious education. With increased interest in education for peace and justice, praxis theories of education, and education for liberation, the role of political ideologies in religious education needs both clarification and analysis.

Since this study is a preliminary and limited investigation of ideology and religious education, my main task is to clarify terminology and to suggest a number of directions. Thus I will attempt to clarify the meaning of various concepts, review literature on ideology in a number of fields of study, and examine the limited inquiries that have been done in religious education. A number of conclusions about the relationship between religious education and ideology are offered.

Ideology

The word *ideology* has a vagueness in meaning. Its usages move along a continuum from a false justification of a political, economic, or social situation to a logically and empirically defensible justification. In Marxist social and political theory, the term is used in a pejorative sense to refer to the false consciousness that legitimates institutions which maintain and foster the interests of the dominant class of society. Religion and capitalism are primary examples of such false consciousness in orthodox Marxist theory. Non-Marxist social and political thinkers usually use the term to describe coherent belief systems which are related to the social, political, and economic life of society.

An analysis of the concept of ideology highlights certain usages. The term is used to describe the beliefs of a group, to evaluate these beliefs, or to predict how people will act in accordance with their beliefs. The context of an ideology is action in social, political, and economic life. An ideology is held by a group and it is acted on by a group. What distinguishes ideology from a belief system is that an ideology bespeaks beliefs in application to situations of social and political action (Pratte, 1977, p. 29).

Though various disciplines such as philosophy (Pratte, 1977), sociology of knowledge (Berger and Luckmann, 1966; Mannheim, 1936; Habermas, 1975; Gadamer, 1975), economics (Marx, 1844), and social psychology (Rokeach, 1963) have produced analyses of ideology, my preference in this study is for an analysis that comes primarily from political science. A political ideology includes basic assumptions about persons, society, and the economic system. Political theories also maintain clearly the dimension of action in social and political life that is crucial to the concept of ideology. I view the different analyses from the various disciplines as complementary to one another. A comprehensive analysis would incorporate the different aspects of ideology that are uncovered by different fields of study.

A classic work on political ideologies describes three distinct components of political ideologies (Dolbeare and Dolbeare, 1971). Ideologies include a *world view* or general perspective on how economic and political systems work, why they function in this manner, and whom the systems work for best. Secondly, ideologies encompass *central values and goals* that are considered most desirable. Thirdly, ideologies have an image of the process of *social change* and the particular *tactics* deemed appropriate for achieving change according to the world view, values and goals, and images of change.

Every ideology has a world view or an understanding and explanation for what is happening in the society: whether the social order is egalitarian or stratified; what brought about this situation and what keeps it in place; how social classes relate to one another; how the economy is organized and run; who benefits from such an organization; what is the distribution of power in society and what sustains this arrangement; what are the interrelationships among class, wealth, and power. Though these issues appear to be factual ones, they are open to different points of view in American society today. Ideologies, thus, are based on assumptions and interpretations of selected facts. These assumptions and facts are organized in coherent, interpretative schemes that constitute the dominant American ideologies of capitalism, liberalism, conservatism, and reform liberalism.

Underlying the world vision of ideologies are *central values* and their interpretation. Equality, freedom, justice, due process, law, and social order are examples of such political values. It is rightly pointed out that the critical questions are: "the way in which such values are understood or defined . . . and how they are ranked in priority when they conflict with each other (Dolbeare and Dolbeare, 1971, p. 7)." Basic questions concern the demands of freedom and equality—of due process and order on individual freedom and national security. The distance between values and perceptions of the existing condition of society constitute the *goals* of an ideology. Goals are therefore the conditions, institutions, and policies that will realize the most important values of ideologies.

Ideologies are action and change oriented. A process of *social change* is necessary for achieving the goals and values that are central to a particular world view. All ideologies grapple with such issues as the scope, direction, and tactics for social change. While the *scope* is concerned with the amount of change envisioned, *direction* may be viewed in terms of a conservative-liberal continuum. A wide variety of *tactics* for social change has been espoused by various ideologies: electoral politics, judicial proceedings, lobbying and legislative action, violent and nonviolent resistance, mass demonstrations, boycotts and protests, and revolution.

A critical problem concerning ideologies is their justification. Though some understandings of ideology seem to presume that they are necessarily inadequate and incapable of justification, I prefer to emphasize that part of the continuum of word usage that considers ideologies as susceptible to adequate justification. The justification of an ideology is, in part, similar to the confirmation of a hypothesis or theory. The world view, values, and beliefs can be examined for internal coherence. One can argue whether or not the results of the ideology are capable of being realized and are morally acceptable, as well as whether or not the assumptions about what is valuable can be supported by appropriate evidence. Other dimensions of justification include an examination of assumptions about the nature of knowledge and the validity of the empirical base.

Political Ideologies

In the United States today there are a number of competing political ideologies. Major ideologies include capitalism, liberalism, conservatism, and reform liberalism. These four ideologies constitute the mainstream of ideological positions. Each of these political ideologies makes certain assumptions about the economic, social, and political order. Certain elements are shared among these positions, and this consensus has made serious ideological conflict rare in American history. These ideologies are in basic agreement in approving the existing social, economic, and political structures.

The dominant ideology in the United States has been *liberal capitalism,* a combination of capitalism in economics and liberalism in social and political theory. Capitalism is concerned with how and why the economy should be organized. Liberalism is concerned with the social and political values that should motivate civic life. Though the two are independent, they share basic assumptions about human persons and human society. The combination of these two ideologies has dominated American history since its very beginning.

Though part of the mainstream of American ideologies, *conservatism* has until recently had a marginal role to play in the history of this country. Two forms of conservatism have been identified. *Individualist conservatism* insists on a completely free market and a hands-off attitude of government. Property rights are considered of more value than equality. Equality is seen as the opportunity for involvement in the quest for economic success. A second strand of conservatism, *classical conservatism,* has few proponents in this country. In this theory the needs of society are superior to the needs of individuals, society is an organism distinct from individuals, and government should be conducted by an elite of talent.

A third ideology within the mainstream of American life is *reform liberalism*. Reform liberals share the ideological values of liberals but differ from them in placing a greater emphasis on equality. They also see a reduced role for property rights and individual self-interest. Reform liberals are willing to try new programs for social improvement, usually under the sponsorship of the government. Change is to be sought through the established legal and political system.

Besides these mainstream ideologies in American society, a number of other ideologies have been identified by social and political scientists. These ideologies are usually referred to as *radical ideologies*. Presently, there are a number of ideologies that can be classified as radical: populism, socialism, Marxism, anarchism, radical feminism, and radical minority liberation. *Populism* is an individualistic and communitarian protest in behalf of the common person against the entrenched power elites. *Socialism* opposes the capitalistic system and calls for a system which is egalitarian and communitarian. *Marxism* goes beyond socialism in prescribing the revolutionary praxis by which a new society is to be established. *Anarchism* emphasizes both individual goodness and the value of community life and calls for an elimination of government. *Radical feminism* works for a reconstruction of values and structures in society to achieve full social and political equality. *Radical minority liberation* calls for a separate society within American society that is constituted by blacks, native Americans, or another minority group.

It is clear that these radical minorities are not separate but, rather, related ideologies. The influence of these radical ideologies has been greatest in times of social, economic, cultural, and political unrest. These ideologies also serve the purpose of pointing out the weaknesses and limitations of the mainstream ideologies.

Theology and Ideology

Recent developments in theology have brought the issue of ideology to the forefront. Political and liberation theologies have taken up the challenge of Marxist and neo-Marxist thought to the power of ideologies in all aspects of life, including religious faith and theology. The earliest thrust of Marxist thought was to criticize religion under the guise of a criticism of ideology. This effort exposed religion as an ideological superstructure that supported particular types of oppressive relationships in society. It is only recently that theologians have taken up the challenge of analyzing the ideological presuppositions which are present in theological doctrines.

The relationship between faith and ideology is a fundamental issue, for example, in the theology of the Latin American theologian, Juan Segundo. For him, ideology is: "the system of goals and means that serves as the necessary backdrop for any human option or line of action (1976, p. 102)." Segundo's ideological position is a critique of capitalism and the adoption of certain elements of Marxist social and political thought. The relationship between faith and ideology is extremely close in his theology. The major distinction between the two, in his view, is found in the absoluteness of faith and the relativity of ideologies. A faith, however, that does not have ideological commitments is considered a dead faith.

Theologies of praxis deal specifically with ideologies. Practical theologies presume a commitment to, and an involvement in, social or political movements. Ideologies found in Christian theology range from conservative to liberal reformism to radical Marxist revolutionary praxis. Most forms of liberation or political theology employ some aspects of Marxist critique of society. This critique usually puts them into conflict with prevailing ideologies in church and society.

Though the political nature of much of third world theology is recognized, the political and ideological nature of North American theology is often overlooked. The dominant American philosophical tradition of pragmatism is noted for its emphasis on sociopolitical praxis, especially in the thought of John Dewey (1963 ed.). Reinhold Niebuhr (1952) exposed the economic, racial, and national interests masked in much of Christian theological thinking. John Courtney Murray (1960) argued for a concept of society in which religious freedom was an essential element. His work found acceptance by the Roman Catholic Church in its Vatican II Declaration on Religious Freedom. Theological visions permeated the political thinking of Martin Luther King and Abraham Lincoln. Recently, we have been made aware of the influence of radical religious socialism on the theological system of Paul Tillich, who toned down his radical political theology at the advice of Reinhold Niebuhr, when the latter convinced him that a radical socialist ideology was less appropriate to the United States in the 1930s and 1940s (Stone, 1980).

Ideological analysis has also been present in the work of more contemporary North American theologians. The Canadian theologian Gregory Baum has given explicit treatment to the role of ideology in New Testament polemics against the Jews, the development of theology surrounding Vatican II, and the rise and decline of Christian Socialism in Canada (1975; 1981). Holland and Henroit (1984) have done an incisive social analysis of the United States. A number of feminist theologies have exposed patriarchal biases within Christianity.

The connection of theology with ideological positions has come under criticism on a number of grounds. There is always the danger that politically committed theologians may consider certain forms of social, political, and economic organizations as ideal embodiments of Christian principles. Christian civilization, the Social Gospel Movement, Christian Democrat or Socialist Parties, the Secular City, and the Christian Right can easily become idols that distort religious faith. A critical theology that constantly examines the ideological assumptions of faith is needed to guard against absolutizing any ideological arrangement. One approach to this issue, an essentially faulty one, is the denial that there is a relationship between faith and ideology. Religious persons can relate to broader issues of the social order only by critically taking certain ideological perspectives. The risk of being wrong or inadequate must be taken in order to make faith relevant to the full human situation.

The theological discipline of social ethics is rightly concerned with the question of theology and ideological positions. The approach to this problem taken by Philip Wogaman (1976) is commendable. Christian moral presumptions are utilized in investigating the suitability of ideal forms of social organization. This investigation leads to certain presumptions about political and economic ideologies. Positive presumptions of Christian faith include the goodness of created life, the value of individual life, the unity of the human family in God, and the equality of persons before God. Human finitude and human sinfulness are negative presumptions. Polar values to be balanced are the individual and social nature of the person, freedom and responsibility, subsidiarity and universality, conservatism and innovation, and optimism and pessimism. Though Wogaman's conclusion that the presumptions of Christian faith point to some form of democratic socialism as ideal may not be acceptable to all, his work is a model of theological thinking in this complex area.

Ideology and Education

Before drawing implications for religious education from this discussion of ideology, political ideologies, and theology, it may first be helpful to look at work that examines the role of ideology in educational theory and practice. The role of ideology in public education has become a major issue among some educationists. A study of religious education through examining ideological positions would provide valuable understandings of past practices and present developments.

The issue of ideology and public education came to the fore in the 1970s when revisionist historians questioned the traditional view on the development of public schooling in the United States. The growth of public schools is closely connected with changing political, social, and economic ideologies. Both liberal and conservative ideologies have left their marks upon the schools. The most powerful ideology influencing education has been industrial capitalism. According to some revisionist historians, the most powerful and lasting changes in schools have come from their adaptation to large-scale corporate capitalism. Administration and organization, curriculum and teaching, as well as predominant values and visions come out of this ideological position.

Though various political ideologies have helped shape the contemporary school, with the advent of industrial society schools have increasingly adopted the value and methods of corporate capitalism. Revisionist historians David Cohen and Marvin Lazerson concluded that: "the ideology of school management was re-cast in the mold of the business corporation, and the character of education was shaped after the image of industrial production (1973, p. 355)." One of John Dewey's major educational thrusts was to modify some of the harsh elements of capitalism by infusing society and the school with politically liberal ideals, which would include:

"the use of government action for aid to those of economic disadvantage and for alleviation of their conditions (1963 ed., p. 21)."

Social and political ideologies are part of the thought of many educational theorists. Richard Derr (1973) has used a formal classification scheme to analyze educational theorists according to their social thought. An earlier work by Merle Curti (1966) had presented a more substantive treatment of the social thought of American educators. Derr proposes two main classifications, each with subdivisions: (1) *education for the maintainance* of existing societal arrangements through either (a) *stabilization* or (b) *reproduction;* (2) *education for the improvement* of societal arrangements through either (a) *modification* or (b) *replacement.* Though useful as a formal classification scheme, Derr's work needs to be extended to treat ideologies not within the mainstream of American educational thought and to treat the more political dimensions of ideologies.

The most recent writings on ideology and education have come from sociologists of knowledge and have focused on an examination of the technocratic consciousness that permeates educational theory and practice. The ideological dimensions of such practices as behavioral modification, programmed instruction, educational administration through management objectives, career education, and behavioral objectives have been analyzed by Michael Apple (1979) and C. A. Bowers (1977; 1978; 1980a; 1980b). Apple has focused on the political nature of school knowledge as part of the ideology of the dominant social class. His critique is from a Marxist perspective in that he keeps in the foreground the primacy of economic activity in determining class relationships and the distribution of knowledge in society. The critical social theories of Jurgen Habermas and Alvin Gouldner are the starting point for Bowers's analysis of the technocratic ideology that he sees as pervasive in schooling.

The essence of the work of Apple, Bowers, and others is analysis or interpretation of curriculum. They make the valid point that schools and curriculum are essentially governed by predominant ideologies in society. What one misses in their work is any clearly defined political and economic theory relevant to the American situation. Focusing on the curriculum of the schools as they do, they offer proposals for reform only within the context of the school. As is well known, school reform alone is inadequate to deal with broader issues of social change, as the debate over the issue of equal opportunity in the schools in the past decade has amply demonstrated. Just as John Dewey and other educators were compelled to treat school problems in the context of broader societal issues and ideologies, so educators who analyze the impact of ideology in schools need to move to broader ideological considerations.

Ideology and Religious Education

Though the study of the relationship between ideology and religious education has received little scholarly attention, work in this area has begun. A number of decades ago George Coe's social-cultural approach to religious education contained a reformist-liberal social ideology. The aim of Christian education for Coe was a "mature and efficient devotion to the democracy of God, and happy self realization therein (1917, p. 55)." The specific social aims Coe advocated were social welfare, social justice, and world society. Coe is only the chief example of religious educators who have theorized about religious education within the reformist-liberal ideological tradition.

A number of contemporary religious educators have shown a sensitivity to ideological criticism. Gabriel Moran's (1974) proposals for a reform of religious bodies were an effort in trenchant prose to undermine the reigning ideology of a religious education that focused on church, preaching, faith, liberation, and man. Moran suggested that "instead of talking endlessly about the liberation of man in the future, a religious body would be a place for men, women, and nonhumans to experience the present (1974, p. 99)."

A practical approach to doing what Moran suggested may be found in William Kennedy's suggestions for "a counter education" to unmask middle-class ideologies. In this form of education, ideologies are clarified by attempting to move persons from a concern for personal values to a concern for social/political values, from private to public behavioral patterns, from a local to a global scope of concern, and from an ethical motivation based on charity to one based on justice (Kennedy, 1979).

What is needed to supplement the treatment of ideology in Moran and Kennedy is a concrete encounter with particular sociopolitical ideologies that might inform theories of religious education. Brian Wren, the British adult religious educator, rightly contends that religious educators should take a stand on political ideologies and bring their own ideologies to bear on educational theory and practice. Wren goes against the value-free approach to education common among many philosophers of education in his country by calling for ideological commitment on the part of educators. In this position he is dependent on the example and writings of Paulo Freire regarding the impossibility of neutrality in educational theory and practice. In the British situation Wren's choice is for a radical socialism that focuses on equality, redistribution of wealth, and the inevitability of conflict. He contends that in the struggle for justice "the Christian knows he cannot be neutral. It is necessary to decide *for* some people and *against* other people (1977, p. 114)."

The dangers of ideological commitments in education have long been the subject of debate among educators. A heated debate over the issue took place in the 1930s between George Counts, John Dewey, and others within the Progressive Education Association. Analytic philosophers of education have given extensive treatment to the distinctions between education and indoctrination into particular ideologies (Snook, 1972). An analysis of possible positions in this argument is found in Brian Hill's careful study. Hill contends that educators may validly attempt to achieve a position of committed impartiality. In this position teachers would foster a critical analysis of beliefs, values, and ideologies and "exhibit their own beliefs as additional data for analysis, provided that their procedures for teaching and assessing remain neutral (1981, p. 334)."

Religious Education as Ideology-Critique and Ideology-Commitment

To summarize the main points developed in this study, I should like to suggest that two essential functions of religious education, and of all education, are to critically unmask ideologies and to foster commitment to ideologies. I contend that these two functions need to be better highlighted in the theory and practice of religious education.

Religious education should *foster a suspicion of ideologies* (considered as false views of reality that support current understandings and practices). A dominant mode of religious education is hermeneutical—focusing on the disclosive power of stories, myths, symbols, rituals, parables, and doctrines. Though this is a valuable component of religious education, an approach to religious education that simply discloses a tradition is in danger of merely affirming a tradition and thus not challenging the status quo within church and society. Uncritically affirming the Christian tradition may mask, for example, ideological justification for anti-Jewishness or antifeminism. Religious education needs to be sensitive to the particular world views found in religious stories, myths, and symbols. Religious education also needs a healthy suspicion of ideologies found in contemporary culture. The mass media are a fertile field for such ideological critique as has been shown in an earlier study in this collection.

Religious education should also *foster a commitment to ideologies* (viewed as justifiable views of reality that contain central values and images of social change). It is not enough to say that religious education should include action or praxis. Religious education must also foster commitments to visions of society that are ethically, politically, and theologically powerful. To do this properly it must require analysis of the mainstream political ideologies presented earlier in this study. It should be recognized that creative religious thought has often been associated with radical political thought.

My recommendation that religious education should foster ideological commitments is subject to a number of qualifications. My primary focus in religious education is upon the religious education of adults. Obviously, the danger of indoctrination is less in adult religious education than in the education of children and youth. Furthermore, political commitments are relative and in need of constant critical correction. The same can be said of certain aspects of religious commitments. Finally, there is room for honest differences of opinion among religious persons concerning the adequacy of a particular political commitment. Political commitment as well as faith commitment entails making judgments and choosing actions that involve high levels of risk.

Notwithstanding these qualifications, it is my contention that religious educators must explicitly aim to promote both suspicion of ideology and commitment to ideology. Recent developments in both theological and educational thought impel us to move in this direction. The truth is both to be known and done. Ideology critique and commitment to ideology enable us both to know and to act upon the truth.

CHAPTER 12

RELIGIOUS EDUCATION FOR POWER AND LIBERATION

We cannot avoid using power, cannot escape the compulsion to afflict the world, so let us, cautious in diction and mighty in contradiction love powerfully.

Martin Buber

Power and liberation are two central themes of the Bible. The chief event in Jewish history was the Exodus which liberated the people of Israel from the bondage of slavery, a movement made possible by the powerful intervention of God in human history.

From the outset of his public ministry Jesus saw his mission in the words of Isaiah:

> The Spirit of the Lord has been given to me,
> for He has anointed me,
> He has sent me to bring good news to the poor,
> to proclaim liberty to captives
> and to the blind new sight;
> to set the downtrodden free,
> to proclaim the Lord's year of favor
> (Luke 4: 18–19).

Jesus' call for freedom became a great threat for the oppressors and a challenge to the oppressed. The gospel accounts give a picture of a charismatic figure who met opposition from the establishment when he attempted to free the people from the Sabbath "blue laws." Jesus proclaimed that the Sabbath was made for man and not man for the Sabbath. He took issue with other laws which unjustly infringed on human freedom. Jesus also defended his disciples when they contravened conventional practice, an action which served concretely to subvert the authority of the legal tradition.

A reading of the Gospels shows that Jesus challenged the various social institutions which legitimized and maintained the dominant values of his society. He attacked the very principles on which prestige, privilege, and authority rested. In Marxist terms, he attempted to change the basic class structure. Jesus' assault on the legal tradition and what it supported was made in an effort to give people power over their own lives and to liberate them from needless and oppressive burdens. By what authority or power did he do this? The Gospels show him again and again justifying his power. Jesus asked people to trust him, to remain loyal to him, and to participate in his work. He appealed to the authority of God for the legitimation of his work.

THE POWER OF EASTER

The source of Jesus' power to liberate people remained a problem even to the end of his ministry. His closest disciples harbored doubts and ambiguities. It was only after Jesus' death that his followers began to understand the source of his power. It was only after they themselves, empowered by the Spirit, became free themselves, free from fear of themselves and others that they truly realized that his power was the power of God. One modern author explains this new power in terms of the Easter event:

> The empowering of the powerless is at the heart of the Easter miracle, not some spectacular occurrence whose principal significance is to evoke amazement. . . . All [New Testament traditions concerning Easter] point concretely in the same direction—to the liberating, energizing power of the cross in human life (Ogletree, 1971, pp. 192–93).

Easter is a force which has continued in the life of the Christian community. It carries within itself the dynamics for human liberation in every age. The import of Easter is not that everything has been done for us but that we ourselves are empowered to labor with all our resources for the liberation which this event opens for us. It is this Easter event which has revealed in most dramatic form the explosive power of God operating in the world to enable the creative growth and the liberation from oppression which is the goal of many contemporary social movements.

Christian faith still empowers men and women in today's world to achieve genuine liberation from all forms of oppression. A thorny problem arises, however, when we must determine in advance, and even after the event, which movements are of God and which are not. Christians make different judgments about the women's liberation movement, Latin American revolutionary struggles, the black power movement, the consumer movement, the pro-life campaign, the nuclear disarmament movement, and other contemporary social, political, and economic problems. There are no simple rules-of-thumb that guide decisions in the concrete order of things, but what must be clearly asserted is that God is somehow involved in the ambiguity, the uncertainty, and the contingency of the historical process. Contemporary struggles are critical expressions of God's activity. They offer concrete possibilities for overcoming bondage and oppression, and of actualizing ways in which the true gospel of freedom can be realized. Decisions must be made; mistakes will no doubt take place. To have faith in God is to run the risk of taking sides in the concrete problems of this world. The world is, after all, unfinished. Its liberation is not assured. God wants us involved in struggles where, after both prayer and study, we believe that the liberating power of God is involved.

In recent years a political theology has developed which attempts to relate the Christian gospel and tradition to political struggles for liberation. The issue of power is a central theme within this theology. Rubem Alves, one of several Latin American theologians whose influence extends well beyond the southern hemisphere, sees the creation of history as possible only through power. For him, power is the form which human freedom takes. Politics is:

. . . the vocation of man, because every man is called to participate, in one way or another, in the creation of the future. Politics thus becomes for this consciousness the new gospel, the annunciation of the good news that, if man emerges from passivity and reflexivity, as the subject of history, a new future can be created. It challenges man: "Seek first the kingdom of politics and its power, and all these things shall be yours (Alves, 1972, p. 16)."

Alves's stance is one of a Christian revolutionary who feels that violent use of power is almost a necessity in the struggle of Latin Americans for liberation. Another contemporary Christian, Martin Luther King, took a stand in favor of nonviolence as the only practical way to struggle against evil because it alone is based on a right understanding of reality. King wrote that:

. . . the use of violence in our struggle would be both impractical and immoral. To meet hatred with retaliatory hate would do nothing but intensify the existence of evil in the universe. Hate begets hate; violence begets violence; toughness begets greater toughness. We must meet the forces of hate with the power of love; we must meet physical force with soul force. Our aim must never be to defeat or humiliate the white man, but to win his friendship and understanding (King in Richardson, 1969, p. 182).

The abuse of power and the quest for freedom are not new in human history. What is novel in today's social and political concerns is the overt way in which the gospel message is being presented as a liberation manifesto. In the following pages I will examine the implications of this development for the work of teaching and education within the churches. The General Catechetical Directory of the Roman Catholic Church, in speaking of the "special functions of catechesis for adults," says that they should learn "to evaluate correctly, in the light of faith, the sociological and cultural changes in contemporary society." It adds further that adult catechesis should "explain contemporary questions in religious and moral matters," and "shed light on the relations between temporal action and ecclesial action (GCD, 1971, No. 97)."

One way to approach contemporary questions of power and liberation is through the work of Paulo Freire, the noted Latin American educator. While his work provides a starting point for education for power and liberation, others must be willing to participate in this process. My own attempt to describe this evolving form of religious education, which can be termed liberating, consists in viewing education as immersion, dialogue, conscientization, and politics.

RELIGIOUS EDUCATION AS IMMERSION

A liberating religious education must be an education of immersion into the life of the people it attempts to educate. I believe that this characteristic is best described by the pastoral letter of the Appalachian bishops, *This Land is Home to Me* (1974). The letter speaks of closeness to the people as an essential element of the social apostolate. To be close to the people means that:

> . . . we must
> continually take time and invest creativity
> into listening to our people,
> especially the poor.
> For it is they who,
> out of their frustration, dreams, and struggles,
> must lead the way for all of us.

Throughout this whole process
of listening to the people,
the goal which underlies our concern
is fundamental in the justice struggle,
namely, citizen control,
or community control.
The people themselves
must shape their own destiny.
Despite the theme of powerlessness,
we know that Appalachia
is already rich here
in the cooperative power
of its own people.

Closeness to the people is also a fundamental principle in the pedagogy of Paulo Freire. He speaks of the need for communion with them at every stage in the educational and political process. The words that illiterates were taught were taken from the people. In the Freire method investigators must spend a long period of time listening to and recording their language and expressions. Freire warns against those educators and teachers who come to the people with ready-made programs. For this reason Freire refused to use existing books and materials. In his view each cultural situation demanded its own resources.

Many programs in religious education fail because educators plan programs without close consultation with the people to be educated. I attended a meeting of adults once who were deciding what type of religious education to offer to the children of their community. I suggested that no program be started until we heard from the children and young people themselves. We later heard from them and jointly prepared a program, for them and with them. To our surprise the younger children wanted a program in basic fundamentals of the faith; the older children wanted a course on the Bible. A nine-year-old boy, to the consternation and distress of his parents, asked on three separate occasions for a course in sex education. Education as immersion will bring some surprises and perhaps embarrassments.

A dramatic example of education as immersion were the successful Street Academies of Harlem. Because of the great number of students who did not attend school there, a group of specially trained teachers roamed the streets of Harlem looking for students, listening to their problems, providing educational experiences for them, and, in general, discovering the prevalent attitudes of these young people towards the schools and society.

Perhaps we religious educators should take seriously the advice of Jesus when he told us to *go and teach*. Too often our approach is *come and we will teach you*. Religious educators must find and develop ways in which to meet people where they are: their homes, places of work, places of leisure and entertainment. Meeting people where they are is one thing; the next task is to listen seriously to them and become immersed in their lives.

RELIGIOUS EDUCATION AS DIALOGUE

Authentic dialogue between teachers and students is at the heart of a liberating and powerful education. This statement is accepted as an obvious truism in educational circles, but I honestly feel that only lip-service is given to this truth. After all the words and efforts of progressive educators about the necessity of interaction in the classroom, and after all the efforts of Third Force psychologists to promote the use of personal encounter in the educational process, it has to be sadly admitted that a great majority of class time is still taken up with teacher talk.

Paulo Freire practiced and advocated a dialogic education. He also trained the coordinators of his circles of culture to listen to the concerns and interests of people and to make these the focus for educational dialogue with them. The basic form of education that he advocated was the group discussion on relevant cultural themes in the lives of the people. In his writings he criticized "the banking concept" of education where teachers make periodic deposits into the safekeeping minds of students and then make occasional withdrawals from them in exact words and phrases. In his treatment of dialogue Freire was greatly influenced by the philosophers Martin Buber and Gabriel Marcel. It was Buber who emphasized that all real living is the meeting of persons. Marcel developed his philosophy in terms of the presence of one person with another when engaged in dialogue.

A religious education which uses dialogue as a basic process is one that will give power to students and teachers. It will give students the power to be themselves, to develop their own religious faith, to fashion their own values, and to make their own commitments. We all know the tremendous power that we exert when we say our own words. It is a creative experience far different from the experience we have when we merely repeat the words of others, no matter how eloquent another's words are and how uneloquent ours may be. If teachers, also, speak their own words in dialogue, they will experience their words as powerful expressions of their own faith and religious commitments. Dialogue is a powerful tool for challenging teachers and students to manifest the power to be and the courage to be, which Paul Tillich places at the basis of religious faith. Dialogue is important in education, for we tend to distrust words that do not communicate a person, words that do not involve a person. We are all aware of the potential of words for corruption when they do not express personal truth and power.

A religious education that focuses upon dialogue is also a liberating education. It can liberate a person from his or her own cultural biases, from the pressures of peer groups and family, from slavish adherence to a faith that has merely been received from others, and from the sometimes overly influential personality of a teacher. A dialogic religious education can also be liberating for teachers by forcing them to move a little out of the official roles which they play as teachers of religion. As we all know, it is in dialogue with others that we often forget the roles we play and lose the masks we wear.

Authentic dialogue demands a number of things. It demands listening to and hearing what another has to say. It demands the often humbling realization that others have things to say which we ourselves have not thought of and are not capable of. It demands interest in, and concern for, others. Though dialogue between teacher and students is not on a par with the dialogue among friends who are equal in all respects, the effort should be made to make the relationship as much as possible one of equality, as students grow in years and maturity. The task of education is ultimately to enable students to liberate themselves from the power and authority of teachers.

Ways must be found in religious education to promote small-group discussions and face-to-face encounters on religious issues. Here is an example from my own teaching. The trend in higher education, for financial reasons, is towards larger and larger classes. What I have decided to do in this case is to give a number of large-group lectures and have an almost equal number of small-group discussions. On some weeks in the sixteen-week course I meet only with small groups of students to discuss a particular issue. It has been my experience that these small-group dialogues are most fruitful. Of course they have been prepared for by the lectures and readings. There is in my mind nothing sacred about how many times a student attends class. A short intense experience in learning may give insights and open the students for further self-development. A brief intensive session is often a powerful and liberating one. Teaching, as I view it, is not a matter of the number of times a class meets, the length of sessions, the number of books read, the number of pages a report extends—it is rather a matter of waiting for the right moment, the time of insight, the feeling of power and liberation. These I believe come more often than not in the moments of genuine dialogue on real-life issues.

RELIGIOUS EDUCATION AS CONSCIENTIZATION

A religious education that attempts to empower and liberate people has as one of its goals the process of conscientization which is closely identified with the educational theory and practice of Paulo Freire. Conscientization is the term that Freire used to describe the process through which a group of people become critically aware of the concrete conditions—political, social, economic, religious—in which they live, see the problems and contradictions in this situation, and accept their responsibility for participating in efforts to change these conditions. In the setting in which Freire worked, in Brazil and later in Chile, the condition was one of oppression—illiteracy, denial of the right to vote, the lack of organized labor unions, a magical view of religion, and a fatalistic attitude towards the possibility of bringing about change. Freire's educational effort was directed at giving people a sense of personal and collective power to shape their own lives and to eliminate the oppressive elements within their social situation.

The educational process of conscientization is one that gives people a genuine sense of power. It gives them the realization that they have *the power to be*—that they are autonomous beings with minds and wills of their own. It gives them *the power of self-affirmation:* their cry for recognition is heard by teachers and by other students. People begin to affirm their own being and their own significance. Self-esteem is increased. Conscientization also gives people the power of self-assertion—the power to express themselves against opposition, the power to demand from others that they be recognized as persons.

Religious education as conscientization attempts to make people aware of the problems and contradictions which exist in their social reality. The starting point for this educational process is the concrete situation in which people find themselves. Groups may examine from a religious perspective institutional racism, political corruption, abusive use of power by authorities, practices which offend public morality, the rights of conscience, educational systems, the care of the elderly, or the entire health system. The process of conscientization would entail a study of repressive elements within these areas of human activity, a study of the causes of these conditions, and the acceptance of responsibility to work to bring about changes.

The teacher who wants students to arrive at critical awareness has to be one who is truly daring. I tend to judge teachers by the questions they ask and, more importantly, by the questions they allow students to ask. Oppressive elements within Christian churches must also be the subject of critical examination: for example, the ordination of women to the Roman

Catholic priesthood. In churches which proclaim the need for reconciliation there is need to take a critical look at the oppression under which various groups in the churches live: divorced Christians, women, married priests, homosexuals, black and Spanish-speaking Christians. Discussion of reconciliation with God will bear little fruit unless it is accompanied by a critical look at many sensitive problems still unresolved within the churches.

At this junction, it is important to emphasize that I speak of religious education as conscientization primarily in the context of adult education. Other considerations have to be weighed in the education of children. Developmental psychologists have pointed out that a truly critical consciousness is not within the capabilities of children and many adolescents. The religious education of children is in many ways a non-critical initiation into the Christian community and its life. Religious educators of children must be careful to deal only with essentials of life and faith and to develop attitudes that foster future growth and development.

In the religious education of adolescents a more critical approach can be taken, but this must be done with great prudence. The natural questioning of many adolescents of what they have previously learned will lead to a questioning of religious beliefs and practices. The developing critical capacities of adolescents must be respected; an atmosphere of trust and openness should characterize religious education efforts. The religious and moral life must be presented as a matter of free choice and responsibility. A serious questioning of problems in the world and the church can be begun, but teachers need to be aware of the great differences which can exist among adolescent groups, and the need of adolescents for some secure base from which they can question and search for a more authentic religious faith.

RELIGIOUS EDUCATION AS POLITICAL EDUCATION AND POLITICS

A religious education that provides people with a truly liberating power in their lives must seriously face the issue of power and politics. In Latin America today there is a growing realization among theologians and educators that even conscientization is not enough. Education, they contend, must take the next step—a daring and risky one—the step of politicization. In their view religious educators have been heavy on rhetoric and theological theory but light on sacred and secular politics.

In examining Paulo Freire's pedagogy of the oppressed it seems clear that he did not originally attend sufficiently to the issue of the political struggles which would have to follow upon conscientization, if oppressed people were to truly liberate themselves. Freire appears to have fallen into the idealist trap of thinking that somehow people will spontaneously see the ways to bring about necessary changes in society. The raising of people's consciousness will have value only if they can then see ways to bring about these necessary changes and actually organize themselves to bring them about. Working for political change demands close attention to goals, strategies, organization, and tactics.

Religious education as politicization will attempt to bring people beyond the point of critical awareness to the point of action against injustice. Unless a person is willing to strike out in some way against injustice he or she cannot be termed truly human. Truffaut in his film *The Wild Boy* illustrates this point. The boy, Victor, learns to speak and to count. But the doctor wants to find out if he is fully human; he poses the problem: will the boy fight back when he is unjustly punished? The doctor locks him in a closet even though the boy has done his task exactly as prescribed. The doctor waits. Victor puts up a good fight. The doctor is relieved and asserts that there is present in the boy the central element which constitutes the human being—the capacity to sense injustice and to take a stand against it in the form of "I will be destroyed rather than submit."

Part of the curriculum for a religious education for power and liberation is a study of the levels of power that Rollo May (1974) has described: the power to be, the power of self-affirmation, the power of self-assertion, aggression and violence. Each of these levels must be examined in its psychological and sociological dimensions. Also to be examined is the power in nonviolent resistance to evil which Jesus, Gandhi, and Martin Luther King proposed. Power is to be viewed in the lives of individuals and societies.

Nietszche, I believe, was wrong in looking at Christianity as a religion which preached only humility and weakness. One has but to read the Gospel of Mark, or view Pasolini's film *The Gospel of St. Matthew*, to see that Jesus was a person who was involved in power struggles. He exercised power and advised his disciples to use power and authority to preach the Kingdom of God.

Religious education can also help one to analyze the various forms of power which are exercised by some individuals over others. Rollo May's (1974) discussion from a psychological point of view is a good place to start. (1) Power is *exploitive* when it is identified with force and attempts to subject a person by violence or threats of violence. (2) It is *manipulative* when it uses control *over* other persons to get them to act as we think they should. (3) It is *competitive* when it is power *against* another; this may be either helpful or harmful depending on whether it brings out the best or worst in people. (4) A *nutrient* power is exercised *for* others; it takes the form of care for others, especially for children and friends. (5) Power is *integrative* when it is exercised *with* others. This is cooperative power in which one works with others for a common good. *Nonviolent power* is a form of integrative power which appeals to the moral sense of the other person to cooperate with us in achieving some moral purpose.

A religious education for power and liberation is truly a political education in the sense that it will make people knowledgeable about social, political, and economic realities and will urge and aid them to act on this knowledge. The task of religious education as I see it is to emphasize the gospel commandment to love all persons—even the humblest—and to seek justice before all else. Universal kinship and oneness should be the goal in our interior spiritual life, and our quest should lead us to concrete attitudes and decisions as we deal each day with particular persons, ideas, and situations. For some Christians this message has led to revolutionary efforts. Others have been inspired to work for gradual changes in society. Still other Christians see the need for working for the maintenance of existing social structures. It appears that in many instances there is no clear-cut action mandated by the gospel. Differences of opinion and varieties of action will occur. But the gospel definitely does not appear to state that there is to be no relationship between the Christian gospel and a Christian decision in political, social, and economic matters. Jesus' teaching is political teaching, concerned with how men and women are to live and act together, not with men and women in isolation.

A religious education for power and liberation will present the arena of politics as an important Christian ministry. Sister Clare Dunn's view of politics as a "ministry of justice—or better yet, the great arena where justice is won or lost" convinced her to run for the Arizona state legislature. She saw politics at the heart of a renewed religious life, and her work was essentially the same kind of service her Order, the Sisters of St. Joseph of Carondolet, has always given, caring for the sick, the poor, and the homeless. When Father Drinan ran for Congress, the Jesuit General Pedro Arrupe, in granting permission for this candidacy, commented:

Often political decisions and actions in the secular world violate and harm fundamental rights, thus frustrating the true meaning of human existence for the individual and the community. How, for instance, can a Jesuit priest remain impassive in the face of racial injustice, or in the face of institutionalized violence. To remain inactive would mean betraying our calling in life. (Arrupe in Beckwith, 1975)

Father Drinan's decision to resign this position because of pressure from the Vatican can be viewed as an unfortunate development, restricting the ministry of ordained ministers and also religious sisters from the area of politics. This ban has not prevented a number of priests from serving in government positions in Latin American countries. These decisions do not, however, affect the responsibility of lay Christians to become deeply involved in the political struggles of their countries.

In recent years the United States bishops, or their political-social action arm, the United States Catholic Conference, have made rather strong statements on political and social issues. They endorsed the United Farm Workers' boycott of lettuce and table grapes until union elections took place. They opposed capital punishment and suggested prison reform. They urged a new United States-Panama treaty, with Panama reaping most of the benefits of the canal. They proposed a ban on the import of Rhodesian chrome to protest that country's racist policy. They supported conditional amnesty for conscientious objectors who evaded the draft during the Vietnam War.

The most dramatic entrance of the bishops has been in the debate over the morality of war, especially nuclear war. Their pastoral letter on this subject has been the subject of widespread discussion. Within the letter itself a strong endorsement is given to educational efforts for enlightening members of the Catholic church on issues pertaining to peace and war.

The United States Catholic conference, through Monsignor George Higgins, gave guidelines a number of years ago for the place of politics in the church. The guidelines stated that while a priest should never use the pulpit for partisan politics he has a serious duty to instruct the faithful on the moral implications of social and political matters. Preachers were urged to approach political issues positively and to deal with specifics in a give-and-take dialogue after church services. The thrust of the directive was that the discussion of the moral implications of specific political issues could follow the homily. I believe that these directions might also be applied in the classroom and in other educational settings.

In reflecting upon power it has become clear to me that any discussion of power is woefully incomplete without a discussion of justice, for the demands of justice determine the legitimacy of the power that is used. A conception of justice which I feel is consonant with the Christian tradition has been developed by the philosopher John Rawls (1971). Rawls argues that the natural inequities of birth, strength, intelligence, and ability are inherently unfair and that justice requires society to compensate for such inequities. In this view some inequities would be permitted in society so long as these benefit the less advantaged members of society. This view leads logically to the elimination of meritocracy, to quotas in education and other fields, and to a drastic redistribution of income.

POWER, LIBERATION, AND LOVE

In the course of this study I have said almost nothing about a human quality which is certainly of the very essence of the spiritual life of men and women—the quality of love. For many people love and power are opposed; a person is either motivated by power or motivated by love. Many go so far as to look upon power as a denial of love and upon love as the renunciation of power. The tendency to do this is especially strong in those who view love as merely an emotional response and power as sheer force or compulsion.

Although I feel that it is necessary to maintain the distinction between love and power, I also feel that it is fruitful to bring out the interrelationships between the two. It is clear that persons cannot love unless they have the power to love. Love alone is not enough, for without power it remains a mere sentiment; it is unable to accomplish anything. On the other hand, power without love tends to become manipulative and exploitive. Power is thus the means through which love is translated into action. But love is the force which directs power to proper ends and objectives. Martin Buber expressed this relationship when he observed: "I do not know what would remain to us were love not transfigured power and power not straying love (Buber, 1967, p. 45)."

Human liberation is a work of love, but it is also a work of power. A religious education, to be truly liberating, must involve itself with both love and power. It clearly asserts that God is love, but it also affirms that God is mighty and powerful. Jesus is the incarnation of God's love; he is also the incarnation of God's power and strength. While Jesus preached an ethic of love, he also found a place for the violence that was necessary for attaining the Kingdom of God. The spirit of God is both a spirit of love who binds people together and a spirit of power who encourages them to act against injustice. Christians should be known not only by their powerful love but also by their loving power. Human liberation is the work of a loving and powerful God working through men and women of love and power.

CHAPTER 13

RELIGIOUS EDUCATION AND THE SOCIAL IMAGINATION

Interest in the imagination is an ever-present phenomenon in the life of many people in society, especially artists, poets, writers, and film makers. Interest in the imagination in the life of many ordinary persons usually comes and goes according to personal and social needs. Today we find many intellectuals and academics, including educators, devoting attention to the nature and role of imagination. This increased concentration on the imagination among many people may well come from the contemporary situation of the world, which moves some persons to see apocalyptic visions of nuclear disaster and others to create hopeful and utopian visions of a future in which peace and justice will dominate human life.

The creation of hopeful visions of the future is in a special way a task for educators who work with both the young and the old. Educators have many reasons for participating in the use of the imagination for developing helpful and hopeful visions of the future. In fact, education has little meaning except within the vision of a hopeful future. Furthermore, among educators, religious educators have special resources for fostering this type of imagination in the myths, rituals, doctrines, and lives of religious communities.

In this study my aim is to propose an understanding of social and political imagination which should accompany the aesthetic imagination in developing images of the real which can become human goals or achievements. I will first describe what I mean by the social imagination. Then I will examine how both theologians and educators have included this dimension in their recent work. Finally, I will present some concrete suggestions as to how religious educators might foster the social imagination in their institutions and teaching.

THE SOCIAL IMAGINATION

Before describing the social imagination, I think that it is helpful to distinguish two forms of imagination, the aesthetic and the social, even though there are connections between them. Although there is a great interest today in the role of the imagination in religious education, this concern usually takes the form of interest in the aesthetic imagination, that is, the power of the person to both appreciate and form images of the beautiful. The role of the imagination in education is usually associated with education in the arts or the aesthetic dimension of education. This type of education takes two forms. We can expose persons to works of art in order to foster certain attitudes, values, and sensibilities. We can also develop the aesthetic imagination by fostering the creative capacity of learners to produce works of art. Art appreciation is a value in itself but art production or creation is considered an even loftier aim. The aesthetic imagination is concerned with the world of beauty and works of art. It attempts to develop those capacities which enable us to understand, feel, and appreciate images in various forms and the abilities which enable us to perform, produce, or create images of the beautiful in acceptable forms.

Besides the aesthetic imagination persons also have a capacity for social or political imagination. This imagination is both similar to and different from the aesthetic imagination. Education has the task of fostering both types of imagination. By social imagination I mean what Buber calls "imaging the real." C. Wright Mills, the American sociologist, in his classic work *The Sociological Imagination* (1959), described social imagination as the power that enables us to understand larger historical scenes and contexts, to understand our experience by locating ourselves within a specific period, and to recognize that we know ourselves and our chances in life only by becoming aware of others in similar or different circumstances.

The social imagination enables us to understand our society and its place in human history, as well as the varieties of men and women in this society. Through social imagination we can shift from one perspective to another: individual to social, psychological to political, family to nation, theology to economics. By this power we hope to grasp what is going on in the world and to understand the intersections of biography and history within society. Other names for this imagination are political imagination and historical consciousness.

Social imagination finds expression not only in the knowledge that we have of persons, historical periods, and present problems, but also in active compassion and personal responsibility to alleviate the pains and sufferings of others. After we get inside persons, communities, and societies we are in a better position to move to concrete imaging of involvement in their struggles.

The social imagination is both similar to and different from the aesthetic imagination. It is similar to it in that it utilizes the world of images. But the images of the social imagination take the form of history, visions, stories, concepts, and theories. It differs from the aesthetic imagination in that it attends especially to the social and political existence of individuals. The aesthetic imagination may deal in images of the political and social, but it draws more on human experience and consciousness and not on knowledge from the social sciences. This is not to say that the aesthetic imagination has not provided powerful social and political images. Great works of art such as the novels of Dickens, Tolstoy, and the contemporary William Styron give powerful social and political images.

It should be clear that my purpose in this study is not to oppose the two forms of imagination but to indicate how the two forms both differ from and complement each other. Social scientists learn from the images of artists. Artists learn from the images of social scientists. The powerful novel and film *Sophie's Choice* was a work of individual imagination and the fruit of extensive study and re-presentation of the events of the Holocaust.

While the aesthetic imagination is fostered by works of art, the sociological imagination is fostered through the social sciences and in a secondary manner through humanistic works. While previous cultures were dominated by a philosophic, scientific, or psychological mentality, it appears that for our age the common denominator of cultural life is social understanding and imagination. This quality of mind presents the opportunity for understanding ourselves and our human possibilities within the society in which we live.

The major problems of our times are social and political. They concern the types of values which we want to foster in a particular society and in the entire world. While social and political problems may be expressed by art—and art at its best does dwell on social feelings—it does not do so with the intellectual clarity required for the understanding of contemporary problems. As Mills (1959) noted:

Art does not and cannot formulate these feelings as problems containing the troubles and issues men must now confront if they are to overcome their uneasiness and the intractable miseries to which these lead (p. 18).

RELIGION AND THE SOCIAL IMAGINATION

Forms of religion at their best are concerned with the social imagination. In all forms of religious expression there is always the sense of a past, present, and future which are valuable for human existence. The *past* continues to have meaning for religious persons. Our relationship to the past is not merely one of memory but also one of imagination. We periodically reconstruct the past. Religious literature is very much a repository of the past experiences of a community. The power of tradition is influential in all religious groups. Religious rituals, symbols, stories, and myths are ways to image the past and to keep it alive. The ritual celebrations of Passover and Easter have a primary reference to events in the past history of Jewish and Christian communities. In religions which put an emphasis on doctrinal statements, contemporary teaching must always take account of past teachings. Great inspiration is drawn from great figures of the past.

The religious imagination also is operative in understanding the *present* condition of persons and communities. Through such doctrines as sin and grace, faith and works, creation and salvation, we can understand the polarities and dialectics of present human existence. Religious rituals attempt to engage persons in contemporary problems of individual and social existence. The images of justice and peace hold out goals that we are to strive for in our present existence. There is always room in living religions for symbols and stories drawn from present experience.

In a powerful way religious images attempt to motivate us to imagine another *future* symbolized in various ways as Heaven, the Kingdom of God, Nirvana, and Paradise. The imaging of these future realities empowers us to work for the future existence contained in religious visions. In the interpretation of religious visions of the future a shift has taken place from other-worldly concerns to this-worldly issues. Such images as salvation and liberation are increasingly interpreted as realities which are to be attained in our present existence. Religious rituals also look to the end state of the religious community.

Besides a recognition of the fullness of religious life in its three-dimensional existence, there has also been a major shift in the study of religious literature, doctrines, and rituals. Recent theological discussion has given increased attention to the social, political, and cultural dimensions of religious myths, rituals, and doctrines. In ages when individualism was a dominant cultural phenomenon, religious experience and its codifications became increasingly individualized. Today, at a time when we are more attuned to social and communal aspects of human existence, we are rediscovering the strong communal and social dimensions of all religious phenomena.

This phenomenon is seen, for example, in the interpretations of the Christian and Jewish Scriptures. For a number of decades an existentialist interpretation of this literature predominated. This was primarily because of the efforts of Rudolph Bultmann, who used the categories of existentialist philosophy to reinterpret the Gospels for our time. Present-day interpreters of the Scriptures are more attuned to the political and social aspects of the Gospels. It is recognized, for example, by many scholars that Jesus was not an apolitical person. His politics appear to have been that of nonviolent resistance to evil. His religious vision included a vision of a society of peace and justice to be brought about by the power of his Father and not the force of arms (Yoder, 1972).

In the field of theology one of the most dramatic developments is the emergence of political and liberation theologies. Both of these forms of theology are in serious dialogue with the social sciences. The social imagination is a powerful theological tool among politically oriented theologians. Contemporary theology has become aware of the cultural contexts in which previous theologies developed and the limitations of those theologies. Attempts are now made to construct theologies which consciously take into consideration the present situation or "the signs of the times," the expression of the Vatican II Pastoral Constitution on the Church in the Modern World. European political theology began by attempting to broaden the categories of neo-Thomist, neo-orthodox, and existential theology to include specifically social and political dimensions. This theology is in close communication with neo-Marxist political, social, and economic theory. It attempts to deal with problems of secularization of life and the reduction of the religious to the private sphere. This form of theology has included a sharp criticism of the bourgeois mentality of contemporary Christianity.

The social and political dimensions of Latin American liberation theology are at the center of controversy in the churches of Latin America. This theology takes as its starting point a careful social analysis. The basic Christian communities and their efforts at working for justice are the contexts for this theology. The attempt to correlate social analysis with Christian faith and theology is an act of social imagination since what is done is not just the condemnation of present social structures but also the imaginative work of proposing what the future society should be.

North American theology has taken up the challenge of these political and liberation theologies in attempting to develop theologies which are more concerned with political, social, and economic dimensions of human existence. It is now clear that the theologies of other cultural situations cannot simply be transported to the North American scene. What must be developed are theological approaches which are relevant to our particular social context. Some groups, such as blacks, women, and native Americans, have modeled theologies along the lines of Latin American liberation theologies. These theologies begin with an analysis of historical and present forms of oppression, discrimination, and marginalization. The religious tradition is then examined to see how it has been used to foster present contradictions in society. These theologies also image a future in which inhuman and immoral situations do not exist.

Other North American theologies have attempted to develop a practical or strategic theology which is more indigenous to the American situation. These theologies attempt to do justice to the pluralism of religious faiths, North American social analyses, and theological understandings. Gregory Baum (1981) has retrieved the tradition of Canadian socialism in an attempt to critique from a theological perspective the social situation in Canada. John Coleman (1981) has made an attempt to outline a strategic American theology that draws on Protestant political theory and on the extensive tradition of social Catholicism. The third volume of David Tracy's monumental work on theological method will be devoted to the area of practical theology, that is, theology as it impinges on the social, political, economic, and cultural spheres. At the Center for Concern in Washington, D.C., Joseph Holland and Peter Henriot (1984) have made efforts to relate social analysis and the Christian gospel to contemporary problems in society. What is clear from the work of these socially oriented thinkers is that theology must enter into closer connections with all strains of social thought and analysis.

Having briefly reviewed efforts in contemporary theology to utilize the social imagination, I can now move to the field of education to argue for a greater involvement of educators in developing the social imagination. It seems that in this area religious educators have lagged somewhat behind developments in general education.

EDUCATION AND THE SOCIAL IMAGINATION

It is my view that educators need to pay more attention to the social sciences other than psychology in developing educational aims and methods as well as in exploring educational contexts. I believe that the fields of education and religious education have too long been dominated by psychological theories and research. Educators are generally familiar with the work of Piaget, Erikson, Skinner, Kohlberg, Maslow, and Rogers. Religious educators also know the work of Goldman and Fowler. Psychology is viewed as helpful in gaining an understanding of how persons develop and learn, and how they might best be taught. Almost all teachers have had courses in educational psychology.

There is no doubt that a significant contribution has been made to education by these psychological theories, even though there have been some critical voices raised recently about the actual usefulness of the great amount of psychological theory and research (Egan, 1979; Moran, 1983).

Other social scientists have also pointed out the cultural biases which are often found in the work of psychologists. The limitations of psychology come to the fore especially when one wishes to take into account social, political, and economic aspects of education.

Few teachers have studied social theory or sociology of knowledge. Few religious educators are conversant with understandings of society that are provided by the classical sociologists Durkheim, Weber, and Marx or the work of more contemporary sociologists Parsons, Berger, Bellah, and Luckmann. For the past decade a group of sociologists of knowledge, both British and American, have examined school learning and adult education from the perspective of the social contexts of this learning (Young, 1971; Apple, 1979; Thompson, 1980). The impact of this work has yet to be felt in the field of religious education.

The work of social scientists is extremely important for religious educators who are attempting to relate religious faith to the contemporary world and to avoid the dangers of teaching and fostering a privatized faith. Educators who wish to deal intelligently with such issues as world hunger, multinational corporations, and nuclear disarmament need the social imagination that comes from a study of the social sciences. Religious education for peace and justice demands the development of the social imagination fostered through a study of the social sciences. The approach to social education and ministry developed by the Center for Concern in Washington begins the pastoral cycle with experience and social analysis. Only after these two phases are completed does a group move to theological reflection and social action.

The field of religious education has recently devoted more attention to social imagination and analysis. Suzanne Toton (1982) has written about the responsibility of the Christian educators to deal with world hunger. Toton uses the methodology of liberation theology. She first presents an analysis of the causes of world hunger. Then she appeals to theological teachings which have to be brought to bear on this issue. In a concluding section she develops her own educational theory and gives examples from her own practice for making students both aware of and active in the problems concerning world hunger.

My criticisms of the failure of religious educators to foster social imagination is directed both at educators and at the institutions in which they are educated. A study of the curricula of graduate schools, institutes, and seminaries where religious education is presented will reveal that extremely few courses are offered in this area. The major thrust in these institutions is toward a general pastoral ministry and spirituality. Institutions that take seriously the social movements in our time will certainly have to devote more attention to this neglected area of study.

If religious educators are aware of the increased social consciousness in theology and in educational theory, they will be in a better position to foster the social imagination of their students. One cannot foster in another what one does not have in oneself. I should now like to make some suggestions to religious educators on ways of fostering their own social imagination and that of their students.

FOSTERING THE SOCIAL IMAGINATION

Fostering social and political imagination is an important task for religious educators. I should like to make some suggestions on how this might be done in the various contexts of religious education. My focus is on the settings of home, school, parish, and community. In order to focus these suggestions I will organize them around three areas: objectives, programs and curriculum, and teachers.

Objectives

All educational institutions and organizations are constantly evaluating their stated philosophy, mission, and objectives. Families are involved in this process in informal ways. Schools often have to formulate a philosophy of education. Parishes go through periodic reassessment of mission statements. Adult education committees review their work and plan for future endeavors. Too often, stated philosophies fail to contain explicit social and political dimensions since they are often couched in terms of individual or personal religious needs.

Statements of philosophy of educational and religious mission need to take cognizance of social contexts and social goals. The tradition of Christian education is not usually a narrow and sectarian one that prepares Christians for an isolated or neutral social and political life. There exists, for example, within the Catholic tradition in this country a long history of Social Catholicism which includes such persons as Orestes Brownson, John Courtney Murray, John Ryan, Dorothy Day, Thomas Merton, and Daniel Berrigan. This Social Catholicism also makes its appearance in the many social utterances of individual bishops and conferences of bishops.

Protestant religious educators also have strong confessional theology in this area. Prominent theologians include Walter Rauschenbusch and the Social Gospel tradition, the Christian Realism of Reinhold Niebuhr, and the Christian Socialism of Paul Tillich. Other Protestant theologians who have contributed to this tradition include John C. Bennett and Paul

Ramsey. The synodal documents of Protestant churches have had a long tradition of contending with social and political issues.

In stating the purposes of Christian education for home, school, and parish these rich traditions should be drawn on. Important questions concern what kinds of citizens we want to develop in our Christian homes, communities, and institutions. I realize that there will be debate on these issues within the pluralistic settings of Christian churches. Statements of philosophy and mission do not have to arrive at total agreement or consensus. The very process of struggling with social purposes is an exercise in collective social imagination. We have recently witnessed the international debate among Christians on peace and disarmament. Although honest differences exist, there are enough religious values to which all persons adhere to unify a community and motivate it to action.

In setting objectives for Christian education, Christians are involved in a task of social imagination in that they are attempting to define the types of persons and communities that they wish to develop. This task demands both a look back at the religious tradition, a look at the present situation, and a vision for the future of individuals, communities, and societies. This task is something which is best done by all persons in the community. Christians bring to it the particular resources which their tradition and faith life provides.

Teachers

It is clear that schools of theology and religious education need to give more attention to fostering social and political imagination in their training of teachers of religion. Curricula in these institutions need to be examined to determine whether historical, social, political, and economic contexts and understandings are included within educational, religious, and theological courses. Social imagination is both a part of all courses in these areas and also a separate function of courses in the social sciences.

The task of fostering social and political imagination among present teachers can be accomplished through study leaves and in-service education. Teachers who have strong backgrounds in the social sciences can be encouraged to make more explicit connections between these disciplines and religious concerns. A creative use of team teaching can bring social imagination to the fore for many teachers through exposure to colleagues who are stronger in the social sciences. Often those religion teachers who have a grounding in the social sciences or another secular discipline bring more creative perspectives to the teaching of religion.

In parish adult education it is helpful, as I have done, to include social

workers and community workers as teachers and organizers in programming and teaching. Since these persons deal with problems of social life
and community organization, they can do a great deal to make members of
the community aware of Christian responsibilities in these areas. It is also
beneficial to develop educational experiences where persons speak from a
variety of backgrounds: theological, sociological, and psychological. A
professional group I was involved with treated a broad range of issues in
this manner: alcoholism, adoption, housing, arms race, and capitalism.

Curricula

There are a number of ways in which programs and curricula of religious
education can be shaped to foster social imagination. The teaching of the
Scriptures and theology should include attention to the social contexts and
the political implications of these studies. Teachers need to be sensitive to
the dangers of applying biblical and theological knowledge exclusively to
the areas of private faith and spirituality. Our religious traditions speak to
us not only as individuals but as individuals within social communities.

Social imagination can be fostered especially through courses and
educational experiences which are interdisciplinary, e.g., theology and
economics. To deal with critical issues of world hunger demands an
exercise of both social and theological imagination. Economic, social, and
political factors are involved in this issue. Different opinions and explanations are offered for the cause of the problem. Some lay the blame for the
problem at the feet of capitalist economies. Others point to a complex
combination of causes and factors. This type of social and political analysis
must be done before one moves to explicitly religious and theological
responses. For these reasons topics such as these are best treated in an
interdisciplinary manner and taught by persons skilled in various disciplines.

Social imagination can be fostered through service programs and pro-
jects which put an emphasis on firsthand experience with social realities. If
the service component of religious education is to have any degree of
seriousness, students need both to experience and to study about the social
reality of various contexts. The Christian responsibility is to understand
and act in the threefold sphere of human existence: personal, interpersonal,
and sociopolitical.

The Challenge of a Socially Relevant Faith

The call to education for social imagination is a call to make religious
values relevant for personal and communal life. This call is not a modern

one but actually an ancient one. Many of the prophets of Israel railed against the failure of the people to do justice to the deprived members of the community. In describing the Last Judgment Jesus spoke of responsibilities to poor, naked, imprisoned, hungry and thirsty persons. Vatican II bade all Christians to read the signs of the times and to fashion a faith in light of human needs and problems. It is a social imagination connected to a political faith which makes us sensitive to both individual and institutional oppression. It fosters in us a feeling for what increases or decreases in others their full human and spiritual development.

No matter what we say of the importance of the social and political imagination of religion, it is also important to realize that this imagination is subordinated to more central religious values. Jacques Maritain advised us that:

Before doing good to others and working for their benefit, before practicing the politics of one group or another . . . , we must first choose to exist with them and to suffer with them, to make their pain and their destiny our own. (Maritain in Doerning, 1982, p. 504)

The challenge of Christians was issued by the humanist Albert Camus: What the world expects of Christians is that they set themselves free from abstractions and look at the blood-stained face of history in our times.

Since many Christians in our country have achieved relatively comfortable middle-class status, it will become even more important to foster a social and political imagination which fosters a relationship of solidarity with the poor and weak of this world. Johannes Metz, the German political theologian, has warned that a church that is engaged in following Jesus has to put up with being despised by the wise and powerful. What the church cannot afford is to be despised by the poor and small, by those who do not have another to help them. For Jesus these are the privileged ones, and they must know that they are represented by us. The Anglican bishop of Liverpool David Shepherd utters the same sentiments in his clearly titled book *Bias for the Poor* (1983).

One natural response to what I have written is that by fostering social and political imagination we run the risk of making people paralyzed in the face of the great problems of this world. This is certainly a danger. But this danger can be avoided, perhaps, by reflecting on two rather optimistic persons, one from an earlier era of church history and one from present-day politics. St. Bernadine of Sienna suggested: "Can you not give a loaf? Well, give a crumb. Can you not give wine? Give water. Can you not help a sick person? Grieve with him at least. Show him your compassion."

The second person is Robert Kennedy. At Capetown, South Africa he spoke these words on June 6, 1966:

Few will have the greatness to bend history itself; but each of us can work to change a small portion of events, and in the total of all these acts will be written the history of this generation. It is from numberless diverse acts of courage and belief that human history is shaped. Each time a man stands up for an ideal or acts to improve the lot of others, or strikes out against injustice, he sends a tiny ripple of hope, and crossing each other from a million centers of energy and daring, those ripples build a current which can sweep down the mightiest walls of oppression and resistance.

CHAPTER 14

LIBERATION SPIRITUALITY: THEOLOGY AND MODELS

In recent years we have witnessed the development of liberation and political theologies. Concurrent with this development there is now, in many countries, a renewed interest in forms of spirituality. My purpose in this study is to explore the possible connection between liberation theologies and forms of spirituality that are derived from or connected with them. It is my view that spiritualities are often connected with theological movements in the Christian churches.

In this study I propose to review briefly the various sources for the current scholarly interest in spirituality. Next, I will focus in a particular way on the sociocultural resources for this study. Following this, I will present classical as well as modern models of a liberation spirituality. I will conclude by presenting some principles for a contemporary liberation spirituality.

By spirituality in this paper I refer to a religious life style, in which a person lives in conscious relationship to God, self, others, nature, and the world. I recognize that this definition has the strengths and weaknesses of its theistic assumptions. I believe that what I say also has some relevance on a purely humanistic or naturalistic level.

FOUNDATIONS FOR SPIRITUALITY

In order to understand the relevance of liberation and political theologies for our time, it is first necessary to understand the various foundations for the contemporary interest in spirituality. Contemporary spirituality has a number of foundational sources: biblical studies, historical studies, theology, psychology, and the social sciences. Liberation spirituality looks to all of these sources in developing its principles.

Christian spirituality finds its roots in the *biblical tradition*. The Jewish and Christian Scriptures—like all religious literature—provide the models, ideals, attitudes, and norms that should characterize the life of religious persons. Biblical studies have important contributions to make for the formation of religious ideals that are present in specific persons and movements. One can speak of a wisdom spirituality, a prophetic spirituality, and various Pauline spiritualities. The biblical tradition gives the examples of many who lived lives of faith in response to God's call. The life of Jesus is obviously the prime example for Christians. Many spiritualities of Jesus have been developed from a study of the gospel traditions.

The study of spirituality also looks to *systematic theology* as one of its foundational sources. Theological views give rise to particular spiritualities. In some theological traditions there are even branches of practical or applied theology called ascetical and mystical theology. One's view of God and primary religious symbols and their interpretations are influential in forming a spiritual life. Different Catholic and Protestant theologies are related to differences in Catholic and Protestant piety. Those committed to more secular and this-worldly theologies have spiritualities which have strong secular foundations and connections.

Part of the renewal in the development of spirituality as a field of study has been the increased attention to the *history and traditions of classical spiritualities*. Classic works in spirituality have been published by two major publishers, Paulist Press and Doubleday. What these classical studies provide is a perspective for the examination of present forms of spirituality. Through such classics we are put into touch with Christians from both East and West and are enabled to enter into the cultural contexts in which they lived their lives.

Contemporary studies in spirituality have been enriched by connection with a number of *psychological* theories. Especially helpful have been works in Jungian and humanistic psychology. Helpful associations have been made between psychological and spiritual wholeness. The works of developmental psychologists such as Erikson and Fowler have provided a framework for understanding spiritual growth.

The one area that has been rather late in coming into the discussion of spirituality is the area of the *social sciences*. It is this academic field that I hope to bring into the discussion of contemporary spirituality. An examination of sociology of religion increases our knowledge of different forms of spirituality within different cultures. This knowledge added to biblical studies, theology, history, and psychology lays a firm foundation for understanding spirituality today, and especially a liberation spirituality.

SOCIOLOGICAL CLASSIFICATION OF SPIRITUALITIES

A classification of spiritualities can be formed by examining the work of Max Weber (1922; 1963) and Joachim Wach (1944) on religious leaders.

What these sociologists have written about religious leaders can be extended to forms of spirituality or religiousness which characterize the lives of ordinary individuals. From a sociological point of view spiritualities can be classified as magical, priestly, prophetic, ascetical world-affirming, ascetical world-rejecting, mystical world-accepting, and mystical world-rejecting. Sociologists present these as ideal forms or types, realizing that the pure forms of any of these are rarely found. Though our concern will be with prophetic spirituality, it is helpful to relate this form to the other types which are presented by the classic sociologists.

Magical spirituality is characterized by attempts to coerce the gods through songs, dances, dramas, or prescribed formulas. The primary aim of these actions is not the invocation or the worship of God but the attempt to make God do something by the power of one's own words or actions. Magical spirituality has some of the same characteristics as genuine spirituality, and the distinction between the two is not always clear. Both arise from similar needs and have comparable emotional atmospheres: awe, respect, marvel, and wonder. Magical spirituality dominates peasant classes which have a fatalistic attitude towards life. It is also found among the poor and the oppressed people who feel determined in their life situation. Magical spirituality is not absent in other classes of society, though it often takes more sophisticated forms.

Sociologists have made strenuous efforts to separate magical spirituality from *priestly spirituality,* which is primarily ritual and liturgical. This spirituality is involved in divine worship and prayer. Priestly spirituality is often highly rationalized around a definite cult, a body of doctrines or theology, an ethical system of values, and a clear-cut organization. Priestly spirituality also includes elements of pastoral care and the education of a laity who present themselves at the priestly worship. Because of the presence of cult there is a danger of this form of spirituality falling into magical consciousness. Other dangers also exist: a rigid doctrinal understanding, an absolute ethical belief, and a primary status for the organization above the individuals within it.

Prophetic spirituality is related to magical and priestly spirituality in a number of ways. It is related to magical spirituality in those cases where prophets appeal to magical powers to authenticate their mission. But the dominant element in prophetic spirituality is its effort to combat forms of magical spirituality when they find their way into the official cult. The prophets of Israel were critical of those who felt that mere participation in cult—without interior devotion and the living out of the implications of divine worship in individual and social existence—was an adequate spiritual life. The prophets thus often found themselves in combat both with the magicians and the priests over what the prophets believed were the inadequacies of others' religious consciousness.

Though critical of priestly spirituality, especially as regards cultic practices, the prophets saw an important role for ritual in the spiritual life of the people. True ritual, in their view, was based on genuine religious feelings and intentions and bore fruit in religious life. True cult was always inclusive of the responsibility of putting into practice the ideals, attitudes, examples, and laws that were ritualized in cult.

From a sociological point of view the chief characteristic of prophetic spirituality is interest in the relationship between the worship of God and the doing of God's justice in the world. Prophets take up their work out of an awareness of personal call. The prophets often call a people back to the fundamental principles of their religious faith. They often announce divine revelation through emotional preaching. They proclaim religious truths of salvation on the basis of a personal call to point to the revelation of God. Prophesy is exercised in an *exemplary* fashion when the prophet announces through a way of life the way of religious salvation. The prophet engages in *ethical* prophecy when, through preaching and teaching, he appeals to ethical principles which should not be violated or which should be fostered (Weber, 1922; 1963, ch. 4).

The treatment of ascetical and mystical spirituality by sociologists of religion is a complex one. A distinction is made between two forms of asceticism, other-worldly and worldly, and two forms of mysticism, other-worldly and worldly. *Other-worldly asceticism* is concerned with mastery over the flesh and the capacity to control worldly motivation, all in the interest of devotional and other worldly goals. The other-worldly ascetic suffers the imperfections and trials of this life in order to achieve the benefits of future life. The world is viewed as a dangerous place to inhabit; in order not to be contaminated by it, a person devotes energies to various spiritual exercises or practices. Prophetic spirituality agrees with the need for discipline but views the discipline as a means of developing spiritual power to work for justice.

Worldly asceticism finds its clearest example in Calvinism. The worldly ascetic attempts to achieve self-fulfillment in a calling in life which is pleasing to God. This spirituality includes both religious duties and one's secular calling. Though Protestantism has been a prominent proponent of this form of ascetical spirituality, Roman Catholic monasticism has attempted at times to combine a worldly with an other-worldly asceticism. A prophetic spirituality has much in common with worldly asceticism in its emphasis on the value of secular activity, but it points out that historically this form of spirituality has been more conformed to the world than prophetic in judgments about given social arrangements.

Mystical spirituality is both other-worldly and worldly. The *other-worldly mystic* seeks to avoid subjective desire because it interferes with the pursuit of salvation, which means dissociating oneself from the world, with a total loss of interest in its concerns. This mysticism is primarily a quest to achieve rest in God alone. *Inner-worldly mysticism* does not attempt to escape involvement in this world but does not give ultimate significance to life in the world. Prophetic spirituality is more closely related to inner-worldly mysticism in its affirmation of the value of contemplation. It differs from it in refusing to make such a clear distinction between this life and a future existence.

MODELS OF LIBERATION SPIRITUALITY

Prophetic or liberation spirituality has received little attention in contemporary writings on spirituality. Great emphasis is given to priestly, liturgical, mystical, and ascetical spiritualities. However, with the emergence of liberation and political theologies, there is need for work on a liberation spirituality in correspondence to these theologies. In developing concrete models of this spirituality, it is important to look to both ancient and modern times. The past tradition is examined in order to show that this form of spirituality has roots in the Jewish and Christian tradition. Contemporary experience is examined to show the relevance of this spirituality for present religious life. Only a few examples can be given, but these will show significant forms of liberation spirituality.

A liberation or prophetic spirituality sees its major purpose in involvement with movements for social, political, economic, and religious changes. This spirituality includes a response to a definite call to take a stand in the face of injustice and oppression and to struggle to erode sinful social structures. Liberation spirituality has been described by Baum in these words:

> Christian spirituality can find a context in the ethos of emancipation. Both Old and New Testament provide a prophetic spirituality that judges the existing system, yearns for the coming of a new order and prays for the transvaluation of values. "The first shall be last and the last first." "Thy kingdom come." "The powerful shall be pushed from their thrones and the lowly will be exalted; the rich shall be sent away empty and the poor will be filled with good things (1978, p. 281).

What liberation spirituality has discovered is a tradition that has often been neglected in Jewish and Christian history.

It is an interesting fact of history that the prophetic spirituality of the Jewish Scriptures has found powerful expression in such a secular liberation movement as Marxism. The younger Marx sounds much like a Jewish prophet in his denunciation of the injustices of the new industrial society. This is a reason why Christians interested in liberation and political theologies have entered into serious dialogue with Marxists who are faithful to the humanistic tradition of Marx.

Prophetic spirituality has a number of models in the Jewish Scriptures. At Moses' death it was said that no prophet equal to him rose up in Israel. Though Moses is not usually considered a prophet in our ordinary understanding, his political efforts and his teaching place him in the prophetic tradition. The Exodus, formation of a people, and the development of the Law were all religious activities in the secular sphere. The only way for Moses to revolt against political and economic oppression was to revolt against the religious order supporting that oppression.

The well-known prophets of Israel such as Elijah, Amos, Isaiah, and Jeremiah were vehement in their denunciation of the social injustices of their time. All political crises were also considered religious crises. In their sermons they made a close connection between the sin of idolatry and the sin of social injustice. Theirs was a spirituality that related worship and life as well as prayer and action. The prophets were ever alert to the connection between how people worshipped and how they related to one another— between their faith and their ethics. For them, what people treated as ultimate in their lives had an impact on all dimensions of life.

No one makes the case for a liberation spirituality more plainly than Jeremiah. He clearly saw that false worship and social injustice were at the basis of Israel's problems. In Jeremiah's view the political defeat of Jerusalem began with idolatry and social injustice. Standing in the gateway of the Temple of Jerusalem, Jeremiah addressed his people with these words:

> Listen to the words of the Lord. . . . You keep saying, "This is the temple of the Lord, the temple of the Lord." This catchword is a lie, put no trust in it. Mend your ways and your doings, deal fairly with one another, do not oppress the alien, the orphan, and the widow, shed no innocent blood in this place. . . . You gain nothing by putting trust in this lie. You steal, murder, you commit adultery and perjury, you burn sacrifices to Baal, you run after other gods whom you have not known; then you come and stand before me in this house, which bears my name and say, "We are safe": safe you think to indulge in all these abominations. So you think that this house, this house which bears my name is a robbers' cave? (Jer 7:2–11).

With these direct but powerful words Jeremiah pointed out that once people compromised the best truth they knew in worship, many could easily compromise the truth in personal and public affairs.

Jeremiah, however, did not leave his people without hope. In a later sermon he spoke of the New Jerusalem which would be established with a new covenant with God. The deported members of the city of Jerusalem took this vision with them into captivity. This new city would be organized around the worship of God. Out of such worship would grow justice, loyalty, and mercy in human affairs. In this city would be heard the sounds of joy and gladness, for the Lord of hosts would restore what was once a waste city (Jer 33:10–11).

Though the prophets are clearly examples of a liberation spirituality, for Christians the strongest model lies in the life and work of Jesus. A reading of the Gospels shows clearly that Jesus' life included a prophetic and liberation dimension. He gave discourses and performed actions which were clearly of a political nature. However his life and death may be theologized, it is clear that political considerations were prevailing factors.

Many efforts have been made to remove the political dimension from Jesus' life and thus to eliminate him as a model for a liberation spirituality. His political stand is viewed by some as an interim ethic, given his belief in the end of the world. For others, Jesus has been reduced to a simple rural figure who talked about lilies and helped lepers and outcasts. Another view is that Jesus' politics are irrelevant for he lived in a world over which he had little control. Another way to depoliticize Jesus is to assert that he dealt only with spiritual matters, being a radical monotheist, and thus saw little value in purely human values and problems. Finally, some have seen in Jesus' death a life given in atonement and justification to restore men and women to fellowship at a purely spiritual level.

An examination of the Gospels, especially the Gospel of Luke, shows that Jesus' mission was truly a political one. Mary announced this political mission:

> He has shown the power of his arm,
> he has routed the proud of heart.
> He has pulled down the princes from their thrones,
> and exalted the lowly.
> The hungry he has filled with good things,
> the rich sent away empty.
> He has come to the help of Israel his servant,
> mindful of his mercy (Lk 1:51–54).

At the beginning of his ministry when Jesus announced his task by citing Isaiah 61, he cast his ministry in social terms:

> The spirit of the Lord has been given to me,
> for he has anointed me.
> He has sent me to bring the good news to the poor.
> to proclaim liberty to captives,
> and to the blind new sight,
> to set the downtrodden free,
> to proclaim the Lord's year of favor (Lk 4:18).

The jubilee year which Jesus proclaimed was a social arrangement by which former relationships were changed. The event was a visible sociopolitical and economic restructuring among the people of God, to be achieved by God's intervention.

The politics of Jesus appears in this analysis to be one of nonviolent resistance to the evils of the social, political, and economic system in which he found himself (Yoder, 1972). Jesus rejected the sword that the revolutionary zealots wanted to take up against Rome. But in rejecting the sword he did not reject the political method of resistance. That this method was viewed as equally dangerous and political is indicated by the fact that Jesus was crucified with the insurrectionist Barabbas. Also, one of Jesus' temptations was to revolutionary violence and he resisted this temptation throughout his life. Yet, even without this resort to violence, Jesus still posed a sufficient threat to the political and social order. The concluding summary by Yoder on the politics of Jesus nicely brings out the distinctiveness of his mission:

> Jesus was not just a moralist whose teachings had some political implications; he was not primarily a teacher of spirituality whose public ministry was unfortunately seen in a political light; he was not just some sacrificial lamb preparing for immolation, or a God-man whose divine status calls us to disregard his humanity. Jesus was in his divinely mandated (i.e., promised, anointed, messianic prophethood and kingship) the bearer of a new possibility of human, social and therefore political relationships. His baptism is the inauguration and his cross the culmination of that new regime in which his disciples are called to share (1972, pp. 62–63).

CONTEMPORARY MODELS OF LIBERATION SPIRITUALITY

The particular form of spirituality that Jesus exemplified has found followers in two contemporary persons: Martin Luther King and Dom

Helder Camara. Both of these men have considered themselves followers of Jesus in their nonviolent struggles to achieve peace and justice in the world. Their witness, however, is not the only type of witness to Christian values, for we must also examine those who reluctantly but decisively followed the way of violence in the pursuit of justice.

The religious inspiration for King's work as a civil rights leader and as an opponent of the war in Vietnam is well known. King was one of the first in this country who linked these two struggles together. It was part of King's vision that an invisible unity existed among men and women which could be called forth in overcoming evil. In describing his work for peace and justice he uttered these words:

> In my weekly remarks as president I stressed that the use of violence in our struggle would be both impractical and immoral. To meet hate with hate would do nothing but intensify the existence of evil in the universe. Hate begets hate; violence begets violence; toughness begets a greater toughness. We must meet the forces of hate with the power of love; we must meet physical force with soul force. Our aim is never to defeat or humiliate the white man, but to win his friendship and understanding (King in Richardson, 1969, p. 182).

The basic inspiration of King's message was *agape*, which he translated as redemptive love, the love that does good even to those who harm us. For King this self-sacrificing love grows out of the love of friendship, which is a gift of God.

As a Protestant preacher King was strongly influenced by the Social Gospel. He believed that:

> The Gospel at best deals with the whole man, not only his soul but also his body, not only his spiritual wellbeing but also his material well-being. A religion that professes a concern for the souls of men and is not equally concerned about the slums that damn them, the economic conditions that cripple them, is a spiritually moribund religion (King in McNamara, 1974, p. 295).

King's view of religion was a powerful one in this country, and it has influenced many contemporary struggles for justice in this country and throughout the world.

Another contemporary proponent of a nonviolent liberation spirituality is Dom Helder Camara, Archbishop of Recife, in northeast Brazil. This courageous archbishop has defied governments, denounced social injustices, and embraced socialism. Yet he still argues powerfully against violent action. Politically Camara began as what he calls a fascist because of fascism's emphasis on God, Country, and Family. But his direct contact with suffering people in the slums convinced him that fascism does not work to combat injustices. He embraced socialism and preached everywhere a peaceful violence:

> That is to say, not the violence of wars, but the violence of Gandhi, and Martin Luther King, the violence of Christ. I call it violence because it won't settle for trivial reforms, but calls for a complete revolution of the present structures, on socialist bases and without the shedding of blood (Camara, 1975, p. 6).

Camara recognizes that his approach is not popular with many persons in the Latin American churches, both on the right and on the left of the political spectrum. Yet he believes that the church is part of the problem because of its connections with oppressive power structures, its investments in commercial enterprises, and its many failures to come to the aid of the poor and oppressed.

In presenting his stand on peaceful violence, Camara recognizes that this is a matter of personal truth. He does not consider the use of weapons against oppressors immoral or un-Christian. But he says that it is not his way to do politics. At the Roman Synod in 1974 Camara was emphatic in his commitment to a gospel of peace and justice. In this century, he contended, charity consists in advancing the peaceful crusade for justice. The obligation for this commitment comes from the gospel and the social teachings of the church. He advocated a liberation approach to pastoral planning. He also identified politics with working for the common good. The vision of the church he presented was that of a conscious minority in service to a majority.

Camara's interest in Marxism and socialism is not an uncritical one. He sees some evidence in recent thought that Marxists are willing to examine their basic assumptions that religion is alienation and that socialism is necessarily bound up with dialectical materialism. He points to the example of Roger Garaudy as one who is willing to question these assumptions. He also has called upon Christians to recognize the existence of a neo-Marxism which rejects the distortions of socialism and can see in the Christian message a strong inspiration for the full socialization of property, power, and knowledge (Camara, 1975, p. 17).

Camara pays the price for his liberation spirituality. He has suffered threats of death, machine gun blasts, bombs, anonymous calls, and calumnies sent to the Vatican. One of his assistants, a twenty-seven-year-old priest, was hung from a tree and riddled with bullets. Extreme rightist groups have made Camara an enemy of the state and government.

The nonviolent stand of Camara in the face of violence and injustice is not the only stand that Christians have taken. Extremely oppressive and unjust situations have led even dedicated pacifists to take up arms against those responsible for these situations. Bonhoeffer joined the officers' plot against Hitler and abandoned a lifelong commitment to pacifism to oppose oppression in Germany. Many Christians in Latin America in past years have made similar decisions. Camilo Torres is one of the best known of the Catholic priests who became committed to violent revolutionary action. He contended that he took off his cassock to become more truly a priest. In the Bolivian situation where he worked, he believed that it was the duty of every Catholic to be a revolutionary. These Christians have appealed to the longstanding teaching of the church, found in Augustine, Aquinas, and others, that one can rebel against a system that is clearly tyrannical with regard to basic human rights.

The revolutionary struggle in Nicaragua has found support from a number of religious leaders. The Trappist poet and philosopher Ernesto Cardenal turned from a pacifist priest to a member of the Sandinista National Liberation Front. Cardenal compared the situation in Nicaragua to Germany under Hitler. He does not feel that in advocating violence he has abandoned his commitment to the ideals of Gandhi and Merton, his teacher. Some bishops in Nicaragua have defended the revolution while others have opposed it. Cardenal does not consider this a case of priests meddling in politics but rather an involvement in a legitimate action of justice to bring about peace in a tyrannized world (Cardenal, 1979, p. 19).

Thus far the models of liberation spirituality presented have been of rather dramatic and well-known persons. Also, the civil rights movement, the peace movement, and revolutionary struggles are dramatic instances which call for heroic activity. These dramatic examples should not let us lose sight of the long tradition of Christian involvement in social issues in this country. The Social Gospel flourished in the early years of this century. Since the beginning of religious history in this country we have had the religious witness of pacifism, especially among Quakers and Mennonites, and more recently among other Christian groups. The fifties saw the development of many social movements: Friendship Houses, Houses of Hospitality, the Catholic Worker Movement, and Catholic Labor Institutes. Many Christians have shown a deep commitment to liberation spirituality over the years. These include Dorothy Day, Thomas Merton, Peter Maurin, Paul Furfey, Bishop Sheil, John Cronin, George Higgins, and countless others. This tradition was continued in this country in later decades. When we consider that such people as these dedicated themselves to social and political activity from Christian motivation, it is clear that liberation spirituality is found in the lives of many Christians.

Adding these developments to recent theologies of liberation, a case can be made for a distinctive liberation spirituality.

PRINCIPLES FOR A LIBERATION SPIRITUALITY

A liberation spirituality for the contemporary world needs a number of theological principles. Some of these principles have been mentioned in earlier sections of this study. But it is now useful to gather some of these principles together in a concluding section.

First of all, a liberation spirituality looks carefully at *the signs of the times*. Social analysis and the social sciences give a good reading of the signs of the times. They tell us what is happening in the world in which we live and attempt to determine the causes for these happenings. The signs of the times that Christians are to look for are the sufferings, injustices, and inequalities that exist in the world. At times Christians have been too concerned with internal signs connected with institutional church life to read these external signs in secular society. The old saying is still a valuable truth: We do theology with the Bible in one hand and the newspapers in the other.

Second, liberation spirituality sensitizes us to *the social meaning of the Christian Scriptures, doctrines, and history*. It is a mistake to fail to read the Scriptures in a social perspective. An example is the notion of sin. The concept of sin in the Jewish and Christian Scriptures has been privatized in much of contemporary religious thought and spirituality. Sin has been reduced to personal actions against God, God's law, or the church.

Sin, however, is social in a number of ways. It affects the lives of others. It can be perpetrated by one group on another. It consists of the injustices which are built into our social, political, economic, and religious institutions. Many do not feel the sinfulness of racism, militarism, anti-feminism, and ageism because they do not feel personally guilty of actions in this regard. Many are involved in institutions whose structures perpetrate injustices on others. Because of this reduction of sin to a private sphere, it is difficult to speak of a nation or church as sinful or unjust and to recognize the unjust structures these contain (Baum, 1975, ch. 9).

Third, liberation spirituality forges *a connection between prayer, worship, and social action*. The prophetic message is this: there is no religion where prayer and contemplation are ends in themselves. The worship and love of God cannot exist without reverence and love of the neighbor. No true worship is possible unless the implications of this worship for life in the world are made clear.

On the other hand, religious persons will not remain committed to social action for justice and peace nor will they maintain a liberation spirituality unless they are committed to a life of prayer. For as Merton put it:

> He who attempts to do things for others or for the world without deepening his own self-understanding, freedom, integrity and capacity to love, will not have anything to give to others. He will communicate to them nothing but the contagion of his own obsessions, his aggressiveness, his ego-centered ambitions, his delusions about ends and means, his doctrinaire prejudices. . . . Far from being unimportant, prayer and meditation are of the utmost importance in America today (Merton, 1965, p. 165).

Fourth, a liberation spirituality utters *a prophetic or critical word* to all institutions of the world and most especially to the churches. The strongest words of denunciation by the prophets were of Israel and her religious practices. Jesus' severest condemnations were of religious leaders and institutions. A prophetic spirituality today will resist the tendency to shift all the burden on society and to absolve the churches of responsibility. It will continue to hold the churches in judgment for their identification with groups and practices in society which oppress people. It will not fear to examine critically the collective life of the churches, which often fail to apply the principles of social justice to all areas. This may be through opposition to the ordination of women priests, opposition to development of labor unions in church institutions, neglect of the rights of the divorced, maintenance of a middle-class clergy through the imposition of a rule of celibacy which is intolerable for many, or by investments in corporations that have taken morally reprehensible stands.

CONCLUSION

The basic vision that is found in liberation spirituality is that of faith in Jesus, the transformer of human culture. This vision was first presented by Richard Niebuhr (1951) and developed by G. Baum (1975). This spirituality attempts to overcome the dualism between mankind and God, between the gospel and the world. God is affirmed as the mystery present in history and as the very foundation of world events.

This spirituality has a contemplative dimension. It contends that the active struggle for justice and peace in the world is more than faithful obedience to the commandments of God. It is actually a redemptive activity in behalf of the reconciliation of the world. The spirituality that is appropriate for this transformist vision of faith does not draw people from the daily political struggle, but it is the contemplation of the divine mystery of human life calling for us to join in the common action for peace and justice.

Liberation spirituality is critical of all forms of individualism. It does not view salvation solely in personal terms, but as a personal relationship to God with others. Salvation comes through people, by fellowship, by life in community, and by the common effort to create a better social order. This liberation spirituality sees our final destiny as collective. The vision of a final collective destiny gives us power to struggle for peace and justice in our present existence.

CHAPTER 15

FROM MILITARISM TO PACIFISM: EVOLUTION IN THE AMERICAN CATHOLIC CHURCH

INTRODUCTION

The American Roman Catholic church has never been identified as a peace or pacifist church. Rather it has been notable for its support of government war policies through the activities of its leaders and members. The past two decades, however, have seen a momentous change in the Roman Catholic church in the United States in its attitudes towards peace and war. Since Roman Catholics make up the largest religious group in the United States, the Reagan Administration has shown active interest in the development of the bishops' recent document on peace and war.

In this document there is clear evidence that a rather significant change has taken place among the American Catholic people, leaders, and theologians. The document clearly legitimates the pacifist position in the church, without abandoning the traditional teaching on the just war theory. This episcopal legitimation is a remarkable position for a church which has traditionally found the pacifist position unacceptable on theological grounds. It is also significant in the context of current debates in the United States about the conduct of nuclear and conventional warfare.

In this study I intend to describe the developments and underlying causes that have led to this change from militancy to the legitimation of pacifism. The study examines the just war theory in post-Reformation Catholic social ethics, the emergence of pacifism in American Catholicism, and the bishops' legitimation of pacifism. In a concluding section I will offer some speculations about tensions in Catholic ecclesiology and social ethics that are implied in the process of evolution.

II. POST-REFORMATION SOCIAL ETHICS

The traditional position of the Roman Catholic church with regards to pacifism is summarized in an excerpt from the article on pacifism in the *New Catholic Encyclopedia*:

It is clear from what has been said that absolute pacifism is irreconcili-able with traditional Catholic doctrine. Catholic exegetes commonly reject the pacifist interpretation of Christ's teaching. His pronouncement on nonresistance to evil is taken as a *counsel* rather than as a *precept*, and for *private individuals* rather than *public authorities* since these would fail in an essential duty were they to offer no forceful resistance to violent aggressions from within or without. His warning to those who "take the sword" is commonly understood . . . to refer to those *who usurp the function* of rulers. . . . Nor is there any intrinsic contradiction between a just war and Christ's command that *we love our enemies. A just war expresses hatred of the evil deed rather than of the evildoer* ("Pacifism," Vol 10, p. 856. Italics in original).

Post-Reformation Catholic theology inherited an elaborate theology of just war. This theory originated with Augustine and was further developed by Thomas Aquinas. Augustine drew on both Roman and Christian sources for developing a moral argument which legitimized the use of force as a means for implementing the gospel command of love in the political order. Aquinas systematized the criteria for a just war and added the right of self-defense as a legitimate reason for war.

Post-Reformation Catholic theologians rejected pacifism by an appeal to the unity of the Scriptures. Since the Old Testament must be in unity with the New and since the Old shows war as blessed and commanded by God, it was clear to these theologians that the pacifist interpretation of the New Testament was not an accurate one.

The methodology of traditional Roman Catholic social ethics—a natural law ethic which contended that right and wrong could be known by all persons—reinforced the position against pacifism. Through the natural law ethic the post-Reformation theologians were able to appropriate the Greco-Roman doctrine of just war and give it greater refinements. This tradition discussed the conditions under which war could be waged, how war should be waged, and what should be done after war was over.

As the just war theory has developed, it has been based on a presumption in favor of peace over war. Through this theory one can arrive at a defense of conscientious objection. According to the theory there is a *Jus ad Bellum* if there is a just cause, a competent authority, comparative justice in the means used, the right intention, the exhaustion of other means to resolve difficulties, a good probability of success, and a proportionate good to be expected from the war. The just war theory also includes criteria for determining *Jus in bello* (strategy, tactics, and individual actions). These criteria relate to proportionate and discriminating means.

The social context in which this teaching was originally developed was one in which war was a limited phenomenon. It was also one in which the

Roman Catholic church was interested in the maintenance of certain regimes which were friendly to the church and gave the church certain privileges. In the United States the social context, until recently, was one in which Roman Catholics attempted to prove a patriotism which was often put in question by certain religious and nonreligious groups.

In their treatment of pacifism, post-Reformation Catholic social ethicians also saw in the pacifist position the dangerous assertion that the individual's conscience was supreme, not only in matters of faith and morals but also in the political sphere. This appeared to place the individual above the community and the duly constituted authority of that community. Although it was recognized that individuals could disagree in particular cases with political authorities, one could not, it was asserted, ignore them in advance.

The just war theory has always been the accepted position among episcopal leaders and Catholics in the United States. There has even been among American Catholics a special reason to appear loyal to the government and its policies: the history of anti-Catholicism, which portrayed Catholics as owing allegiance to an authority outside the nation. This has produced in the past a certain militancy among Catholics in times of war. The militancy of the American Catholic church is shown in the support of the American hierarchy for Franco's revolution in the 1930s and its opposition to American arms shipments to the Loyalist government. When the pacifist and anarchist *Catholic Worker* and the liberal *Commonweal* adopted a neutral stance on the war, they were condemned by major church figures and suffered a great loss in circulation. (*The Catholic Worker* lost one-third of its 150,000 readers.)

During World War II Catholic bishops gave their moral sanction to the war. There were only a few conscientious objectors and these were associated with Dorothy Day's Catholic Worker Movement and the Catholic intellectual Gordon Zahn. A Catholic camp for conscientious objectors existed in New Hampshire under the auspices of Day and Zahn. This camp has been identified as the first corporate witness to pacifism in American Catholicism and as a source of some roots or antecedents of a very visible movement against the Vietnam War (Cornell, 1980, p. 202). During the war only a few theologians questioned the morality of saturation bombing and the use of nuclear weapons.

III. EMERGENCE OF PACIFISM IN AMERICAN ROMAN CATHOLICISM

The legitimation of pacifism within Roman Catholicism is the result of a number of developments. First, there has been the presence of a grassroots pacifism which has persisted for five decades. Second, there has also been a more acceptable attitude toward pacifism in papal teachings and in the teachings of theologians, as both of these sources look more to Scripture and to the nature of modern warfare. The Vietnam War and the proliferation of nuclear arms have been powerful forces leading to the legitimation of pacifism within the church.

Papal and Conciliar Teaching on Peace and War

There is a certain irony in the fact that as popes and bishops have become increasingly opposed to war and favorable to a pacifist position, their moral authority among Catholics has lessened. Yet papal and conciliar teaching are still influential and authoritative sources in the American Catholic theological world and in the life of the church.

Pius XII (1956) is clearly within the dominant tradition of Catholic just war theory. Three themes are found in his writings. First, he called for an international authority of some sort to coordinate the interaction of sovereign states in an increasingly independent world. This call has often been found in papal documents. While it might be suspected that some popes were putting themselves forward as such an authority, Pope John XXIII spoke of the potential of the United Nations in filling such a position. Second, he attempted to assimilate nuclear weapons within the just war framework by arguing that they were only quantitatively and not qualitatively different. Third, he refused to provide a Catholic position supporting conscientious objection.

The legitimation of the pacifist tradition with Roman Catholicism began with John XXIII's encyclical letter *Pacem in Terris* (1963). In this letter he condemned the arms race and the terror upon which it rests. He called for an international authority. The document provided no explicit endorsement of the right of self-defense for peoples and states. War was condemned as irrational and immoral: "Therefore in this age of ours, which prides itself on its atomic power, it is irrational to think that war is a proper way to obtain justice for violated rights (No. 80)."

This document is seen by James Doughlass (1966) and other pacifists as an affirmation of pacifism. Paul Ramsey (1968) and Bryan Hehir (1980), however, do not see it as a departure from the traditional teaching on self-defense since later documents include the right to self-defense and make no effort to correct or emend *Pacem in Terris*. This document did not make a significant impact on American Catholic social ethics until rather recently. This is also true of the Pope's encyclical *Mater et Magistra* which called for a dialogue with Eurocommunism.

The first explicit affirmation of the pacifist position is found in Vatican

II's *Gaudium et Spes* (1966). This document looked more to Scripture, and it moved away from reliance on principles of just war toward an evangelical stance of prophetic judgment on peoples and nations. The document strongly condemned the use of nuclear arms, with some important qualifications. These qualifications came from the pressure of some American bishops who urged the council to allow participation in the military, legitimate self-defense, and the possession of nuclear weapons as part of a defense strategy. The new attitude which it takes toward peace and war resulted in a qualified endorsement of nonviolent philosophy and a guarded support for conscientious objection. On the former it states:

> We cannot fail to praise those who renounce the use of violence in the vindication of their rights, and who resort to methods of defense which are otherwise available to weaker parties too, provided that this can be done without injury to the rights and duties of others or of the community itself (*Gaudium et Spes,* no. 78).

In addressing the issue of conscientious objection, the council states that "it seems right that laws make humane provisions for the case of those who for reasons of conscience refuse to bear arms, provided however, that they accept some other form of service to the human community (no. 79)."

Statements from later Popes, Paul VI and John Paul II, appear to be within this teaching of the Council. The present Pope has addressed the issue of peace and war on numerous occasions, notably before the United Nations, at Hiroshima, and at Coventry Cathedral. His message has been especially concerned with the prevention of nuclear warfare. In his talks he has utilized the findings of many scientists and physicians who have spoken about the horrors of nuclear warfare.

The pastoral letter of the American bishops comes within this broader Catholic tradition. While it cannot be said that the Catholic church has become pacifist in an absolute sense like the Quakers or Mennonites, it is clear that the pacifist position has become legitimized and that movement is toward a position of nuclear pacifism in official teachings of the church. In the United States this movement toward pacifism was fostered by public debates in the 1960s and 1970s about American involvement in the Vietnam War.

The American Church and the Vietnam War

The Vietnam War was a major watershed in the legitimation of the pacifist position in the American Catholic church. Catholic opposition to the war began as early as 1965. A Catholic Peace Fellowship was formed which took the path of antiwar activism. Prominent Catholics included David Miller, who burned his draft card in 1965, and Tom Cornell, who founded the Peace Fellowship. The fellowship also included the Berrigan brothers, Thomas Merton, and James Forest. Daniel and Philip Berrigan joined with Robert McAfee Brown and Abraham Heschel to form Clergy and Laity Concerned about Vietnam. By 1968 the liberal Catholic weekly *Commonweal* changed its mind on the war by declaring that the war was unwinnable and that its conduct had passed moral constraint. The *National Catholic Reporter* had opposed the war from the mid-1960s. It called for American withdrawal in 1967. In its editorial it stated:

> We believe that the war in Vietnam is now clearly immoral. The commanding reason for this judgment is that the ends for which we are fighting the war cannot be achieved except by the nearly total destruction of our enemy in North and South Vietnam (NCR January 3, 1967).

Opposition to the war was based both on a pacifist position and on an application of the principles of the just war theory. The judgment on the Vietnam War made by Catholic liberal intellectuals also came from the principles of ethical realism of John Courtney Murray and Reinhold Niebuhr. For an increasing number of Catholics opposition was based on a pacifist reading of the New Testament, as witnessed by the number of Catholics involved in public demonstrations and activities against the war.

Within the Catholic peace movement a number of divisions took place which may well presage future debates and differences of opinion among Catholics as they begin more seriously to oppose military buildups in the country. The oldest Catholic pacifist group is associated with the work of Dorothy Day and Gordon Zahn. Since 1933, as we have seen, the Catholic Worker Movement under the direction of Peter Maurin, Dorothy Day, and Ammon Henessey had made a powerful and influential witness to a pacifist Christianity. A small group of Catholic conscientious objectors to World War II joined the ranks of the Catholic Worker Movement. This group carried a peace witness throughout the war, through the cold war, and into the 1960s. With the war in Vietnam this witness began to bear fruit. Many young Catholics began to associate themselves with the pacifist witness of this movement.

During the course of the Vietnam War a division developed among the Catholic resisters. Some continued to press for the witness of pacifism through nonviolence, through the building of a politically relevant pacifism, and through establishing a political strategy which focused on the theology of the Cross but did not retreat from political responsibility (Day, Doughlass, Zahn). For them the church was a community of witness, bearing testimony to a higher truth, risking all—wealth, influence, even membership—to be a sign of contradiction amidst the war making and violence of the age. These persons were more prepared to trust their faith as a guide to policy for church and state. The church should make a courageous witness, forsaking mediocrity and compromise. The state should recognize that violence leads not to peace but to destruction (O'Brien, 1980, p. 138–39).

The other wing of the resistance looked more to the reality of America: racism, poverty, imperialism, and materialism. The break with the nation over the war was only a step toward a new commitment to radical social change. These pacifists were driven both by conscience to active resistance which could border on violence and by a willingness to accept military action to change the status quo. This faction of the resistance pushed towards the limit of nonviolence and asked how far they could go without crossing the threshold to violence. Thus this group moved close to the position of justifying force as a last resort. This group had obvious sympathies with the Catholic revolutionaries in Latin America.

Those who preferred a pacifist witness rather than active resistance found objectionable the secrecy surrounding the raids on Army recruiting offices and industrial plants. In their view nonviolence was not a secretive or conspiratorial activity. They wanted to be faithful to the Gandhian principle of openness and truth. They argued that nonviolence must invite the participation of more and more people in its planning and execution and that the agenda for nonviolence should be open to all to scrutinize. However, in their many trials the resisters had the full support of those who embraced the pacifism of witness.

Besides these strategies for opposing the war, there developed another approach that went beyond just war, pacifism, and resistance approaches. It ignored these categories and spoke in general terms of the need to be peacemakers, but left the means to individual consciences. In this view the church should seek a more explicitly religious ground, evaluating current policies, defending human freedom and human dignity, and urging all to pursue peace and justice. The danger of this approach, taken by many bishops (most especially, Thomas Gumbleton), was that it tended to remove the church from involvement in policy-making decisions. This was acceptable for some but not for many others.

Episcopal Leadership and the Vietnam War

Episcopal leadership during the Vietnam War took various forms. In the mid-60s Cardinal Spellman and Cardinal Cushing represented many bishops when they spoke forcefully in defense of American policy. General episcopal sanction for the war ended when Spellman, in a Christmas message to American troops whom he was visiting at the front, exclaimed that "less than victory is inconceivable." In 1966 Cardinal Sheehan of Baltimore outlined in a pastoral the teachings of Vatican II on self-defense and conscientious objection. His letter was viewed as opposition to the war, which he later denied. In the years to come many individual bishops did become vocal critics of the war (Hallinan, Shannon, Reed, Dougherty) and called for immediate negotiations.

In 1967 there was mounting pressure on the bishops as a body to make a statement on the war. No Catholic bishops appeared at a clergy rally in Washington in mobilization against the war. McAfee Brown asked, "How are we to interpret your almost total silence?" Bishop James Shannon replied that bishops were in a different position than individual theologians such as Brown. The bishops did, however, call for negotiations in their November 1967 meeting. In their 1968 pastoral letter, *Human Life in Our Day,* the bishops noted their earlier conclusion that the war was justified. Antiwar bishops such as James Shannon and Bernard Kelly, both of whom later resigned from the episcopacy, had difficult times. Kelly was disturbed that American bishops were more interested in sending recommendations on the priesthood to the Roman Synod for 1971 than in discussing the war issue.

In 1971 the bishops finally condemned the war. Gumbleton, a peace bishop, became a major spokesman for opposition to the war. The task, according to him, was to work through persuasion and not prescription to educate the church and the nation. Gumbleton has served as the link between opposition to the Vietnam War and the present position on nuclear war. He served as a member of the five-bishop committee which developed the pastoral.

The Change Among Theologians and Intellectuals

The movement of Catholic theologians and intellectuals to a more pacifist position is illustrated by two major books on peace and war written twenty years apart. In 1960 William Nagle edited a book on *Morality and Modern Warfare: The State of the Question.* All the contributors to this volume were Roman Catholics, and all but one espoused the just war theory. The authors included three prominent Jesuit theologians (John Courtney Murray, John C. Ford, John R. Connery), distinguished academicians, and specialists in military affairs (Thomas Murray, James E. Dougherty, William O'Brien). The one pacifist was the sociologist

Gordon Zahn, who had done extensive research on the Roman Catholic response in Hitler's Germany. In 1980 Thomas Shannon edited a volume entitled *War or Peace? The Search for New Answers*. Significantly, in this volume dedicated to Gordon Zahn over half of the articles are by pacifists. The volume also includes contributions from Protestant theologians and historians.

Among Catholic theologians one can find defenses both of the just war theory and of various pacifist positions. The new thing is that pacifism is taken seriously. Roman Catholic social ethicians look not only to natural law but also to distinctively Christian teachings. Doughlass has argued that at the heart of the Christian message is the call for transformative suffering for oneself and others. Pacifism is argued for out of a religious vision and out of a contemplation of what war has done and will do to human society. Joseph Fahey (1980), a theologian and influential member of Pax Christi, argues for a total rejection of war. He even rejects the deterrence argument which many theologians have accepted. Two types of pacifism are presented: a pacifism of witness and a pacifism of resistance. Charles Curran, a prominent professor of Theology at Catholic University, thinks that the pacifism of witness is not a serious option for most Roman Catholics (In Lammers, 1980, p. 99).

A pacifism of resistance calls for a new understanding of the act of refusing to participate in war. This is usually a decision with regard to a particular war (relative pacifism) or to all wars (absolute pacifism). One thing, however, is clear, Roman Catholic ethicians now give much more serious study to the arguments of pacifists.

Some Roman Catholic ethicians, such as Doughlass and Fahey, argue that the just war ethic is no longer tenable. Bryan Hehir, however, argues for its viability partly from the fact that it provides guidelines for arriving at the position of nuclear pacifism. This position has its basis for Catholic theologians in the Vatican Council's condemnation of acts of war aimed at total destruction. The main moral issue for the nuclear pacifists thus is not the use of nuclear weapons but the threat to use them in a policy of deterrence. The moral issue of deterrence was a major issue in the American Bishops' Pastoral Letter. This letter also summarizes the various positions in the Roman Catholic community with regard to peace and war.

IV. THE AMERICAN BISHOPS' PASTORAL ON PEACE AND WAR

The pastoral of the American bishops takes a further step in legitimating the position of pacifism within the Roman Catholic church. It took three years and three published drafts to complete this significant document. Widespread consultation took place among bishops, theologians, military and political experts, administration figures, and European bishops (at a final stage in development of the document). The pastoral, in coming very close to a nuclear pacifism, utilizes both just war theory and a pacifist theology of peace.

Pacifists will find much in the document that legitimates their position. Yet, if the document legitimates a pacifism, it is nuclear pacifism. The legitimacy of the pacifist position is maintained in terms expressed by the Second Vatican Council. But the major argumentation in the pastoral is around the deterrence issue, raised by the continued existence of nuclear weapons for purposes of preventing war.

The bishops' pastoral recognizes a number of forms of nonviolent pacifism. It recognizes a religious pacifism in which persons are motivated by an understanding of the gospel and the life and death of Jesus as forbidding all violence. Religious pacifism is also motivated by the will to give personal example of Christian forbearance as a positive and constructive approach toward loving reconciliation with enemies. A third form is an active nonviolence in which there is programmed resistance to thwart aggression or to render ineffective any oppression attempted by force of arms.

The bishops' pastoral briefly and succinctly makes the case for a pacifist position, thus going beyond the two statements of the Vatican Council. It appeals to the teaching of Jesus, the teachings of Justin, Cyprian, Martin of Tours, Francis of Assisi, Mohandas Gandhi, Dorothy Day, and Martin Luther King. (The mention of Dorothy Day in the pastoral is particularly moving for those who know the suspicion and rejection she experienced from Catholic officials in her lifetime).

The bishops, in the clearest statement on pacifism issued by official church authorities, assert that:

> While the just-war teaching has clearly been in possession for the past 1,500 years of Catholic thought, the "new moment" in which we find ourselves sees the just-war teaching and non-violence as distinct but interdependent methods of evaluating warfare. They diverge on some specific conclusions, but they share a common presumption against the use of force as a means of settling disputes (p. 12).

In the bishops' view both theories have roots in the Christian tradition and each contributes to a theology of peace. The two perspectives are viewed as complementing each other and as preserving each other from distortion.

They also recognize that in a nuclear age the two theories "often converge in their opposition to methods of warfare which are in fact indistinguishable from total warfare (p. 13)."

The pastoral letter includes a long section on recommending efforts to develop nonviolent means of conflict resolution. These are recommended not only with regard to war but apply to all forms of violence, including insurgency, counter-insurgency, destabilization, and the like (p. 21). It recommends nonviolent resistance through organized popular defense in which:

> Citizens would be trained in the techniques of peaceable non-compliance and non-cooperation as a means of hindering an invading force or non-democratic government from imposing its will (p. 21).

The bishops recognize the risks involved in such a defense but conclude that the results may be less disastrous than armed defense. They contend that the proposal at least deserves serious consideration as an alternative course of action.

Though the bishops' document gives strong legitimation to a pacifist position in the church, it does not reject the tradition of the church which regards some legitimate use of force as being within the limits of moral justification. The document addresses force in the context of nuclear weapons. On just war reasoning it rejects the counterpopulation use of nuclear weapons and also condemns their first use. It remains highly skeptical of the possibility of limited nuclear warfare. The pastoral wrestles with the morality of the possession of nuclear weapons as a deterrent but gives a conditioned moral acceptance of deterrence based on balance, as a step on the way to a progressive nuclear disarmament.

The bishops' pastoral thus reveals the acceptance of a theological pluralism with regard to the church's stand on peace and war. The just war theory has not been rejected but room has been made for a pacifist position. Is the church on the way to a more pacifist position and is the pastoral only a step in that direction? Though a great distance has been covered, there is still a long way to go. Church documents give justification to both positions. These documents carry less weight for Catholics than they did in the past. Published statements have not generally been accompanied by effective action. In fairness, it is still too soon to see the full effect of the pastoral on American Catholics. Presently, a nationwide educational program on the Pastoral is taking place. There is no doubt, however, that pacifism—at least nuclear pacifism—will continue to develop within the American Catholic church.

IV. PRESENT THEOLOGICAL DEBATES

Out of the debate over the pastoral a number of important theological issues have arisen for debate. In the years to come these issues will engage theologians in the church and may also affect the life and practice of Catholicism in America. These issues are broadly concerned with Christian social ethics and ecclesiology.

Catholic Social Ethics

The recognition of the pacifist position in the church is also the recognition of a perfectionist ethic that has not been common among Roman Catholic moralists. The pacifist position is based on the principle that human life has an absolute value and that no conflict of values justifies the taking of human life. If this principle is true, it would also appear to refer to issues such as abortion, capital punishment, and euthanasia. This absolutizing of the value of human life and the recognition of absolute or intrinsic moral evil goes contrary to a tendency among Roman Catholic ethicians to reject such concepts. Catholic revisionists in ethics have moved toward a rejection of the notion of intrinsic evil—the morality of an action apart from its circumstances and consequences. In revisionist ethics a certain flexibility has come into ethical considerations. Moralists are concerned with finding proportionate reasons for justifying prima facie evils. The pacifist, perfectionist position contends that:

> All the old calculations aimed at determining "proportionality," weighing "good" effects against "bad" and making the possible choice of the "lesser" evil are rendered meaningless by the simple refusal to accept any degree of evil as an appropriate Christian response (G. Zahn, 1971, p. 54).

It appears, then, that at least these two forms of moral reasoning will have to be reckoned with in the practice of Christian ethics in the years to come. Common ground is found in cases when the two positions arrive at virtually the same conclusion, such as the issue of noncombatant immunity. Yet, even in this case there would be a difference in that some revisionists would allow indirect or unintentional killing of noncombatants.

The Church in the World

The pacifist position introduces into Catholicism a view which is at variance with traditional Catholic understanding of how the church relates to the broader society. The pacifist view is interdenominational and is expressed by the Protestant theologian Stanley Hauerwas:

> It is the duty of the church to be a society which through the way its members deal with one another demonstrates to the world what love means in human relations. So understood the church fulfills its social responsibility by being an example, a witness, a creative minority formed by its obedience to nonresistant love (1975, p. 211–12).

This view is different from the traditional Catholic view of church documents and theologians, which assumes that the church has a positive responsibility to participate in the process of building a more just and peaceful society. The question is whether the Catholic church can assimilate within itself both views. How much pluralism on this issue can be tolerated? Is it possible to combine a pacifist ethic with a churchly ecclesiology? Denominational churches do not seem to tolerate the pluralism envisaged by the theology that has recently developed in the American Catholic church.

REFERENCES

Abbot, Walter, ed. "Pastoral Constitution on the Church in the Modern World." *The Documents of Vatican II*. New York: America Press, 1966.

Adams, Frank, and Horton, Myles. *Unearthing Seeds of Fire: The Idea of Highlander*. Winston-Salem, N.C.: John F. Blair, 1975.

Allport, Gordon. *The Individual and His Religion*. New York: Macmillan, 1950.

Alves, Rubem. *A Theology of Human Hope*. Saint Meinrad, Ind.: Abbey Press, 1972.

Apple, Michael. *Ideology and Education*. Boston: Routledge and Kegan Paul, 1979.

Aristotle, The Basic Works of. R. McKeon, ed. New York: Random House, 1941.

Bacon, Francis. *The Works of Francis Bacon*. London: Longman and Co., 1876–1890.

Babin, Pierre. *The Audiovisual Man*. Dayton, Ohio: Pflaum, 1970.

Bandura, Albert. *Social Learning Theory*. Englewood Cliffs, N.J.: Prentice-Hall, 1977.

Barker, Kenneth. *Religious Education, Catechesis, and Freedom*. Birmingham, Ala.: Religious Education Press, 1981.

Baum, Gregory. *Religion and Alienation: A Theological Reading of Sociology*. New York: Paulist Press, 1975.

Baum, Gregory. "Spirituality and Society." *Religious Education*, 1978, 73, 3, 266–283.

Baum, Gregory. *Catholics and Canadian Socialism*. New York: Paulist, 1981.

Bausch, William. *The Christian Parish: Whispers of the Risen Christ*. Notre Dame, Ind.: Claretian/Fides Press, 1980.

Beckwith, Barbara. "Should the Church be in Politics?" *Catholic Update*. Cincinnati, Ohio: St. Anthony Messenger Press, 1975.

Benedict, Ruth. *Patterns of Culture*. Boston: Houghton Mifflin, 1934.

Berger, Peter, and Luckmann, Thomas. *The Social Construction of Reality*. New York: Doubleday, 1966.

Bergson, Henri. *The Two Sources of Morality and Religion*. New York: Doubleday, 1935.

Bouwsma, William. "Christian Adulthood." In *Adulthood*, edited by E. Erikson. New York: Norton, 1978.

Bowers, C. A. "Emergent Ideological Characteristics of Educational Policy. *Teachers College Record*, 1977, 79, 1, 33–54.

Bowers C. A. "Educational Critics and Technocratic Consciousness: Looking into the Future Through a Rear View Mirror." *Teachers College Record*, 1978, 80, 2, 272–286.

Bowers, C. A. "Curriculum as Cultural Reproduction: An Examination of Metaphor as a Carrier of Ideology." *Teachers College Record*, 1980, 80, 2, 267–290 (a).

Bowers, C. A. "Ideological Continuities in Technicism, Liberalism, and Education." *Teachers College Record*, 1980, 80, 3, 293–321. (b)

Boys, Mary. *Biblical Interpretation in Religious Education*. Birmingham, Ala.: Religious Education Press, 1980.

Boys, Mary. "The Standpoint of Religious Education." *Religious Education*, 1981, 76, 2, 138–141.

Buber, Martin. *A Believing Humanism*. New York: Simon and Schuster, 1956, 45.

Burgess, Harold. *An Invitation to Religious Instruction*. Birmingham, Ala.: Religious Education Press, 1975.

Campbell, Alistair. *Rediscovering Pastoral Care*. Philadelphia: Westminster Press, 1981.

Camara, Helder. *Helder Camara*. Washington, D.C.: IDOC Series, United States Catholic Conference, 1975.

Cardenal, Ernesto. "Letter to the Editor." *New York Times,* June 30, 1979, p. 19.

Coe, George. *A Social Theory of Religious Education*. New York: Scribner, 1917.

Cohen, S. I. "Adult Jewish Education—1976." *Religious Education* 1977, 72, 2, 143–155.

Cohen, David, and Lazerson, Marvin. *Education and Corporate America*. Andover, Mass.: Warner, 1973.

Coleman, John. *A Strategic American Theology*. New York: Paulist, 1981.

Cornell, Thomas. "The Catholic Church and Witness Against War." In *War or Peace? The Search for New Answers,* edited by Thomas Shannon. Maryknoll, N.Y.: Orbis Press, 1980.

Cremin, Lawrence. *Traditions of American Education*. New York: Basic Books, 1975.

Cupitt, Don. *Taking Leave of God*. London: SCM Press, 1980.

Curti, Merle. *The Social Ideas of American Educators*. Totowa, N.J.: Littlefield, Brown and Co., 1966.

Derr, Richard. *A Taxonomy of Social Purposes of Public Schools*. New York: McKay, 1973.

Dewey, John. *Democracy and Education*. New York: Macmillan, 1916.

Dewey, John, and Dewey, Evelyn. *Schools of Tomorrow*. 1916. Reprint. New York: Dutton, 1962.

Dewey, John. *Human Nature and Conduct*. New York: Random House, 1922.

Dewey, John. *Liberalism and Social Action*. New York: Capricorn, 1963.

Doerning, Bernard. "Jacques Maritain and the Spanish Civil War." *The Review of Politics,* 1982, 44, 4.

Dolbeare, Kenneth, and Dolbeare, Patricia. *American Ideologies*. 3d ed. Chicago: Rand McNally, 1976.

Donohoe, J. W. "Paulo Freire: Philosopher of Adult Education." *America,* 1972, 127, 7, 167–170.

Doughlass, James. *The Nonviolent Cross: A Theology of Revolution and Peace*. New York: Macmillan, 1966.

Dulles, Avery. *Models of the Church*. New York: Doubleday, 1977.

Dulles, Avery. *A Church to Believe in: Discipleship and Freedom*. New York: Crossroads, 1982.

Dunne, John. *Reasons of the Heart*. Notre Dame, Ind.: Univ. of Notre Dame Press, 1978.

Durka, Gloria. "Toward a Critical Theory of Teaching." *Religious Education,* 1979, 74, 1, 39–48.

Durka, Gloria, and Smith, Joanmarie, eds. *Aesthetic Dimensions of Religious Education*. New York: Paulist, 1979.

Durkheim, Emile. *The Elementary Forms of Religious Life*. New York: Free Press, 1965.

Durkheim, Emile. *Moral Education*. New York: Macmillan, 1973 ed.

Dykstra, Craig. *Vision and Character: A Christian Educator's Alternative to Kohlberg*. New York: Paulist, 1981.

Egan, Kieran. *Educational Development*. New York: Oxford Univ. Press, 1979.

Elias, John. *Conscientization and Deschooling: Freire's and Illich's Proposals for Reshaping Society*. Philadelphia: Westminster, 1976.

Elias, John. *Foundations and Practice of Adult Religious Education*. Malabar, Fla.: Krieger, 1982.

Elias, John, and Merriam, Sharan. *Philosophical Foundations of Adult Education*. Malabar, Fla.: Krieger, 1980.

Eliot, T. S. *Four Quartets:* "Little Gidding." In *Collected Poems*. New York: Harcourt Brace and World, 1963.

Engel, David, ed. *Religion in Public Education*. New York: Paulist, 1974.

Erikson, Erik. *Childhood and Society*. New York: Norton, 1962.

Erikson, E., ed. *Adulthood*. New York: Norton, 1978.

Fahey. Joseph. "Pax Christi." In *War or Peace? The Search for New Answers*, edited by Thomas Shannon. Maryknoll, N.Y.: Orbis Press, 1980.

Farley, Edward. *Ecclesial Reflection: An Anatomy of Theological Method*. Philadelphia: Fortress, 1981.

Farley, Edward. *Theologia: The Fragmentation and Unity of Theological Education*. Philadelphia: Fortress, 1983.

Fowler, James. *Stages of Faith*. San Francisco: Harper and Row, 1982.

Freire, Paulo. *Education Como Practica de la Libertad*. Santiago, Chile: ICIRA, 1969.

Freire, Paulo. *Pedagogy of the Oppressed*. New York: Seabury, 1970. (a)

Freire, Paulo. *Cultural Action for Freedom*. Cambridge, Mass.: *Harvard Educational Review* and Center for the Study of Development and Social Change, 1970. (b)

Freire, Paulo. "The Educational Role of the Church in Latin America." Washington, D.C.: LADOC, 1972, III, 14. (a)

Freire, Paulo. "A Letter to a Theology Student." *Catholic Mind*, 1972, 70, 1265. (b)

Freire, Paulo. "Conscientizing as a Way of Liberty." Washington, D.C.: LADOC, 1972, 2, 29. (c)

Freire, Paulo. *Education for Critical Consciousness*. New York: Seabury, 1973. (a)

Freire, Paulo. "Education, Liberation, and the Church." *Risk*, 1973, 9, 1, 34–48. (b)

Freire, Paulo. "Conscientization." *Cross Currents*, 1974, 24, 1, 23–81.

Freud, Sigmund. *Totem and Taboo*. New York: Vintage Press, 1922.

Friedman, Maurice. *To Deny Our Nothingness*. New York: Delta, 1967.

Gadamer, Hans-Georg. *Truth and Method*. New York: Seabury, 1975.

Gangel, Kenneth. "Christian Higher Education at the End of the Twentieth Century." *Bibliotheca Sacra*, 1978, 135, 100–105.

Gaudium et Spes (1966). In *The Gospel of Peace and Justice: Catholic Social Teaching Since Pope John*, edited by J. Gremillon. Maryknoll, N.Y.: Orbis Press, 1976.

General Cathechetical Directory. Washington, D.C.: United States Catholic Conference, 1971.

Geertz, Clifford. *Interpretation of Cultures*. New York: Harper and Row, 1973.

Gilkey, Langdon. *Message and Existence: An Introduction to Christian Theology*. New York: Seabury, 1979.

Goodman, Paul. *The New Reformation*. New York: Random House, 1970.

Gould, Roger. *Transformation: Growth and Change in Adult Life*. New York: Simon and Schuster, 1978.

Greeley, Andrew. *The American Catholic: A Social Portrait*. New York: Basic Books, 1976.

Groome, Thomas. *Christian Religious Education*. San Francisco: Harper and Row, 1980.

Habermas, Jurgen. *Theory and Practice*. Boston: Beacon, 1973.

Habermas, Jurgen. *Legitimation and Crisis*. Boston: Beacon, 1975.

Halbfas, H. *Theory of Catechetics*. New York: Herder and Herder, 1971.

Harris, Maria. *The D.R.E. Book*. New York: Paulist, 1976.

Hartshorne, H., and May, M. *Studies in Deceit*. New York: Macmillan, 1929.

Hauerwas, Stanely. *Vision and Virtue*. Notre Dame, Ind.: Notre Dame Press, 1975.

Hegel, George. *Early Theological Writings*. New York: Harper and Row, 1948 ed.

Hegel, George. *Reason and History: A General Introduction to the Philosophy of History*. New York: Liberal Arts Press, 1953 ed.

Hehir, J. Bryan. "The Just-War and Catholic Theology: Dynamics of Change and Continuity." In *War or Peace? The Search for New Answers*, edited by Thomas Shannon. Maryknoll, N.Y.: Orbis Press, 1980.

Hill, Brian. "Teacher Commitment and the Ethics of Teaching for Commitment." *Religious*

Education, 1981, 76, 3, 322–336.

Holland, Joseph, and Henriot, Peter. *Social Analysis*. Maryknoll, N.Y.: Orbis, 1984.

Illich, Ivan. *Deschooling Society*. New York: Harper and Row, 1970.

John XXIII. *Pacem in Terris*. In *The Gospel of Peace and Justice*, edited by J. Gremillon. Maryknoll, N.Y.: Orbis Press, 1976.

Jung, Carl. *Memories, Dreams, Reflections*. New York: Random House, 1961.

Kelly, Thomas. *A History of Adult Education in Great Britain: From the Middle Ages to the Twentieth Century*. rev. ed. Liverpool: Liverpool Univ. Press, 1970.

Kennedy, William. "A Radical Challenge to Inherited Educational Patterns." *Religious Education*, 1979, 74, 5, 491–95.

King, Coretta. "The Legacy of Martin Luther King, Jr.: The Church in Action." In *Religion: American Style*, edited by P. McNamara. New York: Harper and Row, 1974.

Kluckhohn, Clyde. *Culture and Behavior*. New York: Free Press, 1962.

Kohlberg, Lawrence. "States of Moral Development as a Basis for Moral Education." In *Moral Education: Interdisciplinary Approaches*, edited by C. Beck, B. Crittenden, and E. Sullivan. New York: Paulist, 1971.

Kohlberg, Lawrence. *Essays on Moral Development: The Philosophy of Moral Development*. San Francisco: Harper and Row, 1981.

Knowles, Malcolm. *A History of the Adult Education Movement in the United States*. Malabar, Fla.: Krieger, 1977.

Knox, Ian. *Above or Within: The Supernatural and Religious Education*. Birmingham, Ala.: Religious Education Press, 1976.

Lammers, Stephen. "Roman Catholic Social Ethics and Pacifism." In *War or Peace? The Search for New Answers*, edited by Thomas Shannon. Maryknoll, N.Y.: Orbis Press, 1980.

Lapidus, I. "Adulthood in Islam: Religious Maturity in the Islamic Tradition." In *Adulthood*, edited by E. Erikson. New York: Norton, 1978.

Lasch, Christopher. *The Culture of Narcissism*. New York: Free Press, 1979.

Lee, James M. "Key Issues in the Development of a Workable Definition for Religious Instruction." In *Foundations of Religious Education*, edited by Padraic O'Hare. New York: Paulist, 1978.

Levinson, Daniel J.; Darrow, Charlotte N.; Klein, Edward B.; Levinson, Maria H.; and McKee, Braxton. *Seasons of a Man's Life*. New York: Ballantine, 1977.

Loevinger, Jane. *Ego Development: Conception and Theories*. San Francisco: Jossey-Bass, 1976.

Lonergan, Bernard. *Method in Theology*. New York: Seabury Press, 1972.

McKenzie, Leon. *Adult Education and the Burden of the Future*. Washington, D.C.: Scholars Press, 1978.

McKenzie, Leon. *Religious Education of Adults*. Birmingham, Ala.: Religious Education Press, 1982.

Mannheim, Karl. *Ideology and Utopia*. New York: Harcourt, Brace and World, 1936.

Manno, Bruno. "Distancing Oneself Religiously." *New Catholic World*, 1979, 222, 1331.

Marthaler, Berard. "Socialization as a Model for Catechesis." In *Foundations of Religious Education*, edited by Padraic O'Hare, 64–92. New York: Paulist, 1979.

Marthaler, Berard. "Handing on the Symbols of Faith." *Chicago Studies*, 1980, 1, 19.

Marx, Karl. *The German Ideology*. New York: International Publishers, 1844.

Marx, Karl. "The Critique of Hegelian Philosophy." In *Critical Sociology*, edited by P. Connerton. New York: Penguin, 1976.

Marx, Karl. *Early Writings*. Trans. By T. B. Bottomore. New York: McGraw-Hill, 1964.

Maurice, Frederick D. *Learning and Working*. 1855. Reprint. London: Oxford University Press, 1968.

May, Rollo. *Power and Innocence*. New York: Norton, 1974.

Mead, Margaret. *Culture and Commitment: A Study of the Generation Gap*. New York: Doubleday, 1970.

Melchert, Charles. "Does the Church Really Want Religious Education?" *Religious Education*, 1974, 69, 1, 12–22.

Melchert, Charles. "What is Religious Education?" *The Living Light*, 1977, 14, 3, 339–352.

Merton, Thomas. *Contemplation in a World of Action*. New York: Doubleday, 1965.

Miller, Randolph C. *The Clue to Religious Education*. New York: Scribner, 1950.

Miller, Randolph C. *The Language Gap and God*. Philadelphia: Pilgrim Press, 1970.

Mills, C. Wright. *The Sociological Imagination*. New York: Oxford University Press, 1959.

Monette, Maurice. "The Language of Need in Adult Religious Education." *The Living Light*, 1978, 15, 2, 167–180.

Monette, Maurice. "Paulo Freire and Other Unheard Voices." *Religious Education*, 1979, 74, 5, 543–554.

Moran, Gabriel. *Theology of Revelation*. New York: Seabury, 1966.

Moran, Gabriel. *Catechesis of Revelation*. New York: Seabury, 1967.

Moran, Gabriel. *Design for Religion*. New York: Herder and Herder, 1970.

Moran, Gabriel. "Catechetics: R.I.P." *Commonweal*, 1970, 99, 299–302.

Moran, Gabriel. *Religious Body*. New York: Seabury, 1974.

Moran, Gabriel. "Where Now, What Next." In *Foundations of Religious Education*, edited by P. O'Hare. New York: Paulist, 1979.

Moran, Gabriel. *Education Toward Adulthood*. New York: Paulist, 1979

Moran, Gabriel. *Interplay*. Winona, Kansas: St. Mary's Press, 1981.

Moran, Gabriel. *Religious Education Development*. Minneapolis: Winston Press, 1983.

More, Thomas. "Utopia." In *Famous Utopias of the Renaissance*, edited by F. R. White New York: Macmillan, 1955.

Murray, John C. *We Hold These Truths*. New York: Sheed and Ward, 1960.

Nagle, William. *Morality and Modern Warfare: The State of the Question*. Baltimore: Helicon, 1960.

Nelson, C. E. *Where Faith Begins*. Atlanta: John Knox Press, 1967.

Neusner, Jacob. *Invitation to the Talmud*. New York: Harper and Row, 1973.

Niebuhr, Reinhold. *The Irony of American History*. New York: Scribner, 1952.

Niebuhr, H. Richard. *Christ and Culture*. New York: Harper and Row, 1951.

O'Brien, David J. "American Catholic Opposition to the Vietnam War: A Preliminary Assessment." In *War or Peace? The Search for New Answers*, edited by Thomas Shannon. Maryknoll, N.Y.: Orbis Press, 1980.

Ogletree, Thomas. "The Gospel as Power: Explorations in a Theology of Social Change." In *New Theology No. 8*, edited by Martin Marty and Dean Peerman. New York: Macmillan, 1971.

O'Hare, Padraic, *Religious Education for Peace and Justice*. San Francisco: Harper and Row, 1983.

Oliver, Donald, and Bane, Mary Jo. "Moral Education: Is Reasoning Enough?" In *Moral Education: Interdisciplinary Approaches*, edited by C. Beck et al. New York: Paulist Press, 1971.

Osborn, M., Charnley, A., and Withnall, A. *The Psychology of Adult Learning and Development*. Leicester: National Institute of Adult and Continuing Education, 1982.

Parsons, Talcott. *Sociological Theory and Modern Society*. New York: Free Press, 1967.

Peters, R. S. *Ethics and Education*. Glenview Ill.: Scott, Foresman & Co., 1966.

Piaget, Jean. *The Moral Judgment of the Child*. 1922. Reprint. New York: Free Press, 1965.

Pius XII. *Major Addresses of Pius XII*. Edited by Victor Yzermans. St. Paul: North Central Publishing co., 1961.

Plato. *The Republic*. Translated by F. Cornford. New York: Oxford, 1945 ed.

Position Papers and Recommendations from the Symposium on the Parish and the Educational Mission of the Church. Washington, D.C.: United States Catholic Conference, 1978.

Postman, Neil, and Weingartner, Charles. *Teaching as a Subversive Activity*. New York: Delacorte, 1969.

Postman, Neil. *Teaching as a Conservative Activity*. New York: Delacorte, 1979.

Pratte, Richard. *Ideology and Education*. New York: McKay, 1977.

Ramsey, Ian. *Religious Language*. New York: Macmillan, 1957.

Ramsey, Paul. *The Just War: Force and Political Responsibility*. New York: Scribner, 1968.

Rawls, John. *A Theory of Justice*. Cambridge, Mass.: Harvard University Press, 1971.

Richardson, Hubert. "Martin Luther King: Unsung Theologian." In *New Theology No. 6*, edited by Martin Marty and Dean Peerman. New York: Macmillan, 1969.

Ricoeur, Paul. *The Symbolism of Evil*. New York: Harper and Row, 1967.

Robinson, Edward. *The Original Vision*. Oxford: Religious Experience Unit, 1977.

Rogers, Carl. *Freedom to Learn*. Columbus, Ohio: Merrill, 1969.

Rokeach, Milton. *The Open and Closed Mind*. New York: Basic Books, 1960.

Rousseau, Jacques. *The Emile*. New York: Teachers College Press, 1956.

Schaefer, James. *Program Planning for Adult Christian Education*. New York: Paulist, 1972.

Schmidt, Stephen. *History of the Religious Education Association, 1903-1970*. Birmingham, Ala.: Religious Education Press, 1983.

Scott, Kieran. "Communicative Competence and Religious Education." *Lumen Vitae*, 1980, 35, 1, 76–96.

Scott, Kieran. "Three Traditions of Religious Education." *Religious Education*, 1984, 79, 3.

Segundo, Juan. *The Liberation of Theology*. New York: Orbis, 1976.

Shannon, Thomas ed. *War or Peace? The Search for New Answers*. Maryknoll, N.Y.: Orbis Press, 1980.

Sharing the Light of Faith: National Cathechectical Directory for Catholics of the United States. Washington, D.C.: United States Catholic Conference, 1979.

Shepherd, David. *Bias for the Poor*. London: SCM Press, 1983.

Skinner, B. F. *Walden Two*. New York: Macmillan, 1948.

Smart, Ninian. *Secular Education and the Logic of Religion*. London: Faber, 1968.

Smith, H. Shelton. *Faith and Nurture*. New York: Scribner, 1941.

Smith, J. W. D. *Religious Education in a Secular Setting*. London: SCM Press, 1969.

Snook, I. A. *Concepts of Indoctrination*. London: Routledge and Kegan Paul, 1972.

Stokes, Kenneth. "Update on Adult Education in Churches and Synagogues: Protestantism." *Religious Education*, 1977, 72, 2, 121–132.

Stokes, Kenneth, ed. *Faith Development and the Adult Life Cycle*. New York: Sadlier, 1983.

Stone, Ronald. *Paul Tillich's Radical Social Thought*. Atlanta: John Knox Press, 1980.

Strommen, Merton. *Five Cries of Youth*. San Francisco: Harper and Row, 1979.

Sullivan, Thomas F. "The Directory, the School and Television." *The Living Light*, 1980, 17, 3, 211–219.

The Challenge of Peace: God's Promise and Our Response. The Pastoral Letter on War and Peace. *Origins*, 13, 1, May 19, 1983.

This Land is Home to Me. Pastoral Letter of the Catholic Bishops of Appalachia. Prestonsburg, Kentucky: Catholic Committee of Appalachia, 1974.

Thompson, Jane L. *Adult Education For A Change*. London: Hutchinson, 1980.

Thompson, Norma, ed. *Religious Education and Theology*. Birmingham, Ala.: 1982.

To Teach as Jesus Did. Washington, D.C.: United States Catholic Conference, 1972.

Toton, Suzanne. *World Hunger: The Responsibility of the Christian Educator*. Maryknoll, N.Y.: Orbis, 1982.

Tracy, David. *Blessed Rage of Order*. New York: Seabury, 1976.

Tracy, David. *The Analogical Imagination*. New York: Seabury, 1981.

Turner, Victor. *The Ritual Process*. Chicago: Aldine Publishing Co., 1969.

Vaillant, George. *Adaptation to Life*. Boston: Brown, Little and Co., 1977.

Wach, Joachim. *Sociology of Religion*. Chicago: University of Chicago Press, 1944.

Warren, Michael. "Catechesis: An Enriching Category for Religious Education." *Religious Education*, 1981, 76, 2, 115–127.

Weber, Max. *The Sociology of Religion*. 1922. Reprint. Boston: Beacon Press, 1964.

Wei-Ming, Tu. "The Confucian Perception of Adulthood." In *Adulthood*, edited by E. Erikson. New York: Norton, 1978.

Westerhoff, John, and Neville, Gwen. *Generation to Generation*. Philadelphia: Pilgrim Press, 1972.

Westerhoff, John. *Will Our Children Have Faith?* New York: Seabury, 1976.

Westerhoff, John. "A Call to Catechesis." *The Living Light*, 1977, 14, 3, 354–58.

Westerhoff, John. "Anniversary Reflections: Religious Education: 75 Years." *Religious Education*, 1981, 76, 6, 578–584.

Whitehead, Evelyn, and Whitehead, James. *Christian Life Patterns: The Psychological and Religious Invitations of Religious Life*. Garden City, N.Y.: Doubleday, 1979.

Wilson, John. "What is Moral Education?" In *Introduction to Moral Education*, by N. Williams, and B. Sugarman. New York: Penguin Books, 1967.

Wogaman, Philip. *A Christian Method of Moral Judgement*. Philadelphia: Westminster, 1976.

Wren, Brian. *Education for Justice: Pedagogical Principles*. Maryknoll, N.Y.: Orbis, 1977.

Wright, Derek. *The Psychology of Moral Behavior*. New York: Penguin, 1971.

Wuthnow, Robert. "A Sociological Perspective." In *Faith Development and the Adult Life Cycle*, edited by Kenneth Stokes. New York: Sadlier, 1983.

Yeaxlee, Basil. *Spiritual Values in Adult Education. Vol. I, Vol II*. London: Oxford Univ. Press, 1925.

Yeaxlee, Basil. *Lifelong Education: A Sketch of the Range and Significance of the Adult Education Movement*. London: Cassell and Co., 1929.

Yinger, M. *The Scientific Study of Religion*. New York: Harper and Row, 1970.

Yoder, John H. *The Politics of Jesus*. Grand Rapids, Mich. Eerdsman, 1972.

Young, M., ed. *Knowledge and Control*. London: Collier-Macmillan, 1971.

Zahn, Gordon. "The Great Catholic Upheaval." *Saturday Review*, September 11, 1971, 54.

VITA

John L. Elias, Ed.D. is Professor of Adult and Religious Education, Fordham University, Bronx, New York. He is the author of *Conscientization and Deschooling: Freire's and Illich's Proposals for Reshaping Society* (Westminster, 1976), *Philosophical Foundations of Adult Education* (Krieger, 1980), *Foundations and Practice of Adult Religious Education* (Krieger, 1982), and *Psychology and Religious Education,* (Third Edition, Krieger, 1983). Dr. Elias is also the founding director of St. Mary's Centre for Adult Religious Education, Strawberry Hill, England.

INDEX OF PRINCIPAL NAMES

Whitehead, J., 99, 104, 221
Wilson, J., 49, 221
Winstanley, G., 131
Wogaman, P., 57, 154, 221
Wren, B., 24, 91, 123, 144, 157, 221
Wright, D., 50, 221
Wuthnow, R., 98, 221
Wyckoff, C., 20, 42

Wycliffe, John, 130

Yeaxlee, B., 129, 137, 138, 143, 221
Yinger, M., 65, 221
Yoder, J., 179, 194, 221
Young, M., 124, 181, 221

Zahn, G., 203, 206, 209, 212

INDEX OF PRINCIPAL SUBJECTS